D1443385

THE DEVIL'S
RIGHT-HAND MAN

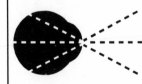

This Large Print Book carries the
Seal of Approval of N.A.V.H.

THE DEVIL'S RIGHT-HAND MAN

THE TRUE STORY OF SERIAL KILLER ROBERT CHARLES BROWNE

STEPHEN G. MICHAUD AND DEBBIE M. PRICE

THORNDIKE PRESS

A part of Gale, Cengage Learning

GALE
CENGAGE Learning

Detroit • New York • San Francisco • New Haven, Conn • Waterville, Maine • London

Copyright © 2007 by Stephen G. Michaud and Debbie M. Price.
The Edgar® name is a registered service mark of Mystery Writers of America, Inc.
Thorndike Press, a part of Gale, Cengage Learning.

ALL RIGHTS RESERVED
Thorndike Press® Large Print Crime Scene.
The text of this Large Print edition is unabridged.
Other aspects of the book may vary from the original edition.
Set in 16 pt. Plantin.
Printed on permanent paper.

LIBRARY OF CONGRESS CATALOGING-IN-PUBLICATION DATA

Michaud, Stephen G., 1948–
    The devil's right-hand man : the true story of serial killer
Robert Charles Browne / by Stephen G. Michaud and Debbie
M. Price.
      p. cm.
    Originally published: New York : Berkley Books, 2007.
    ISBN-13: 978-1-4104-0493-0 (lg. print : U.S. hc : alk. paper)
    ISBN-10: 1-4104-0493-5 (lg. print : U.S. hc : alk. paper)
    1. Browne, Robert Charles, 1952– 2. Serial murderers —
United States — Biography. 3. Murderers — United States —
Case studies. 4. Serial murder investigation — United States.
5. Murder — United States. I. Price, Debbie M. II. Title.
    HV6248.B753M53 2008
    364.152'3092—dc22
    [B]   2007044719

Published in 2008 by arrangement with The Berkley Publishing Group, a member of Penguin Group (USA) Inc.

Printed in the United States of America
1 2 3 4 5 6 7 12 11 10 09 08

THE DEVIL'S
RIGHT-HAND MAN

PROLOGUE

As Scott Fischer remembers it, Robert Charles Browne's name first arose one morning in the spring of 2002 at the Old Heidelberg Pastry Shop, a well-worn Colorado Springs institution on a seedy stretch of South Tejon where the El Paso County sheriff's department cold case squad often gathered to shoot the breeze, discuss the news, and sometimes even get down to business.

That morning's cold case colloquy in the popular bakery-café quickly veered away from practical matters. The three friends settled instead on the subject of serial murder, which was in the news. Another alleged itinerant killer had just been caught. At some point in the discussion Charlie Hess looked over the Formica tabletop at Lou Smit and asked, "You ever work somebody who you just really thought was a serial killer?"

Hess, then in his midseventies, a retired veteran of the FBI and CIA, was the senior member of the group. Lou Smit, a regionally renowned and controversial former police detective about ten years Hess's junior, didn't ponder the question long. "Yeah," he answered, "Robert Browne. I suspected he was a serial killer from the start."

Robert Browne was the sort of exotic and extremely dangerous felon for whom Lou Smit reserved the sobriquet "tiga-gata," a cross between a tiger and an alligator, or the meanest animal anywhere. There had never been any doubt in Lou's mind that Robert Browne was a tiga-gata.

Nor need he explain who Browne was to Hess and Fischer, the third member of the team, a retired newspaper publisher in his late fifties. The cold case squad and practically everyone else around Colorado Springs were keenly familiar with Robert Browne. Seven years earlier, the soft-voiced, green-eyed Louisianan had gone to prison for the abduction-murder of thirteen-year-old Heather Dawn Church. In a plea-bargain deal, Browne had been sentenced to life without parole. The horror of Browne's bold crime, which remained unsolved for three and a half years, shook the community, the state, and the country. Browne ultimately confessed to murdering Heather, but everyone knew that Lou Smit was the real reason Browne was caught; a point of personal annoyance to the killer, who claimed he was framed. Robert Browne bore the detective a deep enmity.

Besides their evident maturity, this unlikely-looking trio of would-be crime busters had three things in common. Each was a friend of John Anderson, the El Paso County sheriff who had brought them together and sworn them all in as honorary deputies. As retirees, each also had a lot of free time. And, as Sheriff Anderson saw it, each had the right personality to be part of a three-person cold case team devoted to solving the hoary old puzzlers that accrete like arterial plaque at law enforcement agencies everywhere.

Sheriff Anderson, who in '02 had one year left in office, was a strong proponent of modern police management and up-to-date forensic investigation. As a young Colorado Springs police detective in the seventies and early eighties, he had partnered with Lou Smit to work cold cases. The sheriff was well aware that cold cases, usually homicide investigations, can turn cold for any number of reasons, then begin to gather dust in the files or get lost altogether (a distressingly common occurrence). Still, he also believed that a lot of cold cases were just waiting for the right investigator or team of investigators to pick them up and solve them. As Lou Smit always liked to say, the leads were in the files.

Anderson felt his old friends would bring complementary skill sets to the task. Scott Fischer, the former corporate executive, was savvy with technology; his double major in college had been accounting and computer programming. After signing on as a sheriff's volunteer in 2000, Fischer also had gone through the deputy training program to become a reserve officer; he was sanctioned to carry a gun and make arrests. Lou Smit brought with him a deep well of investigative experience and a thorough knowledge of the criminal mind. Charlie Hess's forte was analysis; his key virtues were patience and determination. He had had three careers, at least: one, which lasted ten years, was as an FBI agent; during the war in Vietnam, he'd worked for the CIA in the controversial Phoenix Program; and he later became a polygraph examiner attached to the San Diego Police Department. Now, despite a variety of health issues, he was ever avid about his fourth professional incarnation as a cold case sleuth.

Hess kept an ornamental hand grenade on his desk in the cold case room. There was disagreement whether the device was a memento or a metaphor. On the wall above his desk hung a framed copy of his CIA performance review for the first nine months of 1968.

"Subject is impatient with incompetence and with people who are insincere in their work," the final paragraph read in part. "This characteristic occasionally creates an impasse which can only be resolved by removing one of the parties from the scene of action. . . . He is invariably right in his assessment of the situation, and thereby makes it more difficult to criticize him for his impatience."

Hess liked "being at the pointy end of the spear," as Lieutenant Ken Hilte, the cold case squad supervisor, explains.

Sheriff Anderson placed absolute confidence in Hess, Smit, and Fischer, which was necessary if he was going to open some of his department's most sensitive files to them. He would, he says, "trust all three with my life, my wife, and my money."

All three also had an ornery streak, which Anderson appreciated. "They're more apt to ask forgiveness than beg for permission," he explains. "They wouldn't let little things stand in the way."

Plus they worked cheap. For the first two years they were in business, the cold case squad was provided work space and phones and little else. For a local law enforcement agency chronically strapped for cash, the three old friends came at the right price.

In the gospel according to Lou Smit, cold case investigations are 95 percent paperwork, and that was all the squad did at first. They foraged around the department for the files and boxes containing bits and pieces of what turned out to be fifteen or so unsolved cases that still seemed salvageable. Some of the material they needed was where it should be. Some was at the bottom of desk drawers. Some was buried under huge stacks of discarded documents left in the corners of forgotten closets.

Slowly and painstakingly, they reconstructed each case according to Smit's template. "We really studied them," says Fischer. "We'd take every report and face sheet and put them in order by date. We did time lines. Wrote the summaries. Did the indexing. Created a whole set of leads for each one."

Once every jot and tittle was in its correct place, they had 129 black binders, each three inches thick with tidy blue labels, enough books to occupy an entire wall of their squad room. The information in the books was indexed and computerized and ready for detectives to use for follow-up. Except the follow-up didn't always follow up. Detectives were supposed to team together in pairs to work the cold cases, but the responsibility to also investigate the constant flow of new cases made progress on the cold cases very slow. Frustration set in.

Inevitably, the cold case squad members began to think about expanding their franchise to become more proactive and to do their own investigations. "I put all this time into building these books, and I wanted to slam someone into jail," is how Fischer remembers it.

Charlie Hess, who doesn't type and avoids equipment more complex than a rotary-dial desk phone, was both bored with paperwork and eager to engage on the level he knew best, one-on-one contact.

Lou Smit was more patient with the slow progress, yet he, too, realized that a key component to successful cold case investigation was missing. There was no one out there "stirring the pot," as he phrased it. No one was making things happen.

Moreover, all three felt a strong sense of responsibility to the victims of violent crimes and their survivors; in many instances the cold case squad offered these people their final hope for justice or peace of mind. Those who lose relatives, friends, or loved ones to homicide often never know more about the case than the identity of the dead or missing victim. They often are haunted by that ignorance. No matter how horrible the truth of a crime, what a survivor may imagine over and over can be a far greater burden on the heart. The cold case squad wanted to give these people the comfort of fuller knowledge; the what, where, when, how, and why of the crimes, if possible. This thought was very much on their minds that morning in 2002 when Charlie Hess first asked Lou Smit about serial killers.

If Lou was right that Robert Charles Browne's killing career probably had not started and stopped with Heather Church, then they realized that Browne was likely responsible for multiple crimes with multiple victims, all still unsolved. Luckily, Browne was fairly close at hand, serving his life sentence in lockdown twenty-three hours a day, seven days a week at the Colorado State Penitentiary in Cañon City, where the state houses its most violent and dangerous offenders. Over the years, Browne had had lots of time to think. Perhaps he also had something to say, if the questions were posed in the right way.

Why not send this tiga-gata a letter? Charlie proposed.

Scott and Lou agreed. It was time to stir the pot.

ONE

Just northwest of downtown Colorado Springs, where the prairie gathers itself into great, rolling foothills, there rises from the earth a colossal monument: the red-orange Garden of the Gods, a collection of 300-foot-high sandstone and shale monoliths sculpted by the winds over sixty-five million years to resemble cathedral spires, a pair of kissing camels, or Siamese twins.

Rampart Range Road, a rutted gravel washboard, winds away from the mystical stones to within six miles of snowcapped Pikes Peak — Colorado Springs' pink granite citadel, which at 14,110 feet dominates the landscape in all directions — then snakes about sixty miles north along the crest of the Rampart Range to Sedalia, a short distance south of Denver.

Most of the many pickup trucks and jeeps that roar up and down the lower stretches of Rampart Range Road are headed for a popular firing range, where the shooters blast away at paper targets and bags of household garbage (a local quirk) set against the red dirt hillside. This is rural Colorado, where modern-day mountain men grow their beards to their chests and the battered Chevy Suburban parked in the turnout probably is someone's home.

For some, Lower Rampart Range Road serves another special purpose.

Rough and wild, though not too distant from busy north-south Interstate 25, it is a convenient destination for discarding dead bodies. Since the 1970s, nearly a dozen homicide victims have been discovered along Rampart Range Road, and those are just the ones the weather and carrion eaters didn't finish off first.

Seven and a quarter miles up from the Garden of the Gods, the bumpy track runs along the high divide between Williams Canyon to the southwest and Queens Canyon to the northeast. There, the mountain-side falls away in a steep, 400-foot drop to the base of a ravine thick with pine trees and scrub oak. It is a wild yet peaceful place. The wind rushes through the pine boughs, and raptors of several species circle overhead.

It was here that in September 1993 Timothy Belbeck chose to camp in his pickup truck. Belbeck was too short on cash to afford his favorite accommodations, the Pink Panther Motel down in Colorado Springs, but he did have enough money for provisions, including whiskey.

The forty-year-old drifter would later tell investigators how a group of young men showed up and started aimlessly throwing rocks over the side of the cliff. From far below he heard the clink of stone striking metal, a welcome sound for it meant scrap — chrome, aluminum, maybe even some copper — which Belbeck knew he could turn into cash.

It would be tricky to recover anything from the deep ravine, but as Belbeck worked his way toward the bottom of his whiskey bottle, the prospect of running dry emboldened him. Two days later, the whiskey gone, he scrambled down the steep hillside, past a waterbed mattress, until he came to a blue and white 1961 Chevrolet Impala that looked as if it had been rusting away there for at least fifteen years. A front door was open, and the car was filled with dirt from a mudslide. But the old junker still had its radiator, starter, generator, and a battery, all salvageable for drinking money.

Belbeck looked around and saw a derelict

washing machine, a good sign that there was even more junk to be found amidst the trees and dense brush. Continuing with his reconnaissance, about twenty-five feet below the Chevy, he came across a round thing with zigzag marks running across it. The object was smooth and shaped like the other rocks on the hillside, but its color gave him pause. He rolled it over with a stick and saw teeth.

Belbeck realized at once that it was a human skull. Too spooked to touch the thing, he looked again at the sutures running across the top, the eye sockets, the protruding front teeth, just to be sure. Then he bolted and ran — hard — back up the hillside.

Once he got his breath back and his brain straight, he pondered how to proceed. If the skull was connected to the car, he thought, the victim's family ought to be notified. Perhaps there would even be a reward in it for him. Unfortunately, a second trip down the hill yielded no further information. So he thought some more. A friend advised that if he reported the skull, Belbeck might come under suspicion, and he didn't need that kind of trouble. Then again, there might be that reward.

On September 13, four days after he first

found the skull, Belbeck finally went to the Colorado Springs police to report his discovery, which he described as a body.

"Not our jurisdiction," the Springs police said. They sent Belbeck to the El Paso County Sheriff's Office.

"Body in a car? That's an auto fatality," said a sheriff's deputy. He directed Belbeck to the Colorado State Police, where at last he connected with Trooper Ron Quintana.

The thirty-six-year-old Quintana had spent the last eleven years investigating crashes and making traffic stops. He had a habit, he liked to say, of being "an inquisitive trooper." Tim Belbeck struck him as a real banana right from the start, but Trooper Quintana knew better than to dismiss the scruffy transient without checking things out.

Quintana drove with Belbeck to Rampart Range Road, where he and the transient worked their way down a rappel line into the steep ravine and found the old car full of dirt.

"So where's this body?" he asked.

Belbeck just laughed and shrugged.

Annoyed, Quintana walked below the car, thinking that a body could have been carried down the mountain by the mudslide. Glancing at the ground around his feet, he saw that same odd object partially buried in the dirt. The moment he bent down for a closer look, however, Ron Quintana instantly knew, as Tim Belbeck had, that here was a human skull.

The bones were so weathered that at first the trooper thought the skull was a centuries-old Indian artifact.

"I wonder who he is?" Quintana said, holding the skull out for Belbeck to see.

"How do you know it's not a she?" Belbeck responded.

Quintana placed the skull in a brown paper evidence bag and returned with Belbeck to the state police barracks to take Polaroid photographs of the skull and to further quiz its discoverer. He strongly doubted Belbeck's story. The hill was too steep. The car was too far down, too buried in trees and brush to strike with a rock. Then there was Belbeck's repeated suggestion that the skull could belong to a female. The man, Quintana thought, was far too interested in a reward. As a precaution, he fingerprinted and photographed Belbeck.

Since it seemed unlikely that the skull came from the car, the state police lacked jurisdiction. So, with Belbeck in tow, Quintana drove over to the El Paso County Sheriff's Office. There, the trooper sat for two hours with the skull in its brown bag on a deputy's desk before being told, "Old car? Old skull? Auto fatality. It's yours."

Next and last stop of the day: the El Paso County Coroner's Office, where the macabre evidence was accepted and logged in for examination.

Quintana then drove to a Wendy's restaurant for a late dinner with his family. As he arrived, his thirteen-year-old daughter, Rhiannon, walked up to his cruiser in the parking lot and looked inside. Before her father could stop her, Rhiannon spotted the Polaroids of the skull clipped to the case file cover on the seat beside him.

"Dad, what's this?" she asked as she picked up the pictures for a closer look.

She could see that the bottom jaw was missing, but the top front teeth instantly caught her attention. They were very distinctive, two large incisors flanked by two crooked laterals. Rhiannon's eyes flew to a missing persons poster in the Wendy's window.

Over the last two years, the face of this other thirteen-year-old girl with her big glasses and her toothy smile had become a heartbreakingly familiar one to Rhiannon and to nearly everyone else all over the region. The child had disappeared without a trace from her home while babysitting her little brother. There was hardly a person in Colorado Springs who didn't know her name.

Ashen, Rhiannon Quintana pointed to the poster.

"Dad, it's Heather Dawn," she said. "You've found Heather Dawn Church."

Two

As it turned out, on March 17, 2000, two years before Charlie Hess's inspiration at the Old Heidelberg, Robert Browne had opened his own dialogue with the local authorities in a short, handwritten note to the "Office of the District Attorney" in Colorado Springs.

TO WHOM IT MAY CONCERN

In the murky, placid depths,
beneath the cool caressing mire,
lies seven golden opportunities.

Missed opportunities?

Lovingly,
Robert Browne

The district attorney's office forwarded the letter to Mark A. Finley of the sheriff's detective division, who had worked the Church investigation five years earlier.

The one commodity that all inmates have in abundance is free time, and many fill up their idle hours with correspondence. They write their loved ones and families. They write their lawyers. They cultivate relationships with sympathetic strangers who'll send them postage stamps and money. They write to newspapers, hoping to interest journalists in their stories. And they write to the cops.

Their motives for contacting the authorities are as various as their agendas, but a common theme in their letters is the suggestion of hidden knowledge they might be coaxed into sharing. Most veteran detectives are familiar with these types of letters from prisoners — although a rhymed note is unusual — and most are extremely skeptical of them.

Mark Finley subscribed to that point of view.

"I have tried to anticipate what you are wanting to do," Finley replied in a typewritten letter dated March 23, "and believe I have a general idea of at least some of the things you refer to in your letter. I have spoken to other agencies in other states, who asked me to handle things at this end.

"Certainly I am willing to come speak with you if that is what you want."

But Finley warned Browne not to play games with him.

"I will tell you up front," he continued, "no other agencies are interested unless you are willing to provide bona fide information, which will be of assistance to them.

"I took the liberty of writing this letter, rather than make a visit, to assess exactly what it is you want to do. It would be a waste of time to show up and speak in rhymes."

A week later came another handwritten note from Browne. Instead of writing to the district attorney's office this time, he addressed the envelope to Mark Finley at the sheriff's department.

Browne had been back in touch with his muse. On lined notebook paper, he had printed four stanzas of rhyming verse. This time he defined "seven golden opportunities." They were "seven sacred virgins, entombed side by side. Those less worthy, are scattered wide."

Nothing would be gained, Browne rhymed, "Until your minds/have all been drained." More explicitly, he suggested that his reader "dig in deep" to find the virgins.

Browne also hinted at an accomplice

whom he called the "High Priestess."

Tucked behind the verse were two more pages. The first was a taunting note.

"The score is, you *one,* the other team forty-eight!" Then the killer tossed off what would prove to be an actual clue, the first substantive indication that besides the doggerel, he might be peddling something of serious value. It was, however, a very meager, equivocal, and indistinct crumb of a clue. "In addition, if you were to drive to the end zone in a white Trans Am, the score could be *nine* to forty-eight. That would complete your home court sphere."

Browne demanded that no one contact him.

The second page was a crude map of nine states that he had traced from an atlas. Inside each state he had written a number: nine in Colorado, seven in Texas, seventeen in Louisiana, three in Mississippi, five in Arkansas, two in Oklahoma, two in New Mexico, two in California, and one in Washington.

Finley was firmly dubious. He knew that other inmates had made similarly outrageous assertions in the past. Easily the most infamous of these was the late Henry Lee Lucas, a snaggletoothed drifter with an IQ no higher than eighty who in 1983 had persuaded eagerly credulous lawmen all over the U.S. that he'd committed murders — sometimes with his homosexual partner Ottis Toole — in their jurisdictions. Even after Lucas tried to take credit for homicides in Japan, and his victim list climbed to more than 600 people (two or three is a much likelier total count), local law enforcement agencies still were clearing cold cases on his say-so.

By 1984, when *Dallas Times-Herald* reporters Hugh Aynesworth and Jim Henderson exposed Lucas's coast-to-coast hoax, dozens of police agencies had been humiliated and hundreds of detectives discredited. The Lucas case was one of the most embarrassing debacles in the history of U.S. law enforcement, and no cop wanted to be part of a repeat performance.

Still, Finley also knew from experience that his versifying pen pal was both intelligent and crafty, and quite possibly capable of committing such a string of homicides. If in fact Browne had murdered forty-eight people in nine states, he would probably be the most prolific serial killer ever caught in the United States.

Three

If Mike and Diane Church had built their adobe, Santa Fe–style house close to downtown Colorado Springs or the interstate, investigators would have strongly considered the possibility that their daughter Heather's abductor was a traveling serial killer, someone like Ted Bundy, for example, a familiar name in Colorado.

Although serial killers are difficult to characterize generally, those who travel great distances by car usually do not stray too far into unfamiliar territory when hunting for victims. For their purposes, it often is best to stay close to the main highways, where people are more accustomed to dealing with strangers. In case of unhappy surprises, there's always an exit nearby.

But the Churches chose a remote, six-acre plot about eighteen miles northeast of the city and well away from the highway, in isolated Elbert, Colorado, where the nearest convenience store was six miles away and nearly all traffic was local. Whoever snatched Heather hadn't just chanced on their Eastonville Road address. No, logic and experience suggested that the person who took Heather was from the vicinity or was at least familiar with it. Quite possibly he was a neighbor.

Eastonville Road cuts north to south along the edge of a dun-colored prairie that separates itself from a thick band of ponderosa pines known as the Black Forest and rolls off toward Kansas. Hawks feed on the field mice, hairy wolf spiders burrow intricate tunnels through the buffalo grass, and even as the remaining ranches are carved up into five-acre lots, the coyotes yip and bark at night.

In recent years, two-story frame houses with brick-veneer fronts and three-car garages have sprung up like showy milkweed, giving this remote stretch a settled look. But in 1990, when Mike and Diane Church built their horseshoe-shaped hacienda, there were no more than ten houses within a five-mile radius. To the east was a 170-acre cattle ranch. To the south was a 40-acre farm.

Mike, Diane, and their four children, Heather, Kris, Gunner, and Sage, moved into their dream house in July 1990. Diane would recall it was the perfect place to raise a rambunctious young family. All that first summer, the children caught horned toads and built rafts to float them across a nearby pond. Although the house was isolated, Diane felt safe there. She had friends in the area. She and the children were active members of the Mormon church in the town of Black Forest, about ten miles to the south. The Churches had given little thought to security in any event. The house had no garage, no fence, and no burglar alarm.

Their idyll was short-lived. By the fall of 1991, Diane and Mike were living apart and had filed for divorce. Diane and the children remained in Elbert. Mike rented an apartment in Colorado Springs, closer to Atmel Corp., where he worked as a metrologist, a specialist in extremely exact weights and measures.

The house was listed for sale.

About five hundred yards up a hill to the north was 16660 Eastonville Road, the nine-acre Christmas tree farm where thirty-eight-year-old Robert Charles Browne lived in a double-wide "mobile," as he called it, with his fifth wife. She worked for the telephone company, and he looked after his acres of evergreens plus a number of indoor and outdoor dogs and a pond full of ducks.

The Brownes didn't mix much; they and the Churches were unacquainted.

The really private part of Robert's life was a secret from everyone.

Tuesday, September 17, 1991, began in an ordinary way; Diane would struggle to recall most of it.

Heather was small for a thirteen-year-old, five foot one and about eighty pounds, with brown hair and hazel eyes that sparkled behind large, plastic-rimmed glasses. She was an eighth grader at Falcon Middle School, where she had just been admitted to the gifted and talented program. Her goal, as she wrote on a Sunday school survey, was to get straight As and then to go to college. She wanted to be an astronaut. Two summers before, she had attended camp at the U.S. Space & Rocket Center in Huntsville, Alabama. Her parents expected the experience to put a passing fancy to rest, but she came back boasting that she was the only camper who hadn't thrown up after spinning around in a simulator.

She and her brothers caught the school bus as usual at 6:30 a.m. for the hour-long ride to school, where Heather was loading up on math and science courses. She brushed aside concerns that her poor vision might limit her opportunities as an astronaut, saying, "If I can't fly, then I'll be a computer programmer." A family friend who taught at the U.S. Air Force Academy in Colorado Springs promised to sponsor her application to the elite school.

After school that Tuesday, Diane hurried to prepare an early dinner so that she could take the older boys — Kris, ten, and Gunner, seven — to a Boy Scout meeting at the Mormon church. Afterward, she planned to stay at the church to attend a picture-framing class. Heather begged to stay home and take care of five-year-old Sage. There would be nothing for either of them to do during the meetings. Diane agreed, expecting to be back home no later than ten o'clock or so.

As Diane grilled hot dogs, mother and daughter talked in the kitchen. Heather got a sheepish look on her face. There was a school dance coming up. Just that day she'd found the courage to ask a boy to be her date. Would her mother let her go?

"I'll think about it," Diane said, hurrying the hot dogs to the table.

Heather quietly waited and watched.

Finally, Diane could stand it no longer.

"OK. All right, as long as you go with a group," Diane finally said.

Heather jumped up and hugged her mother. "You're the best mom on the planet!" she said, running off to her bedroom to try on clothes for the dance.

Driving away from the house, Diane noticed that the master bedroom window was open. She made a mental note to call Heather from the church with instructions to close it. But when she called Heather at eight thirty p.m., their conversation turned first to the issue of Sage's eight o'clock bedtime and the vaccinations he'd received that afternoon. Heather apologized for letting her brother stay up late, explaining that they had been watching a favorite television show.

"If he's running a fever," Diane said, "give him some Tylenol." Then she hung up, forgetting to tell Heather about the window.

When she and the boys arrived home at about ten fifteen, Diane noticed that the house lights were dimmed and the sliding-glass back door was unlocked. Nothing unusual there. Heather often turned down the lights to watch TV. And the children were always neglecting to lock the door when they let the cats in or out.

Diane tossed her keys onto the kitchen counter and walked back to her bedroom, talking to Heather as she went. The boys went into the bedroom they shared with the littlest Church.

"Mom!" they called out at once. "We can't find Sage!"

False alarm.

Diane hurried to their room, where she found the sleeping boy wrapped up like a burrito in his blankets, wedged between the bed and the wall. This was odd; Sage usually kicked off his covers while he slept.

Moments later, the boys ran down the hallway once again.

"Mom! We can't find Sissy!"

This time she thought they were kidding.

Diane went into Heather's room, intending to kiss her on the forehead, only to discover her daughter's bed was cold. She ripped away Heather's comforter. Nothing! Likewise the closet. She looked around, panicked, then raced through the house with Kris and Gunner, calling for Sissy, all three desperately hoping for a simple, innocent answer to their fears. They looked for Heather in every place they could imagine, even inside the clothes dryer.

Empty.

Diane searched the property, calling for

her daughter in the night.

Only silence.

Then she grabbed the telephone and dialed Mike, who had just returned from a divorce recovery workshop at the First Presbyterian Church.

"Is Heather with you? Do you have Heather?" she shouted.

"No," Mike said. "Have you called her friends? The neighbors? Does it look like someone came in the house? Diane, call 911. Now!"

Within minutes he was speeding in his truck down Platte Avenue toward the house on Eastonville Road. As he fought back tears, Mike told himself that everything was going to be all right, but the premonition of evil was strong. Mike Church knew, right from the start, that someone had taken his daughter.

Diane could not imagine such a thing. She feared that Heather had gone outside to look for one of the cats. Her daughter was afraid of the dark and of the coyotes that prowled at the edge of their property. But Heather loved her kitten Megan above all. In Diane's imagination, Heather had walked too far and had fallen and perhaps broken her leg. Mrs. Church pictured her daughter lying in the draw or somewhere on the prairie, unconscious and in shock.

Panicked calls from distraught parents were common enough for the 911 dispatcher to discount the Churches' worries. The El Paso County sheriff's department generally did not take a missing person report unless the subject had been gone at least a full twenty-four hours, even if that person was a teenager. "Ninety-nine percent of the kids who aren't home when their parents get home are at a party," said the dispatcher, who at first refused to send out a deputy. "Call her friends," she suggested.

"What about the other one percent?" Diane snapped back.

The temperature was dropping; sleet was beginning to fall. Diane called everyone she knew to help her look for Heather. By the time Mike arrived, the house was full of people, their cars and trucks parked around the yard.

She also repeatedly dialed 911 until El Paso County Sheriff's Deputy Les Milligan at last was dispatched at eleven thirty that night. Milligan seemed so young that Diane's heart fell. How could this boy be of any help? He looked barely old enough to be out of high school. But the deputy quickly sized up the situation and took charge, requesting that the El Paso County

Search and Rescue team be sent out as soon as possible.

Mrs. Church would be forever grateful that this apparent kid immediately recognized the seriousness of the situation. Even so, it was daylight before the search and rescue team arrived to begin hiking through the ranchland and knocking on doors along Eastonville Road.

Mike Church stayed at the house that night with his boys. Shortly before dawn, he heard Diane crying quietly in their old bedroom. He went to comfort her, but the gulf between them had widened too far. Even at this, the worst moment of their lives, they could not come together. Later in the day, at the suggestion of police and friends, Mike took the boys back to his apartment to wait.

An eerie morning fog settled over the area as Sheriff's Detective Mark Finley arrived to take charge of the case. Elinor McGarry, a civilian crime scene investigator for the sheriff's office, also arrived to begin her forensic work. McGarry discovered to her deep dismay that all the previous night's vehicle traffic in and out of the Church driveway had canceled any hope of isolating useful footprints or tire tracks. The inside of the house was similarly compromised. Not only had people walked willy-nilly throughout the residence, but Diane herself had tossed around bedding and clothes in her desperate early search.

As searchers, including a pair of volunteers named Diane Kittell and Robert Hunter, fanned out across the prairie, Diane Church and her best friend, Jan Schalk, fidgeted together in the living room. Finally, Mrs. Church could stand the inaction no longer. She got up and washed the dinner dishes, still stacked in the sink. Finished with that, she began to vacuum the carpet.

A deputy heard the roar of the machine and came racing into the living room before any more possible physical evidence, such as fibers or hair, could be sucked up and lost to the investigation.

"What are you doing? Turn that thing off!" he shouted.

It had not occurred to Diane that her home was a potential crime scene.

Diane sat down in the living room once more. She remembers staring out into the foggy morning, when "it popped into my head," she says.

"It" was the sudden recollection from hours before that the master bedroom window curtains "were kinda messed up."

"I had been back in the bedroom and hadn't consciously noticed it," she recalls. "I think I was in a state of shock."

She asked Jan Schalk if she'd noticed the window screen was askew, as well.

"What do you mean, the window screen is askew?" someone asked.

"It just looks like someone has whacked it and knocked it off the track," she explained. "The screen is not in the window properly."

One of the investigators — no one recalls who — overheard the remark and asked Mrs. Church to show them what she meant. "A whole little troop of us," Diane says, walked down the hall together.

At 16660 Eastonville Road, volunteer searchers Diane Kittell and Robert Hunter already had braved a pack of growling, barking chows and shepherds to rouse Robert Browne. They'd recall a quiet man with dark brown hair who said he had no knowledge of anything. Browne did give the two volunteers permission to search his property and even peered under the trailer house himself. But he denied them access to a shed with a distinctive pyramidical roof. He explained that the structure was always securely locked. There was no possibility that a stranger could have gained access to it.

Satisfied, Kittell and Hunter pushed on through the cold mists, thinking so little of the encounter that they did not even file a report. Meanwhile, at the Church residence, Elinor McGarry went to work on the master bedroom window. A polymath who still speaks in the distinctive brogue of her native Scotland, McGarry holds a doctorate in chemistry, which she has taught at various U.S. colleges. She has worked in Canada as a law enforcement toxicologist as well. Among the several other arrows in her forensic quiver is a command of photography and fingerprint technology.

McGarry gingerly lifted the window screen. Then, using a soft brush, she gently dusted black powder across the thin aluminum frame. Odds were that she'd find nothing; according to fingerprint experts, only a small fraction of the objects dusted at crime scenes yield useful prints.

But this time Elinor McGarry got lucky. She smiled. There *was* something there — she could see it — the familiar pattern of lines and whorls. The next step was to very carefully press the special tape down over the revealed print, gently smoothing it to remove any air bubbles. Even the tiniest ripple in the tape could ruin the lift.

Then, holding her breath for steadiness, McGarry peeled back the adhesive and applied it to a white card. *Success.* The prints were exceptionally clear with good ridge detail. Heather's abductor had left a trace of himself, after all.

Now the problem would be finding him.

FOUR

"Robert," Detective Finley wrote Browne by hand on notebook paper on September 23, 2000, after several months of mutual silence, "your last letter reflects in-the-box thinking (no pun intended). It appears you believe other people think in the same manner as you do. I don't believe that is true.

"I am sure it would please you to see news reports of me out hunting geese. It's not going to happen. Should you desire to provide some bona fide details so that I truly know you are not just hallucinating, you will see me act accordingly.

"I find it interesting — the distance you place between yourself and the details I am sure you do know. It would appear to me that the star running back is afraid to play on the home field.

"Cordially, mf."

Put up or shut up was not what the killer

44

wanted to hear. Browne retreated into silence.

FIVE

Colorado Springs — the Springs, as it is known — has always embraced contradictions and surprises. The state's second-largest city, after Denver, with half a million residents in the metro area, it was founded in 1871 by General William Jackson Palmer, a Civil War veteran turned railroad builder who seized upon the idea of creating a tourist resort at the base of Pikes Peak. Twenty years later, after the richest gold field in the world, at the time, was discovered near Cripple Creek, the population of the Springs exploded with rough-hewn miners and new millionaires.

After gold, there was military money: Fort Carson, Peterson Air Force Base, and the North American Aerospace Defense Command Combat Operations Center, built deep inside Cheyenne Mountain. In 1954 came the U.S. Air Force Academy.

Conservatives — religious and political —

have established a powerful base in the Springs, extending their influence across the nation. The Reverend James Dobson, whose organization, Focus on the Family, is headquartered in Colorado Springs, is by some estimates the most powerful evangelical Christian leader in the world. Former Springs minister Ted Haggard was the charismatic head of the National Association of Evangelicals until he was forced to resign in November 2006 after admitting that he bought drugs from a former male prostitute and engaged in "sexual immorality."

Yet, however much residents of the Springs like to view their community as a citadel of piety, prosperity, and preparedness, in many ways it remains as untamed as the terrain that surrounds it.

Back in the 1960s, for example, drifters, runaways, hippies, and bikers flocked to the place, drawn by a variety of Rocky Mountain highs. Soldiers and airmen, headed for or just coming back from Vietnam, could be counted on for adjustment problems. The Springs was getting a taste of big city violence. It needed good cops, and lots of them.

Nineteen sixty-six was a year of reckoning

for Lou Smit. The thirty-year-old Navy vet had tried his hand at a whole range of occupations, from electrician to retail propane distribution to helping his dad run a stump-removal service in Denver. Nothing seemed to work out.

"I was really at a low spot in my life," he recalls. "I had no money, and I had a family I was trying to raise. Finally, one day I just got on my knees and said, 'Look, I'm tired of trying to run my own life.' It just seemed like my way wasn't working out. 'So from now on, I'll just let you handle everything. I'm gonna back off. You just handle it all.' "

Not two weeks later, Smit's cousin, Bill, an officer with the Colorado Springs Police Department, called to say that CSPD was hiring, and that he could probably get Lou on the force. The prayer had been answered. In March 1966 Lou Smit joined the Colorado Springs police as a rookie officer. "I loved the job from the first minute on," he says.

Slight and prematurely short on hair, Smit was no one's idea of the burly street cop who takes down suspects with ease. He laughs when he recalls how once, in his early days, he had to hang on to a lamppost to avoid being pulled across the street by a drunken 300-pound woman who weighed almost twice as much as he did. After such a humiliation in front of his amused fellow cops, Smit began working out, a discipline he has continued, rising each morning before dawn for a trip to the gym.

Smit spent six years working patrol and traffic before lucking into the first important opportunity to show his stuff. After arresting a suspect for shoplifting and impounding the man's car, Lou looked into the trunk. "Oh, for crying out loud!" he said as he spied the head of former president Lyndon Johnson — in wax effigy — peeping out of a sack. The local wax museum had recently been robbed and vandalized, and here was concrete evidence of the culprit.

Sort of.

Opening the suspect's trunk without a warrant or permission was illegal, so neither LBJ's head nor anything else he found there would be admissible in court. Smit tried to convince his captain, Carl Petri, that he'd only been doing an inventory search.

"That's a bunch of bull," Captain Petri said. "But I'll tell you something; you did the right thing in this case, and here's a very important lesson for you. Just because you can't charge him using this evidence doesn't mean you can't charge his friends. It wasn't their car trunk you opened. So go in there and interview this guy and see if he'll tell you who else was involved."

Smit did as he was told and managed to pry three names from his suspect. All three were arrested and charged, and the rest of President Johnson's body was also recovered. Largely on the strength of the initiative he'd shown in solving the wax museum caper, Smit was sent to the detective bureau a few months later.

The bureau was small then, with no separate homicide division, so it didn't take long for Lou to meet everyone around him, including a civilian cadet, eighteen-year-old John Anderson, who worked just down the hallway in the records division. Despite his inexperience, Anderson recognized at once that Lou Smit had a special knack for snooping. "He was analytic where a lot of detectives are very myopic," Anderson remembers. "They'll say, 'Don't bother me, I'm looking over here.' Lou always looked at the larger picture. He also was very good at establishing credibility with violent people — he developed some very good confidential informants — and he had a lot of respect from the other detectives, as well as other agencies. His reputation grew very rapidly."

■ ■ ■ ■

Today Lou Smit is a household name in Colorado in part because of his strong views on the murder of JonBenét Ramsey of Boulder, the six-year-old beauty pageant contestant found dead in her family's basement on Christmas Day 1996. She had been garroted and suffered a massive skull fracture. After assisting the investigation for eighteen months, Smit resigned in protest against its direction. Contrary to consensus opinion among investigators, he believed — and still strongly believes — the evidence showed John and Patsy Ramsey were entirely innocent of their daughter's horrific murder. Smit quit because he felt the Ramseys were being railroaded.

But the cornerstone case of his career as a homicide investigator unfolded two decades earlier, in July 1975, when the body of a young woman was found in a Colorado Springs mobile home park. Cause of death was a single, deep stab wound to the left side of her neck, which severed the carotid artery. She'd been raped as well and had not died easy. The manager of the mobile home park had returned home to find the young woman's body lying outside his door

51

where, in a last desperate attempt to get help, she had reached for the doorbell, leaving a bloody palm print inches below the buzzer. Her blood was on two other trailers where she had also sought help, to no avail.

Police tracked a trail of blood spatters back from the mobile home park to a short, block-long alley where the young woman had been stabbed. The woman, who was beautiful and fresh faced, carried no identification; only a single, ordinary-looking door key was found in a pocket of her jeans. Her physical description was released to the media, which prompted a call to the police. "Hey, that sounds a little like my former roommate, Karen Grammer," said the female caller. "We thought she'd gone back to Florida, because she'd been talking about it." The young woman also provided the police with eighteen-year-old Karen's most recent address.

Lou drove to an apartment on the east side of town, off Academy Boulevard, far from where the young woman had been found, and slid the key into the lock. The door opened. Their victim was Karen Grammer. Her older brother, Kelsey, twenty years old and just starting out on his acting career, flew to Colorado Springs to positively identify his dead sister.

Homicide and sexual crimes detectives commonly strive for emotional distance from the cases they investigate. Otherwise, the heartbreak and anger can consume them like a cancer. Lou Smit is unusual. Because of his deep faith in God, his Partner, as he sometimes puts it, he embraces the pain, considers it part of his job description. Most important, he sees himself not as a technician or artist of crime detection but more fundamentally as the victim's advocate and, by extension, avenger.

"Shoes, shoes, the dead man's shoes, who will stand in the dead man's shoes?" he wrote a quarter century ago for a small law enforcement publication. The article continued:

> I remember something I read long ago: THE DETECTIVE STANDS IN THE DEAD MAN'S SHOES TO PROTECT *HIS* INTERESTS AGAINST THOSE OF ANYONE ELSE IN THE WORLD.
>
> I guess . . . THAT'S WHAT IT'S ALL ABOUT — so many awesome responsibilities are associated with standing in that dead man's shoes.
>
> It means: becoming personally involved in the case and with the victim.
>
> It means: consoling relatives and friends.

It means: caring for the victim's personal possessions and belongings.

It means: respecting that person's body and integrity no matter what race, creed, social upbringing, and past faults or reputation, always remember that something has been taken from him which is priceless and irreplaceable — his life.

It means: closing all doors and answering all unanswered questions.

In Karen Grammer's case, it meant daily visits at the start of his shift to the scene of the crime. It was a ritual he'd already worked into his investigative routine and one with which he has stayed ever since. "Old-timers taught me that," he says. "Go to the scene. Just sit your butt down and watch what is going around." Lou would reflect on the little he knew, and each day he said a little prayer.

About two weeks into the case, still with no useful leads, Smit visited the alley as usual, but this day he suddenly registered something that probably had been bouncing around in his preconscious for quite some time, waiting for his cortex to connect the dots. The alley had struck him as a particularly poor place to commit murder. It was a dead end, which meant that the killer had risked being caught, without an exit, in the midst of his crime. This thought, in turn, led Smit to conclude that the killer *knew* the alley well enough to calculate his risk. Looking up, Lou focused on the apartment complex at the end of the alley. "In fact," he says, "it was close to where the blood spatters began."

Suddenly, a theory of how Karen Grammer was murdered came to him. Smit knew from police reports that on the night of the homicide three young African American males had attempted to rob a nearby Red Lobster just as the restaurant was closing. The would-be hold-up man had plenty of attitude — "militant" was the way the employees described him to police — but he and his buddies, who waited outside, had next to no robbery skills. The Red Lobster employees had already deposited the night's proceeds in the safe and told the robber, sorry, they couldn't oblige his request. He left, cursing the "whiteys."

The investigation had also disclosed that one of those employees was Karen Grammer's boyfriend. What was more, Smit knew Karen occasionally came to the Red Lobster at closing time to pick up her boyfriend. No one in the restaurant had seen her that night; her boyfriend had not even reported her missing, assuming, as her other friends did, that she had simply returned to Florida. What if, Lou thought, Karen Grammer had gone to the restaurant that night and had arrived at the same time as the robbers?

You know, Smit thought to himself in the alley, staring at the apartment complex, *it would only take a second. I'll just go up there and ask the manager.*

"So I got out of my car and walked maybe a quarter of a block. And I asked the manager, 'Do you have any militant blacks who live here?' He said, 'Not now. But there was a group I had some problems with.' "

The problem renters, all associated with Fort Carson in some way, were Michael Corbett, Larry Dunn, and Freddie Lee Glenn.

"Then I asked, 'Did you ever clean up their apartment?'

"He said, 'You know, I haven't. It's still just the way they left it.'

"Do you mind if I take a look?"

"Not at all."

The apartment, Lou recalls, was filled with trash but held little else of interest. Opening a kitchen drawer, Lou found what another investigator might also have discarded as trash — a study guide for a Colorado State driver's license test. Across

56

the cover of the booklet someone had scrawled "Bro Watson." More random bits of information clicked into place.

"Boy, a chill went down my neck," Lou remembers. Winslow Watson, a young black man, had recently been found dead along a local roadside with two bullet wounds in his face.

Lou soon learned from a couple who lived across the hall that Watson, though not on the lease, had shared the apartment with Corbett, Dunn, and Glenn. The couple had complained to Corbett that Watson had stolen a loaf of bread from their refrigerator and now they feared that their complaint had caused Watson's death. The conversation also led Lou in search of a local hooker, who'd been Freddie Glenn's girlfriend. All Lou learned from the couple was that she was black and that she drove a gold Cadillac.

"I looked all over town for that gold Cadillac until I found it one day in front of this bar," he remembers. Knowing it would be fruitless for a white police officer to inquire inside about the vehicle's owner, he called for two traffic cops to start writing tickets on the street. Then Smit sat in his own car and waited. Nothing happened. No one budged.

"So then I walked into the place and yelled, 'Hey, the cops are writing tickets!' Sure enough, here comes this tall, real good-looking black gal."

She gave Lou an alias, not realizing that there was an outstanding warrant for her arrest issued to that same fake name. The detective put her in jail. After reconsidering her options, the prostitute started talking about Freddie Glenn and some of the crimes she knew that he'd committed alone and with others. These included the murder of Daniel Van Lone, twenty-nine, a cook at a local hotel.

Smit ultimately tracked Glenn's former roommate Larry Dunn to New Orleans, where Smit and Chuck Heim, a Colorado Springs prosecutor, interviewed the young man. Promised immunity by Heim, Dunn dumped his erstwhile gang mates in the oil. Though Dunn did no time for the murders, Lou recalls that he did serve a brief federal sentence in connection with a theft at Fort Carson.

According to Dunn, Michael Corbett, a soldier at Fort Carson, was their leader. Corbett, said Dunn, once ran over a rival with an Army tank, severely injuring the man. He also stuck a bayonet in another soldier, just to see what it felt like to kill someone that way. Daniel Van Lone, Dunn said, had been killed for the fifty cents he was carrying. Corbett personally murdered Watson, a member of their gang, for stealing that loaf of bread, just as the young couple had feared.

Dunn also provided an eyewitness account of the rape and murder of Karen Grammer, in which he'd participated. Grammer, Dunn said, had been sitting on an electrical utility box outside the restaurant when he and his buddies pulled up. Dunn told Smit they had kidnapped the young woman because she was a witness to their thwarted robbery, which did not explain why the gang members had then held her in their apartment for four hours, repeatedly raping her. Telling Grammer that they were going to release her, the men hustled her back into the car and drove her around the apartment complex to the dead-end alley.

It was Freddie Glenn, Dunn said, who'd reassured Karen that she wouldn't be killed, then draped a hood over her head and shoved his knife into her neck.

Michael Corbett, who was at Fort Carson the night of the failed Red Lobster robbery and had no part in Karen Grammer's death, was found guilty of three other homicides and sentenced to execution. Freddie Lee

Glenn, who was convicted of killing Grammer, was also sentenced to death. Their sentences were commuted to life terms less than a year later when the U.S. Supreme Court struck down numerous state death penalty statutes, including Colorado's. Both men are eligible for parole; Lou has testified against that and vows to keep doing so.

July 1975 marked a professional milestone for John Anderson, as well.

Crime fighting had fascinated Anderson since early boyhood when his divorced mother — the first meter maid in Colorado Springs — remarried into a family full of cops. Little John grew up listening to his uncles spin their tales of law enforcement derring-do as he dreamed of joining them on the force.

Three days after his twenty-first birthday in July 1975, he got his chance when his uncle Harold Lindsay "Red" Davis, the assistant chief of police, marched his nephew over to the mayor's office. Anderson was sworn in as a Colorado Springs police officer and issued a gun. School and formal law enforcement training would come later. His official career in crime fighting at last had begun.

Within five years, Anderson won a promotion to the detective bureau. Since his early days in the records department he had seen Lou Smit from time to time, usually at crime scenes, and had taken every opportunity to learn from the older man. Now they teamed up.

One of their specialties was working cold cases. In Anderson's recollection, one of the most memorable was the murder of Cheryl McClary.*

The young woman, who worked at a Colorado Springs Walgreens store about a block from Smit's house, had disappeared one night after work, just before Christmas. Several weeks later, her nude body was found in an overgrown section of a local cemetery. She had been raped and stabbed repeatedly. Her clothes and purse were recovered from a Dumpster behind a motel.

For a year, the McClary case went nowhere. Then, after the detective who was working the case left the police department, Smit and Anderson took over in 1982. There were absolutely no local leads to follow, but in the course of reviewing the detective bureau's miscellaneous file, Lou came upon an old teletype from a detective in Florida, alerting Colorado Springs PD

* Denotes pseudonym.

that a vicious sex offender named Joseph Reid* had previously spent some time in their city. The teletype specifically mentioned a Florida case in which Reid abducted a sixteen-year-old girl from a shopping center, raped and stabbed her, and left her, naked, for dead.

There was enough similarity between the Florida case and Cheryl McClary's murder for Smit to take notice. However, the Florida teletype put Reid in Colorado at a time that did not correspond with the date of Cheryl McClary's murder. Nevertheless, intrigued by the similarity of the two sex crimes, Smit submitted Reid's information to the National Crime Information Center computer. There was no match. Not yet quite willing to let go, he then tried local traffic records. Sure enough, Reid had been stopped for a violation not far from the Walgreens just before McClary disappeared.

That night he telephoned the Florida detective, who provided him with a telephone number for Reid's ex-wife, then living in Hawaii. She hesitantly confirmed that they had, in fact, lived in Colorado Springs at the time. Reid had worked for a construction company, while she'd been employed

* Denotes pseudonym.

at the same Walgreens where Cheryl Mc-Clary worked. "Joe picked me up every night after work," she said.

"Joe Reid killed Cheryl McClary," Smit wrote on his calendar that night. He knew he was tracking another tiga-gata.

Next, Smit and Anderson found Reid's car. He had parked it with a cousin in North Carolina, who told Lou by telephone that the vehicle had remained untouched from the day that Reid left it. After some pleading and cajoling, Smit persuaded his department to send him to North Carolina, where the state laboratory processed Reid's car for him. To Smit's disappointment, all they came up with was a speck of mystery blood on the console. In the days before DNA testing, no one could say for certain where the trace had come from.

That left Lou a single long shot chance to close the case. He needed a confession. "I'm down here because I think you killed a girl in Colorado Springs," Lou said to Reid when they first met in a Florida prison interview room. "It would be a lot easier on her parents if you could tell me what happened."

Reid was having none of it. "I could lose my life," he said, reminding Smit that Colorado had the death penalty.

"Do you think they'd send me all this way if I didn't have evidence?" Lou replied. He told Reid that Cheryl McClary was wearing a fur coat on the night she disappeared. "We've searched your car, and guess what we found?" he went on. "I also have a warrant to take hair and blood samples from you."

Smit was, of course, lying, but Joe Reid couldn't take a chance. When Lou got the Colorado Springs prosecutor on the phone, willing to take the death penalty off the table, Reid spoke to him and agreed to the deal.

John Anderson met Smit and Reid at the Colorado Springs airport. Just to make sure a clever lawyer didn't undo the deal, Smit turned to Reid in the car on the way to the police station. "Joe," he said, "you're going to prison for a long, long time. Is there one last thing you'd like to eat?"

"Yes, a taco," said the grateful prisoner.

"Fine," Smit answered, "you can eat it as we drive, and you show me everywhere you went the night you killed Cheryl McClary, and everything you did."

Reid showed Smit and Anderson where he'd parked in the Walgreens lot and how he'd grabbed McClary as she walked by, pulling the young woman into his car through the open driver's-side window. Then he directed the detectives to the churchyard where he'd raped and killed her. Afterward, Reid said, he stripped her body of clothing and identification.

Smit asked what he did with those items.

Reid said he'd disposed of them behind the motel where he and his wife had been staying, and led the detectives to the same Dumpster where McClary's purse and other items were recovered.

Every detail he recalled matched a point of evidence, some that only Cheryl Mc-Clary's killer could have known. There would be no last-minute complications with Joseph Reid's confession and no questions of whether he fabricated any part of it.

John Anderson eventually left the detective bureau with ambitions to build his career on the management side of law enforcement. He finished his undergraduate degree, worked his way up to sergeant, earned an MBA, and waited for his opportunity. Finally, in 1994, he unseated the incumbent El Paso County sheriff, Bernie Barry (who had also been one of his college professors).

One of Anderson's first official acts upon becoming sheriff in early January 1995 was to make Lou Smit an offer he couldn't refuse. Anderson asked Smit to become his detective captain and promised him unlimited resources to accomplish two goals: reorganize the detective bureau and solve the Heather Dawn Church case. Smit immediately agreed.

While the Church case attracted intense national interest — Diane Church did countless radio, newspaper, and TV interviews, appearing on *Oprah* and the *Jerry Springer Show* among other programs, tearfully pleading for anyone with information about Heather to step forward — the investigation on the ground had stalled almost as soon as it started.

None of the forensic evidence gathered at the crime scene had led anywhere, including the fingerprints Elinor McGarry lifted from the window frame in the master bedroom.

There was all the usual confusion and lunacy that such cases generate. Callers reported Heather look-alikes at a credit union in Pueblo, at a Taco Bell in Colorado Springs, and at a mall in Aurora. Diane would remember her missing daughter once was sighted in four states in one day and as far away as Israel.

Investigators checked out a white van, a blue truck, an old green barn where satanic

66

rituals allegedly were held. They even went so far as to research important dates for practitioners of witchcraft and satanism and rode around El Paso County for hours with a mental patient who claimed to have information about the crime.

Psychics popped up. One offered Diane an eerily exact description of the last meal she prepared for Heather and the boys. "You cooked hot dogs because you were in a hurry, and the boys like them," the woman said. "But Heather didn't like hot dogs, and she told you she would fix a peanut butter sandwich for herself." The woman was able to offer Diane little more, other than to say that she thought Heather was dead.

Another psychic, Dorothy Allison of New Jersey, told members of Diane's support group that she saw a property with lots of trees, a building with a triangular roof, a tan pickup truck, and a man named Brown, except there was something unusual about the spelling.

Even the crazy tips eventually petered out until, on the second anniversary of the abduction, authorities made public what Timothy Belbeck had discovered in a ravine off Rampart Range Road, about twenty miles as the crow flies from the Church house, and the case returned briefly to the front page. "IT'S HEATHER," the *Colorado Springs Gazette* announced in enormous headline type on the morning of September 18, 1993.

The grisly discovery extinguished the last of the Church family's hopes. But ultimately it did nothing to advance the investigation.

In the four years since Heather was taken from her home, only a few possible leads on suspects had been developed. Some members of the Churches' Mormon congregation in Black Forest turned on each other. Heather's Sunday school teacher and another family friend were among those whom detectives questioned extensively. In the end, everyone of interest had an ironclad alibi or passed a lie detector test, including Mike and Diane Church.

The FBI committed two dozen agents to the early stages of the investigation. According to Lou Smit, for some unexplained reason the Bureau's search perimeter stopped about a quarter mile up the road from the Church house and just feet short of the mobile home and tree farm at 16660 Eastonville Road.

The FBI did prepare a profile of Heather's abductor. As summarized by Special Agent Danny Joe Harrell, the profile described the UNSUB (for unknown subject) as "a male in his early to late twenties, shy, introverted, and basically a loner. Subject will be unable to achieve sexually whatever he wants with women and has difficulty with women in general. The subject would probably have knowledge of the victim and her family.

"After the crime, the subject would have behavioral changes, which would be noticeable by associates. Individuals close to the subject would notice the changes, which could include an increase in alcohol or drug use, a deterioration in personal appearance, sleeping disorder, a desire to be alone, and possibly fail to show up for work after the abduction."

By early 1995, when John Anderson was sworn in as El Paso County sheriff, the possibility of anyone ever answering for Heather Church's murder seemed remote.

Then Lou Smit went to work. Over the years, Lou had gained respect as a detective's detective. He had famously turned down a promotion to sergeant and the attendant pay raise to continue working murder cases. Whenever he took over a big case, he made it his first job to brew coffee for the squad room, Smit's way of telling others that he knew who was doing the important work.

In a profession where egos often are both

large and frail, Smit's lack of personal vanity was one of those quiet virtues that made him a better leader. He was also a shrewd judge of talent. That is why, after Anderson asked him to head the Church investigation, Smit said he wanted to bring back Detective Mark Finley, who had moved to the Department of Corrections.

Finley commanded his fellow cops' respect as a relentless investigator and tough interrogator, though his occasionally brusque manner also chafed some members of the department. He had led the Church investigation for only a few days before he was redeployed to work another investigation. Some colleagues felt it had seriously hurt the Church case to lose him. Although Smit knew his request would not be popular with some of the department brass, he told Anderson that Finley was an essential addition to the team. Anderson agreed. Finley and Smit were sworn in along with Anderson on January 10, 1995.

Lou began his review of the Church case the same way he approached every investigation. He drove out to Churches' adobe house on Eastonville Road, parked about a half block away, and approached the scene on foot. After a bit, he closed his eyes and prayed to his Partner: "I need a little help on this one."

He met, and prayed, with Diane and Mike Church, just as he would pray with Patsy and John Ramsey a year later after their little girl was murdered. Like the Ramseys, both of the Churches had been suspects in Heather's disappearance, Mike particularly, as some of their allegedly closest friends had quietly shared with investigators their darker doubts about the couple. Smit would have looked hard at the Churches whether or not there were whispers; parents are usually investigators' first focus when a child disappears. But Smit had few reservations after meeting separately with Mike and Diane.

"I really had good vibes from both of them," he says. "It's hard to fake anger."

Diane burst into tears during their meeting at Smit's office. "Diane," Lou told her, "we're going to catch that son of a bitch." He pointed to the case file and added, "The guy who did this is in those books."

Of that Lou Smit was absolutely certain.

"I just didn't think we'd catch him that fast," he says.

Like the other investigators, Smit believed the killer was local and that he was no beginner. He recalled that the window frame, though askew, had been put back onto its track. "That shows thought," Lou explains. "Most criminals would set it aside or leave it on the bed."

Also, "He was smart enough to get rid of the body, put it in an isolated place. I figured he had a high IQ."

Unlike the FBI profilers, he didn't think the UNSUB's first motive was sexual. "In my experience," Smit says, "don't make the crime complicated. It's almost always what it first appears to be. I figured it was a burglary gone bad. I figured she was kidnapped, but I didn't know why."

Smit zeroed in on the window frame fingerprints — very fresh, not degraded at all — that had come back from CBI (Colorado Bureau of Investigation) with no matches. He asked Thomas Carney, a forensic expert with the newly combined city-county Metro Crime Lab, to take a second look.

Carney, a third-generation cop, understood that a failure to match prints stored inside the CBI system did not exhaust the possibilities. All over the world, law enforcement agencies had been installing versions of the Automated Fingerprint Identification System, or AFIS. These digitized databases had lots of advantages and one important drawback: they often weren't integrated with anyone else's fingerprint system, including the FBI's master database. Carney, in fact, was personally familiar with this troublesome kink in the network. He had come to Colorado Springs from Miami, which was the first law enforcement agency in the United States to install AFIS back in 1979.

Since at that time there was no master guide to all the individual AFIS installations, Carney spent about two months compiling his own: a list of all the AFIS systems in North America. He was the first person ever to do so. Ultimately, he identified ninety-two separate systems in the United States, Canada, and Mexico.

Next, he asked the crime lab photographer to make ninety-two sets of black-and-white photographs of the latents taken from the window frame and to mail a set to each AFIS agency. As Lou Smit had noted, the prints themselves were very sharp, really excellent. Carney knew that if the person who left them had ever been arrested and printed, they would find him. He mailed off the packages and waited.

Weeks later, on March 24, 1995, he was standing in his kitchen with his wife when the phone rang. His wife watched anxiously as Carney's expression changed. His eyes welled up with tears.

"What is it?" she asked, fearful that something was seriously wrong.

"We just made a hit on the Heather Church case," he said simply. In his gut, Carney knew at once that the man who left those prints was no ordinary killer. He picked up the phone to make the second call.

At the sheriff's office, Lou Smit, Mark Finley, John Anderson, and the entire detective division were jubilant at Carney's news. There had been two hits in two states, Louisiana and California. Same guy, of course. Robert Charles Browne of 16660 Eastonville Road.

Heather's killer was the Church family's nearest neighbor.

Six

Robert Browne waited a little more than nineteen months before responding to Mark Finley's impatient inside-the-box letter of September 2000. Long silences of this sort would turn out to be a pattern with him.

"Hello Detective Finley," he wrote on May 5, 2002. Browne posed a "hypothetical" question. He wanted to know how quickly a person might be executed after confessing to a homicide committed in El Paso County. "I would appreciate an answer by mail," he added. "No visits. Robert Browne."

Unaware that Browne had broken his two-year silence and that a new letter from him was, in fact, en route to the sheriff's office, the three members of the cold case squad were devising their own plan to contact the killer. They had been thinking very hard about Robert Browne since their meeting at the Heidelberg that same spring. Smit,

Fischer, and Hess reviewed the Church case plus all of the reports generated around the time of Browne's 1995 arrest. They looked at Browne's first two letters from 2000. They talked at length about serial killers; Charlie Hess, in particular, had question after question for Smit on the subject. Then they went to Lieutenant Ken Hilte and Sergeant Brad Shannon for permission to contact the killer.

For Lou Smit, it was an interesting moment of role reversal. Before his retirement as a detective captain, Shannon had worked for him. Hilte had long admired the senior detective. Based on what he'd read so far of Browne's writings, Hilte was doubtful they'd get anywhere with the killer. "We really didn't think Browne was telling us the truth," he recalls. "We didn't believe him. We thought it was an attempt at manipulation, that he was leading us on." On the other hand, "We saw we had nothing to lose by having [them] write him."

Shannon remembers the sheriff's office wanted to see every letter to Browne before it left the building. "We needed to be certain that nothing went out that we didn't want to go out," he says. "There were a few occasions maybe where we said, 'We're not comfortable with this,' but as a general rule they went out as written."

The first letter to Browne went out on May 9, 2002, over Charlie Hess's signature. There were several reasons for choosing Hess as the contact: first, the idea of reaching out to the killer had been his originally; and second, it was believed inside the squad and around the sheriff's office that Hess's experience with the CIA made him best suited to take the lead role. Perhaps most important, Hess — unlike Lou Smit — had no history with Browne. As the public face of the Church investigation, Smit had been widely credited with Browne's arrest, and Browne continued to hold a grudge against him.

Smit, though retired, also had intermittent professional distractions with which to cope, including the continuing and sometimes contentious investigation into Jon-Benét Ramsey's murder in Boulder. Although he'd resigned from the case in 1998, he quietly rejoined the investigation in 2002 and remained an active — though unpaid — investigator for the Boulder district attorney until 2006. Because of these demands on his time and attention, Smit was happy to offer his insights and advice on the letter writing, but preferred to remain behind the scenes. Scott Fischer functioned in a similar way. Plus, he did the typing.

Their first letter crossed Browne's May 5, 2002, note to Finley in the mail.

"Dear Mr. Browne," the letter began. Charlie Hess introduced himself as a "volunteer" who worked on cold cases for the El Paso County Sheriff's Office. But lest Browne mistake "volunteer" for a clerk or typist, Hess devoted the first third of his letter to his background as an FBI agent and then as a CIA agent in Vietnam. He had retired, he wrote, as a polygraph examiner with the San Diego Police Department.

"I must say that I was very intrigued by the correspondence you directed to the District Attorney's Office here," he continued. "The information that you alluded to brings to mind previous high-profile matters I handled and am wondering if you feel it in your interest to grant me an interview."

With this first letter, Hess rejected Finley's confrontational approach to Browne in favor of a more conversational, personal tone. He even threw in a dollop of transparent flattery, noting that "intelligent, unique individuals" were often able to "illuminate matters" that otherwise might remain out of human reach.

Hess also made the unusual decision to give Browne his personal address as a return. Most law enforcement officials would think twice about providing a self-described serial killer with their home address, especially on a letter that might pass through hundreds of hands at Colorado's toughest maximum-security lockup.

It was Hess's theory, however, that if he were to get Browne to open up, he needed to be open, too. He says he never once worried about whether he might be putting himself or his wife in danger.

It was decided that Commander Joseph D. Breister, who was then in charge of the sheriff's investigations division, would answer Browne's May 5, 2002, letter, which arrived shortly after Hess posted his missive. Breister's purpose was twofold. He would address Browne's immediate questions, hopefully to keep the dialogue going, and he would introduce Hess as an agent of the department.

In particular, Breister addressed Browne's "hypothetical" scenario in which the killer had asked how soon someone could be executed if he "identified a murder" and then pleaded guilty "in exchange for a sentence of death."

The investigators surmised that Browne was testing Finley with his hypothetical scenario. But in what way? Was Browne a depressed prisoner who wanted to commit suicide by death penalty? Or was he asking in a very roundabout way whether such a crime would merit the death penalty, hoping, in effect, to learn that execution was unlikely or years away? Or was this just another gambit in his cat-and-mouse game?

Breister played it straight.

"There is no simple answer to your question, but I will synopsize the answers based on a best-case scenario," the commander wrote.

"If the person who committed the murder was hypothetically serving a life sentence for a previous murder, provided credible evidence which led to the discovery of a body and evidence supporting such a crime, represented themselves at trial, pled or was found guilty, was sentenced to death and waived all appeals, the sentence could be fast-tracked and carried out within eighteen months.

"However, before any death sentence is carried out, it is automatically appealed, at least once, to the Colorado Supreme Court," Breister wrote. "This is a best-case scenario."

Then, without specifically naming Hess, Breister told Browne that a letter he had "probably already received" had come from a retired law enforcement officer who worked as a volunteer for the sheriff's office. Mark Finley, Breister added, was no longer with the sheriff's office.

"I thought you should know that he does volunteer his time and reports to me," Breister wrote.

Without saying so directly, Breister had warned Browne that anything he told Hess, Hess would tell the El Paso County Sheriff's Office. It was as close to a Miranda warning as Browne would get for the next four years.

"Hello Charles J. Hess," Browne replied on May 16, 2002. The idea of an interview, he said, was "not acceptable," but letters might be OK.

"What specifically were you intrigued by?" he asked. "What high profile matters were brought to mind? What matters would you like to be illuminated?"

SEVEN

Scott Fischer brought a useful mix of experience and outlook to the cold case squad, beyond his organizational skills, familiarity with computers, and willingness to work as Charlie Hess's typist in their correspondence with Robert Browne.

Fischer was raised with newspaper ink in his blood and crime on his mind. His father, Charles H. Fischer, was publisher of the *Clovis (NM) News Journal,* as well as the civilian head of the New Mexico State Police. "I can remember when I was eight or ten years old, riding up to Santa Fe in a police car, the sirens blowing," Scott recalls.

He started taking sports photos for the *News Journal* as a young boy. In high school, after he'd progressed to snapping every sort of picture for the paper, including traffic accidents and crime stories, the thirty-six-member Clovis Police Department asked him to solve a staff shortcoming by taking photographs for them, too.

"They were forever screwing up crime-scene photos," Fischer says. "So I'd shoot a roll without the body for the newspaper, and then a roll with the body in the picture for the police department."

He found the world of law enforcement deeply appealing — "The most fun I ever had was when I was playing cops" — and soon became a fixture at police headquarters. By the time he attended Eastern New Mexico State University, not far from Clovis, Fischer was a sworn officer, with city-issued gun and badge. He spent one summer running the crime lab for Clovis PD and even went out on patrol for a few weeks.

The county sheriff sent him to crime scene school, where he studied photography, sketching, and fingerprinting. The city police sent him to drug school (operated by the border patrol in El Paso), where he learned to recognize and identify drugs. By the end of his brief career in law enforcement, Fischer was certified as an expert witness both in crime scene investigation and photography.

At age twenty-seven, he succeeded his father at the *News Journal.* From then on, the paper's corporate owners, Freedom Communications, continued to promote him until Scott Fischer was named president of Freedom's newspaper division, as well as a corporate vice president. Three thousand employees reported to him.

Then, in 1998, he jumped off the corporate ladder to become publisher of Freedom's Colorado Springs property, the *Gazette.* All his life he'd wanted to live in Colorado, and now was the chance. But Fischer's tenure at the *Gazette* was brief. In April 2000, he announced his resignation, effectively retiring from the newspaper business at age fifty-five.

Fischer had come to know Anderson, first through his newspaper's coverage of a controversy at the county jail and then as a frequent tablemate on the civic banquet circuit. They had established an immediate rapport. After Fischer announced his retirement in 2000, Anderson invited the now former newspaper publisher to lunch.

"You've been in newspapers your whole life. Is there anything else you enjoyed?" Anderson asked, probing Fischer about his plans for the future.

Fischer found himself talking about his early experiences with police work.

"I always wanted to be a cop," he confided.

"Well, then," Anderson said, "I've got a

job for you. You don't have to work hard, you can set your own hours, and we'll pay you nothing."

Anderson introduced him to Charlie and Lou. Fischer was "completely infatuated," as he describes it, with the older men and the prospect of police work, and he immediately accepted the sheriff's invitation to join the cold case squad.

After a while, however, the sometimes tedious work of assembling and annotating old cases began to feel a bit too sedentary for Fischer. He got itchy, as he says, "to throw somebody on the ground and put cuffs on them," so he enrolled himself in the sheriff's academy in order to become a reserve officer.

The deputy training suited Fischer's inner daredevil. He has a private pilot's license and was an avid motorcyclist until a serious crash and his wife's objections put that pastime on ice. A fitness buff, the bespectacled newspaperman eagerly tackled the rigorous physical training designed for men thirty years his junior. It nearly finished him off, especially the part where the lieutenant drops on top of the recruit and says, "I'm going to choke you out. You have forty-five seconds to get me off." Somehow, Fischer did.

As a reserve officer, he pulled regular patrols, in uniform, and made his share of collars. What sometimes annoyed his superiors was his approach to speeding. Scott Fischer tends to overlook it.

"I am not a good driver," he says cheerily. "I tend to speed. And I will not write a ticket for someone who drives the same, or better than I do. You've really got to break the law in my book. If you're not doing fifteen miles over the limit in a forty zone, I won't even look at it."

Fischer, like Lou Smit, is a hard-nosed cop, disinclined to cut tiga-gatas like Robert Browne any slack. Charlie Hess brought a different sensibility to the cold case squad.

Hess was born in 1927 in the Chicago suburb of Cicero, then the most infamously corrupt mobster haven in America and the base of Al Capone's operations. Hess jokes that back in 1952 when he applied for work as an FBI agent, J. Edgar Hoover must not have noticed the birthplace entry on his job form.

Like Lou Smit, Hess is a Navy veteran with a varied résumé. He's taught school, coached basketball and football, and operated his own private investigation outfit on a couple of occasions. When a friend was elected mayor of Industrial City, California, Hess went to work as city manager.

But his most interesting professional interlude probably was spent in Vietnam. As Hess tells the story, he went to southeast Asia in the 1960s as a civilian aide to John Paul Vann (a former U.S. Army officer celebrated for alerting reporters to the failures in the U.S. military's performance in Vietnam, a story brilliantly retold by journalist Neil Sheehan in his Pulitzer Prize–winning book, *A Bright Shining Lie*). While in South Vietnam, Hess transferred into the Phoenix Program, which employed an array of covert means (including assassinations) to help pacify regions of the country; according to Hess, his duties included overseeing efforts to persuade enemy leaders to become double agents.

The old warrior has been banged up a few times over the decades. He has weathered several health scares, but he credits his durability in part to an extended retreat to the Baja peninsula he took in the late 1970s with his second wife, Jo. He told reporter Pam Zubeck of the *Gazette* that he and Jo built themselves a modest house on the Mexican coast and lived simply and happily, fishing and exploring and enjoying the region's serene isolation for several years.

Ultimately, however, Jo's concern for his weak heart led them back to civilization, he told the *Gazette*. In the event he suffered another attack, Mrs. Hess worried that she might not be strong enough to start up their boat's outboard motor to get him to medical treatment.

Along with his hand grenade and CIA performance evaluation, Hess also displayed in the cold case squad room "The Test of a Man," a poem he wrote in 1950 that celebrates various manly virtues. The hairy-chested rhyme might serve as Charlie Hess's credo. But experience has taught Hess other lessons, too.

Shortly past ten on the evening of December 23, 1991, his forty-year-old son-in-law, Steven Vought, received an emergency telephone call from his son, Steve Jr., who — along with a couple of friends, Ryan Bartos and William Sparks — had just driven past his uncle Don Vought's house on Peaceful Valley Road in an unincorporated part of El Paso County, southeast of the Springs. The three friends had seen Don Vought's garage door closing when they knew no one should be in the house. Uncle Don was out of town.

Steven rushed over to his brother's place. His son, Bartos, and Sparks followed close behind in their car. When they pulled up in front of the house, they saw Steve's father run into the now-open garage. Just as they started toward the house themselves, Steven Vought emerged from the front door, shouting, "They shot me! Get out of the way! Run!" Then he collapsed. Gravely injured by bullets to his left arm and abdomen, Vought was evacuated by helicopter to a nearby hospital where he was pronounced dead shortly after midnight on Christmas eve.

Charlie and Jo Hess flew immediately to Colorado Springs to be with their stricken daughter, Candice, and her family.

One of the three suspects in the robbery-homicide, seventeen-year-old Adam Cooper, was picked up the night of Steven Vought's murder and later confessed to his role in the crime. Cooper's accomplices, Thomas DeGraffe and William Clinton Mangham, also both seventeen years old, turned themselves in on Christmas Day. All three eventually pleaded guilty. Cooper and DeGraffe received twenty-year prison sentences; Mangham was sentenced to forty-eight years in prison.

The Hesses subsequently moved to the area in order to be near their daughter and grandchildren. Three years later, Charlie met and befriended John Anderson when Candy Vought managed Anderson's first successful run for sheriff.

The shock of losing someone dear so suddenly and senselessly is permanent; it leaves a psychic scar that never heals completely. When the cause of death is murder, the survivor's pain is compounded by the often slow, fitful, flawed, and sometimes failed process of finding justice and discovering the truth.

Charlie and his family endured just such an ordeal. His son-in-law's killer went to prison, as did his two associates, but keeping them there has required time, money, work, and constant, enervating vigilance. Inevitably, the ordeal colored his approach toward handling cold cases.

"Charlie had a little different take on what he wanted to accomplish," Fischer recalls. "Because of his past experience, if someone was already in jail, doing time, he became an advocate for, 'Let's just get these things cleared up. Give 'em a letter saying they won't be prosecuted if they'll tell us where the body's at.' He was far more interested in telling the survivors what had happened to their loved one than he was in adding to the misery of somebody in jail."

As Fischer recalls, Hess frequently cited

Ted Bundy as an example of how not to handle an incarcerated killer who is ready to tell his story. Bundy, the handsome, articulate, onetime law student and Republican campaign worker from the state of Washington, is believed to have murdered approximately thirty young women from Seattle to Tallahassee, Florida, during the 1970s. In 1989, with his death warrant signed and the clock ticking toward electrocution, Bundy suddenly started giving up cases to detectives he summoned from law enforcement agencies all over the West. He hoped to trade information for a delay of his date with Old Sparky at the Florida State Prison, characterizing himself as a unique trove of information not only about his own crimes, but also the minds of deviant offenders in general. Like many such criminals, among whom narcissism is quite common, Bundy felt he had much of importance to say. However, neither the governor nor any of the detectives who came to Florida to talk to Bundy spoke up for his proposal. Most said the victims' survivors wanted Ted dead as soon as possible. Most doubted that Bundy had much more to share in any event. He was electrocuted on schedule.

"If they hadn't executed him," Hess often

insisted to his fellow cold case squad members, "we might still be solving murders."

Fischer remembers that he and Smit at first balked at the idea of giving Robert Browne any sort of special treatment in return for what he might know. Seeking justice was one thing; trading favors with a killer was another. "At times, it got a little testy," he says. "You can imagine Lou Smit would just as soon see him get the needle. I tended to go in that direction, too."

Hess continued to argue that the information Browne might share was more valuable to his victims' survivors than any satisfaction they might derive from his execution. Smit and Fischer finally decided to go along. "Lou said basically he wasn't going to do anything to make life any easier for Browne," Fischer explains. "But he understood Charlie's point of view and certainly would hold no animosity if Charlie wished to pursue that. From that point on, we all discussed everything before we did it."

EIGHT

Foremost in everyone's mind in March 1995 had been the fragility of the case against Browne. There was a pair of his fingerprints on the Churches' master bedroom window frame, and that was it. Nothing more to tie him to the house or to the homicide. If he offered any sort of innocent explanation for the prints — say, he could have left them while doing some handiwork around the Church place — the whole prosecution would go into the toilet.

Accordingly, Lou Smit and his detectives cooked up a subterfuge. First, they rigged the dashboard of an old truck with a video camera, then positioned the vehicle at a construction site about half a mile from Browne's trailer so as to continuously monitor his comings and goings.

They planned to send Mark Finley, along with several other detectives, into Browne's neighborhood on foot to knock on doors and interview people as part of a mock canvass. Their mission would look routine enough to anyone, just some deputies out knocking on doors and asking questions.

If everything went according to plan, Finley and Hodges would make their unhurried way to Browne's front door, explain that the department was revisiting the Church case, and would he answer a couple of questions? Before their prime suspect could decline, they'd get to the point: *Have you ever been on the Church property?*

"If he said no — bingo! — that's what we wanted," says Smit. "We were going to arrest him."

But the plan unraveled even before Finley and Hodges arrived on the scene. As everyone was taking their places, Browne suddenly strode from his front door, jumped in his pickup, and headed for town.

Driving toward Eastonville Road, Smit and Sheriff Anderson were faced with a snap decision. "If we arrest him and he lawyers up, we're in trouble," Smit explains. "So do we arrest him right away and give him all that time to think on the way to the police station?"

The answer was no. They followed Browne to downtown Colorado Springs, where he stopped to shop at Meininger Art Supply.

Smit radioed detectives Finley and Hodges to be waiting in front of the store, only blocks from the sheriff's office, to arrest Browne when he came out.

There's no telling how a subject will respond to an arrest; if Browne were packing, he could very well start shooting. To their relief, Smit and Anderson arrived just in time to watch the very routine-looking collar occur at ten seventeen in the morning, according to Finley's later police report. Within ten minutes, Browne was seated in a sheriff's office interview room with Finley and Hodges. Textured soundproofing material lined the walls. The video camera behind the room's one-way mirror began rolling at ten twenty-six a.m., March 28, 1995.

Since Browne had surfaced as their prime suspect only four days before, Finley had not had time to build much of a dossier on him. The detective had paid a brief visit to Browne's hometown, Coushatta, Louisiana, and knew from his suspect's arrest record that he'd been convicted of burglary and once did hard time for stealing a vehicle. During the interview, Browne would discourage discussion of either crime. Finley had also gathered what information he could by telephone with authorities in

Coushatta. Still, Detective Finley had only the sketchiest mental picture of the surprisingly unruffled tree farmer seated across a small table from him, dressed in jeans and a white T-shirt under a New Orleans Saints windbreaker.

Robert Browne was certainly an unusual murder suspect. Though his head snapped when Finley showed him the arrest warrant for homicide, he never betrayed a hint of indignation, confusion, defiance, or remorse. When at one point Browne volunteered, "I am not a calm person," Finley replied, "You look like a pretty calm guy to me, Robert."

Browne was responsive and respectful throughout and spoke in full, mostly grammatical sentences. Strangest of all, he would endure a full six hours of questioning before finally asking to see a lawyer.

Finley took off his suit coat for the interview but kept his tie in place and his shirt sleeves unrolled. Experienced interviewers understand that business dress conveys significantly more authority than a casual look. Finley smoked menthol cigarettes and fetched a pack of Marlboro Light 100s for Browne. Both men consumed several cups of black coffee.

The point of the exercise, of course, was

to elicit from Browne the full facts of Heather's death. The sheriff's investigators needed to know if he had an accomplice, for example, but they had other concerns in mind as well. Though there was no doubt that Robert Browne had left his prints on the Churches' bedroom window frame, twelve jurors might well expect more evidence than that to find him guilty of murder beyond a reasonable doubt. Since there was no other physical or circumstantial evidence connecting Browne to Heather Church, a confession would come in very handy.

The men discussed Browne's family, beginning with his father, Ronald, who had been a sharecropper, a school janitor, and finally a sheriff's deputy. As Robert told the story, his ancestors first came to the New World from England in the 1630s, and "ended up being plantation owners in Louisiana." He said his father had once been prosperous as well, the owner of several thousand acres of ranch and dairy land that he somehow lost when Robert was four or five. Finley didn't press for details of the episode.

Robert explained that he was the youngest of Ronald and Beulah Browne's nine children, all born within nine years. Six of the kids were twins. The oldest child was sister Virginia, born in 1943. Two years later came Mary. Two years after that, Ronald and Donald. After only eleven months, Ruby and Ray. Two years more, Will and Vera. Robert was born two and a half years later, on Halloween 1952.

The Brownes apparently were not strict parents, although Ronald Sr. occasionally took his belt to the children, according to Robert. "There was very little control at home," he said. "Probably not enough."

Detective Hodges joined Finley in the interview room. She would try the good cop role with sympathetic, personal questions. Her presence also permitted Finley to leave the room from time to time, occasionally to confer with the sheriff's officers, who at that moment were tossing Browne's trailer.

Was it tough being the youngest? Detective Hodges had asked.

"Being youngest can be hell," he answered. "It rolls downhill, and you're the youngest." Although there's no evidence for it, Browne consistently described his childhood as a succession of horrors and humiliations suffered at the hands of his older siblings, and tacitly condoned by his mother.

They reviewed Browne's marital history, which began with his wedding to thirteen-year-old Terry Laverne Ward of Coushatta in 1970, when he was seventeen years old, and had since progressed to his fifth and then-current wife, Diane Marcia Babbitts, whom he had married in Colorado Springs in 1988. Before Babbitts, the longest any of his marriages lasted had been four years. Hodges asked why.

"I don't think there ever was any deep involvement," said Browne, who had trouble recalling most of his ex-wives' names. The only exception was wife number two, Tuyet Minh Huynh, a Vietnamese immigrant. She was mother of his one child, Thomas, who was born in 1974.

"Only reason there was a marriage in the first place was hot sex," he went on. "That fizzles after a while if you don't have anything else." The durability of his almost-seven-year marriage to Babbitts proved the point. "She's calm. She's rational," he said. "There's not all these uncontrolled emotions going all the time."

Calm would not characterize Diane Browne later that day when she learned her husband had been arrested for murdering their neighbor's child, Heather Church.

Did Browne attend church? Finley wanted to know.

Yes, as a child, he said. "But puberty kinda took that outta my mind."

He repeatedly described himself as a loner.

"I'm almost a hermit, not quite. I could become a hermit pretty easily if I had a chance."

"Don't like people?" Finley asked.

"I like certain people at certain times," Browne replied. "It's just an effort to deal with people."

Later, he returned to the subject.

"I'm not close with nobody."

"Don't have any buddies?"

"No."

This need for distance extended even to his family, he explained. Older brother Ronald, for example, also lived in Colorado Springs at the time, yet Browne said he saw Ronald rarely, usually on holidays, and couldn't remember his address.

Browne repeatedly denied ever having been to the Church house for any purpose whatsoever. The closest he ever came, he said, was about a month after the young girl's disappearance when he gave a florist delivery truck driver a tow out of the Churches' snowed-in driveway. Finley made sure to cover this subject thoroughly. He didn't want Browne to later invent some innocent explanation for the prints.

Browne also denied owning any firearms — which was illegal for a convicted felon —

even though he knew deputies probably were searching his trailer house and would certainly find abundant guns and ammo. The seized firearms included a Model 57 Marlin .22 Magnum lever-action rifle; a Model 1022 Ruger rifle, plus a Ruger bolt-action 2.32; a Czech-made .22; a Browning twelve-gauge shotgun; and a large amount of ammunition.

Finley asked about kiddie videos discovered in the trailer. They belonged to his wife, Browne said. She had a weakness for Disney fare. There was no discussion about the pornographic movies or the bag of children's clothing and the jewelry also discovered in the trailer.

About an hour into the interview, Finley decided to bring up the fingerprint evidence. He briefly told Browne of receiving positive fingerprint hits from Louisiana and California and the special care that was taken to be certain of the match.

"Two of your fingerprints match the latents we picked up out there at the scene," Finley told him.

"Well," Browne replied without a flicker of hesitation, "you're gonna hafta check 'em again."

"Wait a minute!" Finley said, as if Browne hadn't heard him. "Three court-certified people, fingerprint analysts down there [in Louisiana] directly compared the latent fingerprints to your fingerprints."

He held up both his hands.

"It's this index finger and this index finger," Finley explained. "Not only that, then they mailed me their inked finger-prints, and we took them over to the lab and had an expert there take a look at those and compare them to the actual lifts that were done — same two fingers.

"In the meantime, the prints got out there to California, where apparently you were picked up and they brought you back to Louisiana. Their fingerprint system does the same thing. *Ba-bing!!* on your fingerprints. Why are your fingerprints out there, Rob-ert?"

"My fingerprints aren't out there," Browne answered evenly.

"I am guaranteeing you that I'm not lying to you," said Finley adamantly. "Your fingerprints are there. Do you want me to show you the document that identified your fingerprints?"

"What I want you to do," Browne said, "is fingerprint me again and have someone who knows what they're doing compare."

"We've had four people who know what they're doing compare."

"Then you need to do it again. These are the same fingerprints I've had all my life."

"We don't argue about that."

"Fingerprint me again, and check what's on me with what you find. That's all I ask."

"Believe me, Robert. It's your fingerprints. We wouldn't have had them checked that many times and have everybody be wrong. It's your fingerprints that are there at the house."

"Check again. There's no way. No way."

Browne seemed so certain that his fingerprints could not be on the frame — and so genuinely surprised when it was proven otherwise — that sheriff's investigators, including Lou Smit, later surmised that his certainity was based on the fact that he probably had worn gloves the night he abducted Heather Church. He may have removed his gloves to pry the slender window frame off its track and then forgotten that he had done so. More likely, Smit believes, Browne came by the house at least once before to reconnoiter and left the telltale prints then.

He had several possible motives for taking an interest in the Church house. Browne may have been a peeper. Deviant offenders characteristically exhibit multiple paraphilias, or perversions, as they once were known. These include such practices as placing obscene phone calls, flashing, picquerism (sexual gratification through rapid, repeated stabbing), necrophilia, and voyeurism, which is quite common among deviant offenders. While his initial interest in the Church house possibly was burglary, as Lou Smit surmises, Browne was almost certainly aware that a young girl lived there: Heather and her brothers waited for the school bus at the corner near their house every weekday morning.

Thieves and deviant offenders also frequently conduct scouting missions for the practical purpose of checking out the inhabitants' comings and goings, as well as points of entry and exit. Among sexual criminals, there can be an added motive: for some deviants, to surreptitiously enter a would-be victim's place of safety and then to occupy it undetected — often to stand silently over a sleeping form before departing, still undetected — stokes deep fantasies of God-like omnipotence. It is not a rare phenomenon. Bundy did it.

Another unexplained detail of the case was a smooth river rock discovered inside the Churches' house the morning after Heather disappeared. No one in the family recognized the stone. District Attorney John

Suthers told the *Gazette* that similar rocks were found inside Browne's trailer, piled up on a counter near the telephone. There was loose speculation about the rock's significance, if any, but no definitive explanations.

In the interrogation room, Mark Finley steered the conversation away from the print evidence until about 1:30 in the afternoon, when he handed Browne the typewritten report to read. Finley was three hours into the interview, and so far, Browne had been calm and cooperative if disbelieving of what the detective told him. Remarkably, he had not asked for a lawyer but had continued to talk, even after presented with the fingerprint evidence.

"It don't seem real," Browne said as he studied the pages. "It don't seem real. It's all too real. I know that. But it don't seem real."

"It is real, Robert," Finley said, reminding Browne that *his* prints were found on the frame, no one else's. "There's got to be an explanation. In time we'll find it, and it's not what you're saying."

Nevertheless, the sheriff's office gave way to Browne's insistence and brought a fingerprint analyst over to roll his fingers once more, and to take his palm prints as well. At the same time, Finley asked him if he'd take a lie detector test.

"Let me think about it," said the suspect. "I don't know if I trust those things or not." An hour later, polygraph examiner Danny Riley came into the room with his machine. "I'm the best damn examiner in this state, as far as I'm concerned," Riley told Browne by way of introduction. "I'll know after this test if you're being truthful with me." Riley also advised Browne not to agree to the test if he was guilty.

It was a fairly transparent ploy that apparently worked. Browne was experienced and smart enough to know that he should refuse to take the test; an attorney would not have let him do it. Nevertheless, and in spite of Riley's caution, Browne underwent the examination. Perhaps he thought he could outsmart it.

Afterward, Riley delivered the bad news. "I know based on those charts that you're not being a hundred percent with me," he said and added that the newly inked fingerprints had come back positive, too.

Speaking loudly and forcefully, the examiner tried to seize the initiative with Browne, hoping that at this low moment he'd crumble into a confession. Riley said that he'd met some stone killers in his work, but in his opinion, "You're not that type of guy.

Something happened out there that made you do what you did. Something happened. You're not that type of person, OK? *Listen,* if I thought you were, partner, I wouldn't even have come back in here. I'd have left."

Browne made no response.

"Robert," Riley went on, "I'll tell you what I think happened. I think you went in there to take something, or went in there to look around, and she was there. And I think it probably scared you if nothing else. I know it would me. Then something snapped.

"I've seen that many, many times in my career. The person tells me afterwards, 'Hey, I didn't mean to do what happened.' And I believe him, sincerely, OK? If I didn't think you were that type of guy, partner, I would never have walked back in this door. I would have kept going. That's why I'm here right now. I'm here for one person. His name's Robert Browne."

Still nothing.

"You're gonna have to tell me the truth, goddamn it!" said Riley, his voice rising a notch. "The truth will reign, Robert."

"Apparently not," Browne replied quietly.

"Oh, it will." Riley persisted. "Tell me what happened out there."

"There's nothing to argue about."

"I'm not arguing with you. I'm trying to

help you, OK?"

Browne wasn't buying.

"I knew I shouldn't have taken that damn test," he said.

"No, you should have. You know why you did?"

"Because I was —"

"Because you *care.* It's because you care."

At about 4:30 p.m., Browne finally aborted the discussion.

"I should have asked for a lawyer before I agreed to take that," he said, glancing at Riley's machine.

"Listen —"

"I want a lawyer. You gotta do what you gotta do, but it went against my better judgment by agreeing to that. So now I need a lawyer. Obviously, if that thing said I lied, I need a lawyer. There's no other choice."

Riley, who had taken the precaution of reading Browne his Miranda rights before the polygraph examination, realized that Browne now was leaving him no choice.

"OK," he said, "I'll go talk to the people."

Left alone in the interview room, Browne lit a cigarette and puffed on it disconsolately, surprise and despair in his eyes. Then he buried his head in his hands and slumped onto the table, silent and unmoving.

A few minutes later, Detective Finley, now

wearing his suit coat, purposefully strode back into the interview room.

"Howdy, partner!" he said. "You want another cigarette? That's the last one you're gonna have."

NINE

Charlie Hess wrote Browne again on June 11, 2002. He immediately set about trying to build rapport with the killer. Browne had spent time in Vietnam; so had Hess. Perhaps their separate experiences in Southeast Asia would provide enough common ground to develop a regular correspondence.

Hess also knew enough about Browne's military career to know that the killer had received several commendations, including a Bronze Star for service in Vietnam in 1972. By merely mentioning the Bronze Star, Hess could stroke the killer's ego *and* let him know that he had done his homework.

Hess told Browne that he had directed the CIA Phoenix program in III Corps, spending most of his time "in Cu Chi, Tay Ninh, and Long An: headquarters in Bien Hoa." The investigator added that he, however, had not earned a Bronze Star. "A worthy accomplishment," Hess wrote.

He continued that he was "intrigued by the unique manner in which you originally chose to communicate, the map, the poetic verse, etc." He was, he said, reminded of Ted Bundy, Henry Lucas, and other killers who had carried on dialogues with authorities.

"It did appear," he wrote, "that you wished to provide details, by virtue of the information you provided. I feel you do have a desire to clear up some pending matters."

Hess hoped he might lure Browne into a personal dialogue from which, eventually, would flow hard facts, possibly to confirm the astonishing assertions of Browne's verse, letter, and map of March 30, 2000. There was the taunt, *the score is you one. The other team forty-eight,"* which suggested Browne was claiming to have committed forty-eight murders. And then there was the cryptic poem: *"The seven sacred virgins, entombed side by side / Those less worthy, are scattered wide."*

Browne's reference in his verse to "caressing mire" and the need to drain the grave framed the cold case squad's central dilemma. Had this inmate in fact murdered seven young girls and consigned them, one by one — or all at once — to some watery grave in Colorado? What of the forty-one other victims? Or was he simply weaving a tapestry of lies, or half-lies and half-truths? There were no easy answers to these questions.

Presuming that Browne in fact had committed these murders as he alleged, how could Charlie Hess draw him into a discussion? If he was telling the truth, Robert Browne was, by definition, a remorseless sociopath incapable of guilt or empathy — although, like most sociopaths, he could fake it when necessary. His victims had significance to him only as objects, not as people.

There is no foolproof way to engage such a criminal, one who approaches all relationships as a contest for power. It is possible in some cases to exploit their grandiosity and paranoia. Or they might be willing to trade information, as Bundy unsuccessfully tried to do to save his life.

Charlie Hess hoped he could appeal to Browne's conscience.

He wrote of his son-in-law Steve Vought's murder, and that while "the void . . . can never be filled," he had found "there is great solace in closure." His mission, Hess said, was to help others find closure, too. He suggested that maybe Browne also would "experience a form of relief" by providing details about the murders he hinted at.

"Perhaps we both can achieve our goals," Hess concluded. "Mine, closure. Yours?"

TEN

Even before Detective Finley concluded his arrest interview with Robert Browne that March morning in 1995, a portrait of a deeply disturbed and dangerous individual was emerging from the search of Browne's trailer. As the picture gradually came into focus, the more worrisome Robert Charles Browne looked.

Besides all the guns and ammo, X-rated videos, and the pillowcase containing girls' clothes and jewelry, deputies found a collection of newspaper stories about the Church case and a stolen Bobcat mini earthmover worth $18,000. Robert's wife Diane told investigators he had first used the Bobcat to dig a big hole, then buried the machine in it. They also recovered electronic equipment and personal effects belonging to a local family who had lost their house to arson two weeks previously and whose dog had been poisoned with strychnine. Browne kept a supply of strychnine handy, allegedly to control tree-farm pests.

Among his papers they found an August 1993 contract from a Colorado Springs pawn shop, indicating that he had received $1,000 for a $6,000 necklace and set of matching earrings that had belonged to his wife. Diane Browne's mother gave the jewelry to her daughter when Diane married Browne in 1988. Diane later explained to investigators that when she noticed the jewelry was missing and asked her husband about it, he suggested that a houseguest must have taken it.

The searchers also noted with interest an insurance policy on Diane's life. It paid up to $120,000 — and double that amount if she died accidentally. Mrs. Browne told detectives she originally planned to make Robert a fifty-fifty beneficiary with her adoptive daughter, then twenty-three years old. But in the last year her husband had repeatedly pressured her to make him the sole beneficiary. He promised to take care of her daughter in the event Diane died. In the end, she relented.

The sheriff's department later concluded that Browne's keen interest in his wife's insurance was connected to one of the numerous hidden corners of his life. For an unknown period of time, perhaps months, he had been conducting an AOL chat room romance with a single mother. A search of his computer turned up pages of dialogue between Browne and QT*, most of it sexually suggestive.

On March 22, six days before his arrest, Robert and QT talked of exchanging their photographs. QT fretted that Browne might not like her picture, that he might already think she was "ugly and desperate." But she urged him to send her his photograph "right now."

In part of the exchange, QT talked of how he had aroused her and of mailing her fluids to her virtual lover.

RC Browne: Transporting it across state lines could be a misdemeanor.

QT: Sweetie, I insist . . .

RC Browne: Do you know hat [sic] a misdemeanor is??????

QT: What is a misdemeanor?

RC Browne: Da more I miss da meaner I get.

QT: I like that!!!!

Browne suggested that QT deliver her

* Denotes a pseudonym.

package in person. She said she knew the way to Colorado Springs, and then teased that the road "goes both ways."

Acknowledging the implied invitation, Browne asked, "Do your kids know you met a pervert on AOL?"

Much of the rest of the conversation was devoted to her travails as a single parent. Browne sympathized. "How did the kids beat up on you today?" he asked at one point. When QT said she was drained from giving to her children, Browne replied, "That's called being a parent."

According to investigators, the art supplies Browne purchased at Meininger on the morning of his arrest weren't for Diane, as he told Finley. It was cartooning gear, probably meant for his online girlfriend's son.

Soon after his arrest interview with Browne, Mark Finley was dispatched once again to Browne's hometown of Coushatta, Louisiana, in search of anything that might help flesh out El Paso County's so far meager dossier on their killer. With the fingerprints on the window screen being their only evidence to connect Browne to the murder of Heather Church, sheriffs' investigators were looking for anything that might strengthen their case. Though it seemed unlikely, they theorized that Browne might have confessed his crime to a family member or close friend. His former wives, too, might be able to shed light on his psyche — or so investigators hoped.

At first, Finley found the residents of Coushatta, the tiny seat of Red River Parish, closemouthed and openly dubious that their native son could have kidnapped and murdered a young girl in Colorado.

The town of 2,500 people, many of whom are related by blood or marriage, sits amidst humid cypress swamps, ancient oxbows, "chutes" — a local term for fast-running streams — and exceptionally rich farmland on the left bank of the Red River, about forty-five miles south of Shreveport. Founded during the Reconstruction and named after an Indian tribe, Coushatta has struggled with the loss of farming and manufacturing jobs in recent years. A local hospital, two sawmills, and the yellow pine tree farms that feed the mills are almost all that is left of the town's employment base. Sunbeam's Coushatta appliance assembly plant, where Robert Browne once worked, closed years ago, taking 700 jobs from the local economy. Most of the small businesses, too, have disappeared, leaving the low-slung brick storefronts in the block-long downtown boarded up and empty.

Red River Parish is poor, even for a state that perennially ranks among the poorest in the country — a fact that local law enforcement officers cite when explaining why modern crime-fighting technology is in short supply. Parish voters only approved funding for an enhanced 911 system during the last election, becoming the last jurisdiction in Louisiana to do so.

The crime rate has remained relatively low, except for those years in the 1970s and 1980s when cocaine came to town, along with crystal methamphetamine. Robert Browne would be part of that problem. And though homicides in Red River Parish are relatively few, Coushatta has witnessed some shockingly brutal killings and bizarre suicides, including two such deaths in Browne's own family.

Robert Charles Browne may have claimed descent from a long line of Louisiana planters during his interrogation — a boast no one ever substantiated — but the earliest Browne family recollection anyone in Coushatta shared with Mark Finley was of Browne's maternal grandfather, Melvin J. Bamburg. Finley found that Sheriff Buddy

Huckabay knew the Browne family well; he'd served as a deputy sheriff with Robert's father in the early 1960s and was personally acquainted with both Robert and his older brother Donald, a former state policeman. Huckabay told the Colorado detective that Browne's grandfather was mentally unstable. He'd once dug himself a cave under the family house. Bamburg, a retired farmer, later committed suicide on New Year's Eve 1961. Robert was then eight years old.

Under the headline, "Melvin Bamburg Takes Own Life in Well on Sunday," the January 4, 1962, edition of the weekly *Coushatta Citizen* reported that Bamburg, sixty-seven, had scribbled a note to his wife, Ettress, telling her where to find his body, then draped himself in a length of heavy logging chain and jumped down his twenty-seven-foot water well.

Macabre misfortune struck the family again on September 19, 1963, when the stabbed, dismembered, sexually mutilated, and partially incinerated remains of Earlene Bamburg, Melvin's thirty-six-year-old daughter-in-law and Robert's aunt, were found in her burned-out house near Coushatta. Mrs. Bamburg's killer, a sailor named Clyde Giddens who had once been married to her niece, was sentenced to life in prison and sent to Louisiana's maximum security prison at Angola.

Raymond Browne, an accountant and one of Robert's older brothers, reported that as the youngest child in the family, Robert was often excluded from the older children's activities, which he deeply resented. Raymond conceded that Robert took some teasing, but nothing extraordinary for a family of nine kids. He remembered that on one occasion when Robert was eight or nine, his older brothers had prevented him from tagging along with them by stripping Robert and throwing his clothes up into a high branch of a pine tree.

Ray also claimed that Robert was the brightest child in the family.

His sister Mary, seven years older than Robert, agreed with Ray that the youngest member of the family always seemed to hold a grudge against the rest of them. She told Finley that puberty hit her little brother hard. "She recalled her mother saying Robert felt like he should have everything," the detective wrote, "that they could not give him enough to please him."

Two of Browne's ex-wives would later tell investigators that Robert's mother was emotionally troubled, like her father, Melvin

Bamberg, and given to fits of rage, a description Robert himself confirmed. His mother would on occasion "go off," he told investigators. She once came after him with a knife.

Browne's first wife, Terry Ward, was a petite, thirteen-year-old redhead with freckles when they married in Coushatta in September 1970. Robert, a laconic, lanky serviceman home on leave, wasn't quite eighteen. Terry recalled Robert to Detective Hodges in 1995 somewhat more fondly than his other ex-wives, though Terry, too, had witnessed the "scary side" of her husband. According to an investigative report, Terry told Hodges that Browne never hit her, though he angered quickly, punched objects, and once teasingly dangled her over the side of a hotel balcony.

Overall, though, Terry spent little time with her husband, Hodges reported. Two days after their marriage, Browne shipped out for Vietnam. When she next saw him the following February — Browne in truth had returned in January to Texas but had kept his presence a secret for several weeks — he was changed in ways she could not articulate.

As Hodges reported, Browne had taken an apartment in San Antonio, where Terry joined him. He told Terry that he didn't love her anymore, but that he didn't want to give her up altogether, either. So Terry was to be his daytime wife, responsible for domestic chores. But at night he would leave to see a "girlfriend." According to Hodges' report, Terry believed her husband's girlfriend to be an Asian woman whose picture she found among his possessions in a closet.

They divorced in 1973. The next and last time Terry saw her ex-husband was at his father's 1976 funeral. He was then the same "friendly Robert," she recalled.

Browne met his second wife, Vietnam-born Tuyet Minh Huynh, in San Antonio and married her in October 1973. A son, Thomas, was born in July 1974. By this time, Robert had reenlisted and returned to Vietnam, where he served as a clerk typist, legal clerk, and claims investigator, rising to the rank of E-6. He saw little or no combat. Colorado investigators did not interview Tuyet, whom they were unable to locate during the brief period between Browne's arrest and subsequent guilty plea.

This marriage might have lasted, Browne would later say, but after he shipped out to Germany in 1975, Tuyet, who'd remained behind in San Antonio, informed him that she wanted a divorce. It became final in 1976.

According to available records, Browne was an exemplary soldier from his enlistment in 1969 until his marriage to Tuyet disintegrated. He was awarded the Bronze Star for "outstanding service in connection with military operations against a hostile force" on September 21, 1972. He also received Good Conduct medals for "exemplary behavior, efficiency and fidelity" in June 1973 and October 1975.

While posted in Germany, Browne met the wife of another serviceman, when they both were members of a military theater group. Marjorie Miller[*] and Robert became intimate; she left her husband for him. Marjorie subsequently departed Germany for the Colorado Springs suburb of Manitou Springs with her young daughter and son.

In spring 1976, Browne began actively working for a discharge. He stopped making his bed; his regular drug tests came back positive. When his supervising officers tried to counsel him, Browne defiantly admitted his drug use and said that he had no intention of stopping. The drugs, he later said,

* Denotes a pseudonym.

were part of a campaign to get out of the military, and he did not in fact have a drug use problem. Whatever the case, it worked.

He was discharged on July 12, 1976, and barred from reenlisting. Back in the States, his first stop was Manitou Springs and Marjorie Miller. After he was given custody of Thomas in early 1977, Miller acted as the boy's surrogate mother until May of that year, when Robert and Thomas returned together to Coushatta.

A short while later, it was decided that Thomas needed a more stable environment, so the boy went to live with his aunt Mary and her family in Tennessee, where he was raised.

Browne married wife number three, Brenda Gayle Ware, in September 1977. A pretty, soft-spoken, slightly built brunette with bright blue eyes and a shy smile, Brenda, then just seventeen, was finishing her senior year in high school when she met Robert, then twenty-four, at a Coushatta drive-in. She, too, recalled him as charming — in the beginning — and bright. Extremely bright.

Ware, wrote Mark Finley in his 1995 report of their conversation, "described Robert Browne as being crazy, but not to the point of not knowing what he was doing. She advised that she did not know he was a lunatic until she was married to him. [She] stated, 'He's smooth, like Jekyll and Hyde.' She recalled that Robert Browne had once threatened to chop her up and bury her."

Finley reported that Ware said that Browne always carried a knife in his boot and would explode at "little bitty things," like the time he beat her for failing to put a spoon in the gravy.

After two years of nearly constant abuse — exacerbated by Browne's use of hashish, amphetamines, downers, and possibly LSD — Brenda Ware told the detective that she found the desperate courage to move out.

During the one-year separation then required by Louisiana law in advance of a final divorce, Browne once arrived unannounced at her door as she was speaking on the telephone. According to the detective's report, Ware said that Browne demanded to know who she was dating. He struck her in the face, leaving one of her eyes swollen shut, and departed.

Browne then returned, brandishing a handgun, and abducted her in the orange Ford Fiesta he was driving at the time. Robert took Brenda to a remote waterway known as the Cannon Slough. She remembered he said that if he couldn't have her, no one could. Brenda was absolutely certain she was about to die.

At the Cannon Slough he began beating her fiercely, Ware told Finley. The detective reported that Brenda could not remember how she survived the attack or was able to get back to town.

"She advised that she had blocked out a considerable portion of her memory of this incident," Finley reported.

Brenda told Finley that she filled out a police report, but that no one would pick up her estranged husband. Ware finally sought help from a state senator, who made sure Robert was picked up. Local law enforcement officials say they have no record of the incident.

Brenda told Finley that Browne had bragged that he was an expert arsonist, capable of rigging a hot water heater to start a fire that looked every bit like an accident. While they were separated, a house they once shared where she still stored many of her belongings, including her hope chest, burned completely. Brenda was certain Robert had torched the place.

Their divorce came through in 1980, and Brenda moved on, although she remained terrified of Robert.

"He's the devil's right-hand man," she told Finley. "Call me when you pull the switch."

Browne married his fourth wife, Rita Coleman, a diminutive blond, in October 1980, the same day his divorce from Brenda became final.

"A week after they had been married, Robert Browne attempted to strangle her," Finley wrote. "She advised that her larynx was almost crushed, and that she had to go to the hospital emergency room for treatment." An intern told Rita, then twenty-six years old, to file an incident report to the police. She declined. The reason Robert assaulted her, she explained to Finley, was because he had picked up the wrong set of car keys.

"Mr. Browne was always scheming and felt that everyone owed him something," Finley wrote. "She was very scared of Mr. Browne. She advised that she was afraid that if she was to leave him something would happen to her."

Usually, Rita told Finley, Browne's abuse occurred while they were alone, but she did recall an incident in which Browne had held a handgun to her head in front of one of her friends.

Browne once told her he wanted to be her

property beneficiary. "She told him that wouldn't be a problem, that she would put her vehicle and trailer in his name. He told her he didn't want his name on anything, he just wanted to be made her beneficiary in case something happened to her."

On another occasion, Robert told her "how easy it would be to kill someone and get away with it — 'you just don't know, you just don't know.' [Rita] advised that she took this as a threat against herself.

"She also recalled a 'scheme' that Robert Browne told her about, where he intended to meet a homosexual with a lot of money — e.g., a lawyer — and could get anything he wanted. She took this to mean that Mr. Browne would attempt to blackmail this individual."

And, as other former wives recalled as well, Rita told Finley that her ex-husband would often get up during the night and leave for hours, not returning until daylight. When she questioned him, Browne would say only that he could not sleep and had been drinking coffee at the café.

She told the Colorado investigator of one occasion when, shortly after Browne had returned from one of his nightly forays, sheriff's deputies arrived at their trailer and arrested him for breaking into a construction trailer owned by his employer. "Police found his duffel bag, with the stolen items from the trailer, in their residence," Finley reported. "She believes that a witness had seen her car at the scene of this incident."

Rita and Robert divorced in 1984.

ELEVEN

Robert Browne's letter of July 26, 2002, suggested that Charlie Hess's appeal to his conscience had missed its mark. Rather than address Hess's search for closure with concrete information about possible victims, Browne expressed astonishment that no one had interpreted his previous clues about the seven sacred virgins. He was, he wrote, "dumbfounded" that the "plethora" of information he had provided was not enough. Then he repeated what he apparently considered to be his obvious clues. Instead of verse, this time he wrote a brief list. The place was, as he had written before, a "murky, placid depth." The number was seven. He instructed Hess to "drain-dig." His accomplice was the "High Priestess." Next to the word "motive," he wrote words from his previous poem: "sacred virgins — less worthy scattered."

Then Browne ratcheted up the game.

"Hypothetically," he asked, if someone were holding people in "a concealed chamber," and was then himself incarcerated so that his prisoners died, would he be guilty of murder? Or would the deaths be the fault of the authorities who had prevented the "caretaker" from tending his charges? If so, he wrote, "I suppose three should be added to the nine."

TWELVE

Given the ex-wives' testimonials, Mark Finley was surprised to discover that Robert Browne's recorded criminal history was rather slim and peculiar. The available facts suggested that Browne might have a far darker past than the documents showed.

Finley learned that in March 1983, Faye Aline Self, thirty-three, of the River Towne Apartments in Coushatta, had vanished without a trace. Self was last seen at a bar on Highway 1 across the Red River from Coushatta. Two months later, twenty-two-year-old Wanda Faye Hudson was found brutally murdered at the River Towne Apartments. Hudson was stabbed more than two dozen times with a sharp object, two and a half to three inches long. Her killer also had struck her in the face and throttled her with a ligature before she died. Her apartment floor and walls were covered with her blood.

133

The River Towne Apartments, actually two rows of tiny, white frame cabins near the old Red River bridge, looked more like a collection of fishing shacks than permanent residences. They were owned by Robert Browne's older brother Donald. Robert was also living in one of the River Towne cabins when Faye Self disappeared and Wanda Hudson was murdered, but he was never questioned in connection with the crimes.

Two years earlier, in 1981, Browne had been arrested for stealing three rolls of copper wire from Wireways, Inc., of Natchitoches, which is south of Coushatta. In June that same year, he burglarized a construction trailer belonging to International Paper Co. in Mansfield, where he once worked. This was the case that his fourth wife, Rita, described to Mark Finley. Browne pleaded guilty to reduced burglary and theft counts and spent forty-five days in jail.

He also was charged with stealing a bell in 1985 from a local Baptist church. Authorities later found the bell stashed in his brother's shed.

His first really serious encounter with the law, however, came in 1986. On January 23, he appeared at the Quality Ford dealership in Coushatta, where he had ordered a dark blue '86 Ford F-350 pickup truck. According to the Red River Parish Sheriff's Office incident report, Browne told the salesman at Quality that he needed his new truck to drive to Shreveport "to get the money for the truck and would be back in a few hours."

Instead, he took off on a two-month, cross-country tour. An early stop was Colorado, where he looked up his old lover, Marjorie Miller, who was now married to Jack Mason,* and living south of Colorado Springs.

Browne didn't mention at the time that the brand-new Ford he drove was hot. That's not the way he saw it, in any event. But he did tell Mason that his business was dealing drugs and produced five pounds of high-quality marijuana plus a considerable amount of cocaine to prove it. Browne claimed he'd taken the valuable stash from two drug dealers he'd killed. He said he'd set their bodies on fire in a trailer on his way out of town. If so, Red River Parish authorities have no record of the double murder or the bodies, although they do confirm that a trailer had indeed burned down about the time of Browne's departure.

Browne also had with him a .22 caliber

* Denotes a pseudonym.

Ruger and a 30-06 hunting rifle. Jack Mason sold him two more guns.

After Browne was arrested in 1995 for the murder of Heather Church, Lou Smit and Deputy Walt Scully tracked Mason down at Colorado's Buena Vista Correctional Facility, where he was finishing up a sentence for second-degree burglary. By this time, Mason and Marjorie had been divorced for several years.

Mason told Smit and Scully that he and Browne quickly became tight friends in early 1986, doing cocaine and marijuana daily, wholesaling to street dealers when they needed cash, pulling burglaries by night. One time they lifted 300 rolls of barbed wire from a storage yard; so much wire, in fact, that there was no room in Mason's car for Browne, who was left to get home on foot. Another time, they stole ten saddles and some hardware from a "shack" near Mason's residence.

Mason also said that Browne often went out overnight on his own, frequently returning with jewelry and weapons, which they pawned around town. Sometimes he came back "really wired," as Mason put it.

According to Jack Mason, at one point Browne had let on that he'd committed other murders in Louisiana besides the drug dealer killings. The homicides occurred somewhere near where he lived, and the victims "were down by a stream."

Browne talked about the supernatural a bit, too. Mason recalled mention of the high priestess, but the remark was casual, and the high priestess did not sound like a nearby presence, at least not in Browne's mind.

One time they shot two cows as the animals grazed in a meadow behind Mason's house. Mason recalled that Robert was an excellent shot, hitting his target right behind its ear from a long distance away. The steer dropped at once. They butchered the beeves themselves that night, discarded the hides in a commercial Dumpster, and fed the bones to Mason's dogs. Mason later would add a gruesome detail to his account of the cattle rustling episode. He told the cold case squad members who interviewed him in 2005 that Browne slit the cow's throat and drank the dying animal's blood. He said he declined Browne's invitation to join him.

After several drug-addled weeks, Browne departed Colorado in his blue pickup, making his way around the West until he ended up at a truck stop in Ukiah, California. By this time he was low on cash. At the stop, he met a trucker who took pity on a broke wayfarer, as Browne depicted himself, and offered to let him stay at his home with his family for a while.

Browne by now had been at large for two months and might have remained so indefinitely, had the trucker's son not soon thereafter gotten into trouble for throwing rocks, which brought the state police to the house. An observant trooper ran Browne's Louisiana plate numbers, discovered the pickup was reported stolen, and arrested him.

Browne waived extradition for "unauthorized use of a moveable" — the Ford truck — and was returned to Coushatta by Deputy Captain Larry Rhodes of the sheriff's department. His brother Donald posted a $10,000 bond to keep Robert out of jail until his trial.

In his report of their interview, Mark Finley wrote that Donald complained there had been "a lot of irregularities" connected with the case, including the fact that it had taken Quality Ford a week to report the truck stolen. According to Finley's report, Donald Browne alleged that the dealership knew his brother didn't have a job at the time and was living in a trailer Donald provided him, indicating they should have known Browne did not have the legitimate means to buy a new Ford truck.

But according to what Browne himself later told Colorado investigators, he had made a considerable amount of money dealing cocaine and so decided to order a new truck and pay for it from his hefty proceeds.

When the vehicle arrived on the lot, according to Browne, the salesman tracked him down in a liquor store and told him to come pick it up.

"I said I'd do it tomorrow," he remembered. But the salesman kept pestering him to come drive his big new F-350. So he did, and the next thing Browne knew, he was in Colorado. "The funny thing is," he said with a laugh, "I had the money in my back pocket to pay for the truck."

As Robert's July 1986 trial date approached, Donald began to suspect that his brother was about to flee, so he revoked his brother's bond. This meant Robert had to go back to jail at least until his trial, something Browne was loath to do.

By prior arrangement, on the morning of July 14, he drove himself to the sheriff's office. Once there, however, he refused to get out of his car.

"Robert said he didn't know what he was going to do, that he was thinking," Lieutenant Warren Perkins wrote in an incident report. "I again asked Robert to come on inside and again Robert said he was thinking that he may just make me kill him. I told Robert that it wasn't going to be any of that."

Browne relented, only to balk again at the entrance to the jail.

"Robert said he wasn't going to go behind locked doors again, that he had spent forty-five days down there for no reason and that he wasn't going back," Perkins wrote in his incident report.

Perkins continued, "Capt. Rhodes tried to talk to Robert, but Robert still said he wasn't going to be locked up. Capt. Rhodes told him it was no use making it hard on himself or on us, but he had to go on down. Again, Robert said he wasn't going. Capt. Rhodes got Robert by the arm and Robert jerked loose and said keep your damn hands off me. At this time, Capt. Rhodes and I grabbed Robert and went to the wall. Sgt. Emerson also had Robert. Capt. Rhodes had Robert by the left arm and around the neck; I had Robert by the right arm. I took his right arm around behind his back and Donnie Farley got my handcuffs and put them on him.

"Robert Browne said . . . that someone was hurting his arm and asked who it was.

Robert said that when I get out of here I am going to kill that mother fucker. You don't have to break my fucking arm."

The scuffle netted a split lip for Sergeant Emerson and a resisting arrest charge for Browne.

In September 1986, Browne pled guilty to the truck theft and to resisting arrest and was sentenced to eighteen months in prison on the first count and six on the second, with both terms to run concurrently. He served some of his time in the Red River Parish jail and the rest at the Hunt Correctional Center in Saint Gabriel, where he was paroled on April 13, 1987. Eight days later, he was back in Colorado, where Marjorie and Jack Mason agreed that Browne could use their address for parole purposes. He arrived in a beat-up Datsun and soon resumed his old routine of stealing and doing drugs with Mason.

Smit and Scully wrote that Browne "would shoot dope into his arms, legs, feet, and also into his neck. [Mason] stated that Robert taught him how to really get high and 'take it to the max,' where 'they would flop on the floor and do the funky chicken.' "

One of their favorite pastimes was to drive out to Rampart Range Road, where Heather Church's remains were later found, to shoot their guns and do drugs. Mason said that he and Browne visited the area frequently and spent a lot of time together getting high at the bottom of an embankment. He remembered a rusted-out old Chevy rested nearby.

Mason also told Smit and Scully that one night Browne crept through the window into Marjorie's daughter's room and raped the girl.

THIRTEEN

On the afternoon of Browne's arrest in 1995, his brother Ronald, a welder, and his sister-in-law Rebecca visited the El Paso Sheriff's Office to be interviewed. Ronald Browne essentially confirmed to Michele Hodges and Lou Smit what his brother had told Finley: Robert was a loner. He rarely went anywhere and almost never socialized. In fact, since Donald had pulled Robert's bond back in 1986, Ronald was the only member of the family with whom Robert ever spoke, and that was rarely, even though he and his wife lived in nearby Colorado Springs.

Rebecca Browne was significantly more forthcoming than Ronald in her conversation with Mark Finley. She told the detective she had psychic powers that convinced her Robert had murdered Heather Church and, according to the interview report, that he was "a man with no conscience."

Rebecca Browne was close friends with Robert's wife, Diane Browne. They worked together at U.S. West, and Rebecca had first met her husband, Robert's brother Ronald, at a 1989 dinner party hosted by Robert and Diane, themselves recently married at the time.

Rebecca painted a bleak picture of Diane and Robert's domestic life.

"Rebecca Browne," Finley reported, "indicates that before Diane Browne had met Robert Browne, that she had taken care of her body and was into physical fitness, working out at U.S. Swim and Fitness and socializing. She advised that Diane has put on considerable weight since this time, and does not socialize outside of work."

Finley continued, "Rebecca Browne said that she recalled during the time period that Heather Church had been abducted that Diane Browne had told her that she had done a lot of going to bed alone without Robert Browne. Diane Browne had told her that Robert Browne was going out at night and that she did not know where he was going. Rebecca Browne was certain that Robert Browne was doing this around the time period that Heather Church disappeared. Rebecca Browne stated, 'I just know they were having trouble that way.' She advised that Diane Browne had told her that she thought that Robert Browne had a girlfriend, and that he was drinking considerably during that period of time."

When Detectives David Reisman and Brad Shannon visited Diane Browne at U.S. West in Denver on March 28, 1995, they at first said only that they were investigating the Church case and did not disclose that her husband had been arrested. She was nevertheless nervous and circumspect. According to the officers' report of the interview, Diane insisted that she and Robert were home together the night of September 17, 1991, all night. Had he gone out, she said, she certainly would have noticed. Robert was "a good guy," Diane insisted, and "a wonderful husband" who often cooked and cleaned their house. Although she conceded there had previously been trouble in the marriage, for the past two years she said, "things have been great."

When the officers finally told her that her husband was under arrest for the abduction/murder of Heather Church, "Mrs. Browne's reaction was as expected, shock. She stated that she could not believe he could do such a thing, and asked how we had linked him to the crime." The detectives told her about the fingerprints.

As the interview progressed, Mrs. Browne consulted her memory once again and was not quite so certain about the night of Heather Church's disappearance, according to a police report. Reisman and Shannon returned again and again to the subject. Diane gradually came to recall that Robert may indeed have gone out into the night on September 17, 1991. It was one of his habits to do so, often in the middle of the night, and he always went alone, she said.

At her next interview with Detective Michele Hodges, on April 4, Diane mentioned that Robert was forever altering his appearance; growing and shaving both beards and mustaches, growing and cutting his hair, and changing the way he combed it.

She also touched on the enmity Browne bore his family. "Ms. Browne advised that Robert Browne told her he had a lot of trauma in his childhood. He definitely believed that he was not wanted and his brothers and sisters tormented him. While the other kids would pair off, he would be the odd one out. She stated that he still hates some of his sisters and brothers for what they did to him, that is, tying him up," Hodges wrote in her report of the interview.

He told her that his mother, Beulah, was crazy.

When Robert and Diane argued, typically about money or the constant lies he told her, Robert usually would drive away to go get drunk and not return until the next day, the detective wrote. Diane Browne by now was "almost positive that Robert Browne had gone for a walk on the evening Heather disappeared," Hodges wrote.

A week later, Detective Hodges and Diane Browne spoke once more, by telephone, according to police reports.

Toward the end of the interview, Diane finally conceded that she feared her husband. "Mrs. Browne," noted the detective, "advised that she was afraid to divorce Robert Browne because of his violence." Just as did Terry Ward, Diane told police, although he had not hit her, she had "seen him punch and destroy all of the doors inside their residence." Diane said most of the doors had been replaced, however, "the exterior door still had holes in it where Robert had hit it with a bat. She stated that when he did so, she would think that what he was hitting could have been her head," Hodges wrote.

In light of the AOL transcript and the episode with her life insurance, Hodges wrote, "She now believed it possible that he might have been attempting to get rid of her. She stated that he was the one who cared for her car, repairing brakes, etc. He could easily have made her death look like an accident."

Diane Browne soon thereafter filed for divorce.

Resolution of what the *Gazette* called "one of the most notorious crimes in El Paso County history" brought a mixed measure of relief and anger to Diane Church, who had retaken her maiden name, Wilson, after the divorce from Mike Church. "I feel kind of numb and mad and glad and relieved and just a lot of different things," Diane Wilson told the paper. "Sad. I still miss her like I always did."

But the welcome news also raised a serious question. If the excellent prints Elinor McGarry lifted from the Churches' master bedroom window frame were on file from the very start, what took so long? The explanation illustrates just how imprecise the alleged science of crime detection remains and just how slender is the thread from which the truth sometimes dangles.

The reason that no match was found within the Colorado Bureau of Investigation fingerprint files was that Browne's prints were not there. For some unexplained reason, although he was fingerprinted when he was paroled to the state in 1987, his prints were not entered into the CBI database. The reason that no one had thought to compare his prints with those in the various AFIS databases was just that; no one thought to. The window frame prints *were* regularly resubmitted to CBI over the years. Presumably at some date the Louisiana or California AFIS files would have been integrated with CBI's and a match someday would have been possible.

Eventually. Maybe.

Sheriff John Anderson danced around the issue at the press conference he called to announce Browne's arrest. "I would not call it an oversight," he told reporters, "and I would not blame anyone in the previous administration. I don't believe there was anybody we can point fingers at and blame, particularly when they exhausted every reasonable means they had and then some. I know they did everything they possibly could."

Dan Zook, the county assistant district attorney assigned to the Church case, knew that the prosecution hinged on the strength of two fingerprints and could be a tough sell before a jury. So, as he recalls, the district attorney offered Browne a guilty plea, life in prison without parole.

At a meeting in his office, Zook told public defender Ann Kaufman that the district attorney was not going to give up the death penalty unless Browne was willing to plead guilty. Zook let Kaufman know that Colorado authorities were aware that one of Browne's immediate neighbors in Coushatta had been brutally murdered and another was missing. Zook then added a touch of urgency to the discussion. "I said, 'If you think you want to plead, you better do that right away before we find someone else that he's killed.' "

Looking back, Zook admits, "I was bluffing somewhat."

The prosecutor was stunned by Kaufman's rapid response. Within a week or so, and in advance of Browne's preliminary hearing, "She came in and said, 'We'll take the deal.' That's pretty unheard of, especially in a serious murder case. We were surprised, and it made us think she was pretty worried that something else was going to come up."

By late May 1995, the plea bargain with Browne was finalized; life in prison without the possibility of parole in return for a guilty plea. Mike Church and Diane Wilson OK'd the deal, which was formalized in a thirty-minute hearing on Wednesday morning, May 25, 1995. "He stood up in court today and said he did it," Diane tearfully told the *Gazette*. "I saw it with my own eyes. This is a big relief. If he is willing to say he did it, I'm willing to let him sit in jail for the rest of his life."

A week later, Mark Finley and Lou Smit met with Browne at the Department of Corrections' diagnostic facility in Denver, where he was being processed in advance of assignment to the state penitentiary. They hoped that with his legal jeopardy settled Browne might now share some details of Heather Church's murder. They also asked him about the unsolved March 30, 1983, disappearance of Faye Self and the murder two months later of Wanda Faye Hudson, in Coushatta. The prisoner was told that Red River Parish DA Bill Jones might consider some sort of agreement in return for Browne's cooperation.

"Mr. Browne declined to discuss any details regarding this case," Finley wrote in his report of the interview. He did tell the lawmen that Heather's death had been on his conscience, which was a factor in his decision to plead guilty. He said he hoped

151

he would get some psychiatric help in prison.

"Mr. Browne," Finley continued, "denied he was ever involved in any other homicides."

Five days later, Finley received a telephone call from Susan Lawrence, Browne's placement counselor at the diagnostic center. Lawrence wanted to pass along information that Browne recently had provided her.

"He enjoyed roaming his own neighborhood at night, looking for houses to burglarize," she told Finley. "Sometimes he would take things, sometimes he wouldn't. When he went to the Church residence, there were two lights on inside the house and no cars in the driveway, and he did not think anyone was home. He was surprised by Heather Church inside the house and her killing was unintentional."

Browne said he killed Heather inside the house.

"He placed one hand over her mouth, and one hand on her neck," Finley wrote in his report of the Lawrence conversation. "He demonstrated this to Ms. Lawrence and said he recalled doing this for only a couple of seconds, but now believes it must have been for a longer period of time. He assumed that he had strangled her because she was dead when it was over. Ms. Lawrence asked him if it was possible that he had broken her neck, and he replied that this was a possibility.

"Robert Browne said that he placed Heather Church's body in the back of his pickup truck and drove to the mountains, where he disposed of the body. He denied having any sexual contact with Heather Church.

"Robert Browne said that when this incident first occurred, he believed he was going to be caught, but after a period of time passed, he felt secure.

"Ms. Lawrence said that Robert Browne declined to provide any information regarding any homicide cases in the State of Louisiana. He told her he recalled the incident involving one girl, but did not remember the other. She said he did not seem concerned about providing non-testimonial evidence regarding these cases."

FOURTEEN

Robert Charles Browne faded from the news for a year, until 1996 when he received a note in prison from an anonymous correspondent.

"You got screwed over," the letter said, according to an account in the *Gazette.*

As it happened, Colorado had no death penalty law for a three-month period in 1991. The Colorado Supreme Court had struck down the state's death penalty from July 9 to September 20, 1991, a period in which there were issues with the law's sentencing provisions. As a consequence, anyone subsequently found guilty of committing a capital offense in Colorado during that time could not be made to pay for the crime with his or her life.

Thus there was no death penalty in force on September 17, 1991, the night Heather Church disappeared from her home. According to this argument, Browne's guilty plea of May 1995 — taken on advice of counsel to avoid possible execution — should be set aside.

When Browne personally brought the issue to the court's attention, Colorado Springs attorney Ed Farry was appointed to represent him in the matter. In October 1996, Farry filed a motion to vacate Browne's guilty plea.

Farry argued that Browne had received incompetent counsel and therefore, his guilty plea should be set aside.

"There was not one lawyer or one judge involved in the Browne case who knew what the law was," Farry says.

Assistant district attorney John Zook, among many other Colorado lawyers, thought Farry had a very strong legal point. Zook's only approach, then, was to argue that it was possible, even likely, that Browne had kidnapped Heather and kept her alive for several days before killing her. The actual murder, prosecutors argued, could easily have occurred on or after September 20. The prosecutor advanced as principal proof of this assertion the fact that Heather's body was not found at her house but a considerable distance away. An intruder who unexpectedly encounters and kills someone usually leaves the body behind, Zook argued.

The fact that Browne took Heather — and nothing else from the Church home — suggested that kidnapping and not burglary was the original motive, the prosecutor theorized.

It was "a pretty weak stand," he acknowledges. "I thought we would lose."

Instead, District Judge Gilbert Martinez — who'd accepted Browne's plea in the first place — upheld it. Farry took the matter to the Colorado Court of Appeals and lost there, too. The state Supreme Court declined to review the decision.

FIFTEEN

On August 5, 2002, Hess mused to Browne how "peculiar" he found it that the two of them — "both trained to dispatch human beings" — should find themselves in this situation thirty years later: "You are incarcerated for just that, and I am investigating the who, what and where of it." He added: "The gods must be bewildered."

Hess also explained to Browne, per his "hypothetical" query about victims abandoned in a concealed location, that "the caretaker" would be held legally culpable.

He then moved the dialogue in a new direction with another apparent appeal to Browne's conscience. Hess assured Browne that at his age — then seventy-five — he had no interest in acquiring notoriety or wealth. He only wanted to "make a difference" a few more times before he died.

The old investigator also offered up a bit of bait, proposing for the first time to

Browne that he might find a wider audience for his story. Hess said that a "reporter/author friend" had been intrigued by the few details Hess had shared with him. This potential book project ultimately went nowhere, stymied in no small part by Colorado's Son of Sam law, which prevents criminals from profiting from their crimes. Yet from time to time Hess would return to the subject, seeking to entice Browne into more revealing conversations.

"I believe you are trying to reach out to us," he went on, "and believe me, we are trying to reach out to you. You know what our interest is, and like a quote from a famous movie, 'and what is the quid pro quo.' "

Hess enclosed a snapshot of himself posing with a yellowfin tuna and added a postscript, an evident reference to Browne's previous instructions to "drain-dig."

"We are more than willing to drain the duck pond and 'dig' but are we all willing to generate at this time the publicity that goes along with it?"

The letter touched a chord.

"That's a nice yellowfin in the picture," Browne wrote back three weeks later in a four-page letter.

"With the almost entirely carbohydrate

diet I am forced to endure, the sight of the yellowfin set off a craving for protein. Did the tuna taste as good as it looked?"

Browne's curiosity clearly had been piqued by Hess's mention of a writer friend who might be interested in a book about, or with, Browne. The narcissist is always his own favorite subject. Getting into the spirit, Browne even offered up a lurid, first-person vignette, punctuated regularly with angry exclamation points and question marks, that described the trauma of a small boy suddenly and peremptorily denied his crib. Forced to share a bed with other boys, he is kicked and pummeled night after night.

"I cry and cry and cry," Browne wrote.

The reader is invited to understand this is a story ripped directly from Browne's painful early biography. "The beginning of the endless joy of my childhood," as he put it.

Concluding his account, Browne changed subjects abruptly, telling Hess that the "quid pro quo" — presumably what Browne might receive in exchange for information — was unimportant to him because he did not expect to live much longer. The only thing that might interest him, he said, would be the chance to die "in a remote wilderness," away from other people.

Investigators would puzzle over Browne's

repeated assertions that he did not have long to live. As far as they knew, he was not suffering from a terminal illness, nor did they believe he was truly suicidal. If he wanted to get his affairs in order by unearthing some victims, they could work with that. But that possibility seemed unlikely, as well; psychopaths are not known for their altruism.

Browne's "poor me" plea to die in a remote wilderness seemed to suggest what the killer really wanted — a transfer out of solitary confinement in Colorado's toughest prison.

Finally, in a cryptic postscript, Browne reminded Hess of the High Priestess and told him to ask her "about the chamber."

"I realize that if in fact the matters to which you have hinted have merit," Hess wrote Browne in a September 3, 2002, letter, "that you may have some apprehensions as to how information you furnish may ultimately affect you. Any questions you may have, we believe we can answer."

The letter, more formal than most, had all the earmarks of a group effort. As Hess repeatedly reminded Browne through his use of the word "we," there were other parties interested in their dialogue.

The volunteers floated a couple of ideas apparently intended to nudge Browne along. One was for "someone" to give them hard facts about a murder case, but to do so through a third party — "or some such vehicle" — so as to preserve his anonymity. Hess, the putative author, again offered to visit Browne in prison, alone. "Would this allow us to establish the actual bona fides and help us formulate a mutually acceptable course of action?" he wondered.

The visit, though, would have to come soon because, as Hess told Browne, he was scheduled for surgery on November 4, after which he expected a lengthy convalescence.

Browne wrote right back, carping as before about the injustices he suffered, both in court and behind bars, and warning that the criminal justice system was breeding "monsters" in American prisons who would be "set loose on society."

"These inmates, regardless of their mental state before incarceration, will be angry, vicious, vindictive creatures because of the routine and continuous abuse inflicted on them by evil, sadistic, sanctimonious police and then guards," Browne wrote.

He asked for Hess's opinion on another hypothetical scenario. Would it be all right with Hess if a person were convicted and incarcerated for a crime for which he was not guilty but was, in fact, guilty of "many other crimes"?

Cold case squad members interpreted Browne's question as an obvious reference to his conviction for the murder of Heather Church. Although Browne had pleaded guilty to Heather's murder and had confessed to a Department of Corrections employee that he had accidentally killed the girl during a burglary, he had, on occasion, claimed that he was framed. He clearly was keeping score, as his taunt to Finley suggested: "*The score is you* one, *the other team* forty-eight!"

Then, as in numerous other letters, Browne added his salient information in a cryptic postscript:

December or January 1987 or 1988 (about then maybe)
White Grand Am
Colorado Springs

One of the conundrums Browne's correspondence posed for the cold case squad was his repeated references to a High Priestess. Clearly, she was significant to him, but why?

Scott Fischer set about researching the

symbolism of the High Priestess on the Internet. He also was looking for verbatim references to the "seven sacred virgins, side by side." Foremost in their minds was the possibility that Browne was parroting something he had seen or read. The investigators knew from the inventory of the search of Browne's Eastonville Road trailer house in 1995 that he liked fantasy literature.

While Fischer never found any exact quotes that matched Browne's poetry, he did find dozens of mentions of sacrificial virgins and High Priestess figures. Anyone with even a causal interest in fantasy literature would be familiar with such stock figures, he decided. As he dug through the mountains of occult literature on the Web, he also kept encountering the prime numbers 7, 3, and 11. The number 7 popped up so regularly in occult writings that Fischer concluded that's where Browne likely came up with his seven virgins, too.

"You'll find those numbers come up all the time, so I kind of discounted them," he says.

The possibility that Browne had truly kidnapped and killed seven virgins — or children — also seemed unlikely. The investigators were aware from their reading of the Church case file that investigators in

1991 had looked into reports of satanic cult activity in the Black Forest area. But, as far as they were concerned, those accounts were as reliable as UFO sightings.

"We would go back and forth talking about what was real and what wasn't," Fischer said. "At first, we didn't put much faith in the seven virgins at all. [We thought] it was all bullshit."

Ultimately, Fischer found enough material for the team to craft a letter to Browne on the High Priestess theme.

Hess had correctly intuited that Browne was susceptible to flattery. On September 12, he fulsomely praised Browne's prose sample of August 26. "I sincerely believe it would capture a reader's attention," he wrote. "I am not just trying to flatter you. One thing you can rely on is that I will never lie to you."

Most of the rest of the letter was given over to a series of inquiries about the High Priestess, who had left his mind "awhirl," he said. Hess offered a succession of observations about the High Priestess as a tarot figure, as well as her Biblical incarnations, as if to assure Browne that he took her very seriously, and wished to develop a deeper understanding of her role in the story. Then, after several paragraphs of this, Hess got to his point. "Robert," he asked, "are we talking about a real person, or is the High Priestess allegorical?"

Hess solemnly promised that he was ready to continue their correspondence even if Robert had no useful information to share. He talked about the trust he felt they had already built, and asked, "Do you feel a face-to-face is appropriate?"

After reminding Browne he was slated for surgery soon, Hess closed, "In a mutual search for life's answers to our existence, I wish you well."

Sixteen

In October 2002, Hess sent Browne a birthday card with a picture of a snowy owl on it. Browne, the volunteers knew, was partial to raptors. "Happy Birthday Robert!" he wrote, and signed the card simply, "Charlie." At the bottom he added a postscript. He had noticed from his review of the inventory of items taken in the 1995 search of Browne's mobile home that Browne enjoyed thrillers and fantasy novels. Hess said he wanted to send Browne a book, but had learned that the prison did not allow such gifts.

Browne didn't want Charlie to give up on the book idea. In his next letter he suggested that Hess inquire at the prison library whether he could donate a book that Robert would be allowed to check out first. He had an author in mind, too. Browne was a great fan of the Earth's Children series by Jean M. Auel and was eager to read the latest installment, *The Shelters of Stone.*

In a subsequent note, Browne thanked Hess for the birthday card. "I have long admired the snowy owl," he wrote. "It has an elegant and stoical presence. I take solace in its beauty."

The card had hit its mark.

After inquiring about Charlie's health, Browne signed this letter Derkesthai, another familiar figure from fantasy literature, often used interchangeably with "dragon."

In his letter of November 2, Hess began by returning to some of the wispy clues Browne had offered in previous correspondence.

"Dear Robert," he wrote. "Perhaps you give us too much credit. In searching available records regarding the use of vehicles involved in cases, we are unable to locate any reference to either a white Trans Am or a white Grand Am."

Hess assured Browne that he'd never have anything to do with false convictions, and said he felt lucky to always have been associated "with other investigators who were interested in convicting the right person." In fact, Hess said he remembered numerous cases he'd worked as an FBI liaison to Mexican law enforcement agencies in which felons routinely made false confessions to crimes in the U.S. solely in the hope of escaping the often squalid conditions in Mexican lockups. "So," he wrote, "I spent a great deal of time proving they were not guilty."

As far as the treatment of prisoners, Hess said he had little personal familiarity with the issue. He endorsed doing whatever was necessary — short of torture — to control inmates, and added, "those who enter as child molesters, rapists, and certain types of murderers and those who have committed various 'cruel crimes,' appear to be incapable of rehabilitation. I am sure that is not what you wanted to hear, but as I told you, I won't lie to you."

Then back to the frustrations at hand. Hess pointed out to Browne that *he,* not the sheriff's office, had initiated the correspondence more than two years before, so why this continuing insistence on games and riddles? "If you were just trying to tantalize those responsible for your incarceration, I can understand that," he wrote, "but I can't understand why you would want to 'run me around the bush.' After all, I've put my cards on the table. You know my objectives, which do not include causing you any discomfort . . ."

Hess added that by now he was pretty

much alone at the sheriff's office in thinking that Browne actually had anything worthwhile to share. "Won't you consider laying out just one verifiable instance?" he asked.

He signed his letter, "Charlie, the elder dragon," a reference to Browne's Derkesthai signature. The cold case squad members would never learn what Browne meant by calling himself Derkesthai, and he never used the name again.

The volunteers also sensed that Browne was using postscripts to suggest clues, though no one yet knew what he meant by *"December or January 1987 or 1988 (about then* maybe) *White Grand Am. Colorado Springs."* Hess wrote his own postscript in a more forthright manner, with a piece of information he knew Browne would be glad to have: "The Saints are doing great 6-2!"

"Hello Charlie Hess," Browne replied on December 16. "As far as the holiday season, I wish you a merry merry and a happy happy."

For the first time in their correspondence, Browne explicitly raised the issue that clearly had been on his mind from the beginning. What was his information worth to them? "I will not hand it to [you] on a golden platter with nothing to gain for my efforts," he wrote.

So much for closure.

He needled Charlie, again, for his inability to sort through the various clues — "legitimate information," Browne called it — that he already had provided, especially in view of the department's past experience with finding evidence "where none existed." The Church case had never stopped rankling him, even though he'd confessed to the crime both in court and out.

But the real point of this letter was marketing. Browne was bright enough to realize that he would never be released, as well as paranoid or simply depressed enough to believe he did not have long to live. His letters to Hess were peppered with references to his imminent demise. "You will live much longer than I will," he wrote as a postscript to one note.

So, clearly, he decided to pimp the only asset he had — information — to see what authorities would trade him for it. In this letter, he hinted that a bidding war was possible. Colorado was not the only state with "points of interest," he wrote. Louisiana, he claimed, had seventeen, and he liked the jail food down there better, as well. Moreover, if one considered "procurement" as well as "dispatch and disposal" then, Browne wrote, "the number of states that may be interested more than doubles."

Browne even went so far as to assert that with his help they could "round up" a "whole coven" — presumably the circle around the "High Priestess" — eighteen members of which he said he could identify.

Seventeen

As the new year approached, the cold case team's seven-month quest for an avenue into Robert Browne's psyche had so far hit nothing but dead ends. The killer showed no interest in bringing comfort to his victim's survivors nor did he warm to Hess's implicit invitation to swap reminiscences of Vietnam. If Browne agreed that they were on "a mutual search for life's answers to our existence," it wasn't a front-burner issue for him.

It was frustrating work, with which one of the squad's supervisors, Sergeant Brad Shannon, sympathized. "You're appealing to someone who has no emotion," Shannon observes, "and in that case it didn't work. But while he might not have empathized or sympathized with Charlie, there might have been something that touched Robert. If you want to have a bond or a rapport, you have to find something that you have in common, a common cause. And that cause can't be about Robert's prosecution. He can't get on board with that."

Browne kept throwing out bait — the seven virgins, the map, the white Grand Am, the sample text about his supposedly Dickensian childhood and the escalated body count, now *"at least* 51." But there was no unanimity in the sheriff's department over how to read what Browne was telling them. Mark Finley had guessed it was a sampler of enticements designed to excite, confound, and ultimately embarrass law enforcement. The cold case squad's overseers believed as much, as well. "He was giving us information that couldn't be corroborated," says Lieutenant Hilte, "and that just validated what we suspected, that he was just jerking us around."

Charlie Hess, who'd already confided in a letter to Browne that "I'm about the only one here that believes that you can really put some cases to rest," told anyone who'd listen that he felt he was making progress with the killer. But not even his partners on the cold case squad at this point had much faith that Browne was willing to share anything useful. "I was pretty doubtful," says Scott Fischer.

Hilte says that if the squad were a line

item in the sheriff's budget, their funding would have disappeared by this point. But since the service was free, and as so far the sheriff's office was getting exactly what it paid for, it probably was more prudent to let them keep trying with Browne than to shut down the operation.

The sheriff's office accordingly would continue to treat Browne's claims both skeptically and seriously. Hess, Hilte, Smit, and Commander Joe Breister drove out to Browne's old property on Eastonville Road, where they interviewed the new owner, a former neighbor. She recalled Browne undertaking a strange, nocturnal building project, construction of a little bridge over a culvert. He only worked after 10:30 p.m.

She said he watched other local residents too closely for her comfort; "spying" was her term for it. She also suspected he was responsible when her dogs fell inexplicably ill. After that, she slept with a .38 caliber pistol by her bed.

But the oddness didn't add up to evidence, and the sheriff's office found no indication that Browne buried bodies or built any sort of underground chamber anywhere on his tree farm.

They also searched his property in Fremont County and found nothing there, either. "It's rural, mountain country," says Ken Hilte. "And things are not as obvious as you might hope they would be years later. Also, to think that he would dispose of things on his own property, it's not consistent with what he did with the other victims."

Hilte won't discuss all their investigative initiatives into the "buried virgins" question, except to say they've included an extensive canvass of missing person data banks and inquiries to the other law enforcement agencies. No leads were developed. "With nothing to work with," he says, "you can't produce anything. It's resource management. I don't mean to say that these potential victims aren't important. But I do have other cases to work that have known victims, and people who call and want results."

Still, in their spare time, the cold case squad would occasionally puzzle over Browne's intended meaning. There was a coherence to the clues and hints, rhymed and otherwise, that consistently suggested his alleged victims were underground in some wet, dark chamber, where authorities would have to drain and dig to recover them.

"No advantage will be gained until your

minds have all been drained," Browne rhymed. "Once they're drained it, becomes clear/Dig in deep, for the ones so dear."

Scott Fischer says they initially surmised Browne simply was taunting them, implying that their minds were too cluttered with preconceptions to comprehend his superior scheme. The instruction to drain and dig also suggested the more concrete possibility that Browne had dumped his victims in some body of surface water, such as a lake. Hence the trip to the duck pond.

One other possibility was very specific to Colorado. If read aloud and quickly, Browne's phrase, "Minds have all been drained," sounds like "*mines* have all been drained."

Could the killer be hinting that he'd entombed his victims in an abandoned mine shaft?

Colorado has roughly 23,000 abandoned mines, including hundreds in Teller and Fremont Counties not far from the property that Browne once owned. It is impossible to drive any road in the area without seeing the wooden scaffolding and the piles of tailings that mark the opening to an underground cavity. And as the safety bulletins warn, an abandoned mine is nothing if not a ready-made tomb. Their subterranean chambers typically fill up with water, creating dark, silty pools.

"In the murky, placid depths, beneath the cool caressing mire, lies seven golden opportunities."

Browne's very first clue hints at golden "opportunities" underground. Teller County, an area that he knew well, was home to the Cripple Creek strike, once the largest gold field in the world. He later makes it clear that he's not about to give up his only capital, information, "on a golden platter." Is his repeated use of "gold" a coincidence or another clue?

The investigators did at one point consider mine shafts as Browne's possible dumping sites, but not because of his letters. Yet, with nothing more than idle speculation to go on, the idea quickly was forgotten.

Finally, no theory of the virgins or the High Priestess or secret tombs can ignore Browne's family history of mental illness. Perhaps the whole thing was in his head.

Meanwhile, and more urgently, Robert Browne was wrestling with a mystery of his own. The white Grand Am was a real clue to a real crime — and a very obvious one at that, he thought. He'd also given the sheriff's office an approximate date for this major offense and assumed they'd quickly figure it out.

Instead, he'd been surprised and was openly suspicious that Charlie Hess kept asking for more information. "He was honestly frustrated that we couldn't figure it out," says Scott Fischer. "He wondered, 'How can a woman go missing and never be seen again and her car be stolen and you guys pretend like you don't know what I'm talking about? How can you have no record of that?'"

Easy, it turned out. The record had been erased.

EIGHTEEN

"You know, Robert," Hess wrote on January 7, 2003, "I agree with you. I do not believe I would put the details on a gold platter without first receiving the assurances you consider important. On the other hand, it makes one wonder why you wrote in the first place? You must have been moved by something."

Hess outlined some possibilities that had occurred to him. Maybe Browne was chafing about the Church case and was doing his best to frustrate those he blamed for its outcome. Maybe he'd invented a long list of alleged victims to create more law enforcement interest in him. Maybe he had no outstanding cases to clear; he was simply having a good time causing the authorities trouble. Maybe he was actually being straight. Or, because prison was so boring, maybe he was playing games for amusement and to keep his mind sharp.

"I guess there are a dozen or so possibilities," wrote Hess.

He threw in a typical personal digression. Noting that Browne had said he was an avid outdoorsman, Hess shared some of his fonder personal memories of the outdoors. As a young man, he wrote, he'd worked as a guide at a resort his father owned in Wisconsin. He was a county champion Muskellunge fisherman for three years running. Hess even had a Louisiana experience to tell about. In the early 1950s, after getting to know some local officials with whom he worked a kidnapping case, he was invited back to go goose hunting with them. He said he liked everything about the experience except the chicory-flavored coffee.

Then he addressed Browne's latest queries.

Hess did want to send Browne a book but was waiting for an answer from the Department of Corrections. As far as being transferred to Louisiana, Browne had little chance of that unless he could provide verifiable evidence that he committed a crime in that state.

"So Robert, where do we go from here?"

Hello Charlie Hess,
You were wondering "why I wrote in the first place." I don't know that I could answer that to your satisfaction. I'm not sure that even I know. There was probably a conglomeration of reasons and I was simply exploring possibilities. What my thoughts were at that time, I do not recall.

"Robert," Hess asked on January 21, "what is your suggestion as to how we obtain something tangible . . . that there really are cases out there?"

Hess recommended that Browne consider some potential results. First, what did he expect the "ultimate outcome" to be in Colorado, should the local district attorney agree to work with Colorado law enforcement authorities? Second, what did he expect the other states to do?

"No. 3," Hess wrote. "Are you willing to just lay it all out and let the chips fall where they may?"

Hess's short list of alternative action plans would not please Browne at all, possibly because it implicitly shifted the initiative away from him to the sheriff's office, thereby undermining Browne's control of the situation. Hess would further annoy him with a flip reference to his high-carb prison diet. "I think you will need all the energy this food class provides," he wrote, "as the project at hand will probably be enervating."

Browne specified in a subsequent note that he wanted a medical exam and a transfer out of lockdown if Charlie and "the powers that be" expected him to cooperate.

Hess got right on it, and sent Browne a handwritten letter on January 29, 2003. The investigator said that he was waiting for news from the Department of Corrections before setting up an appointment to visit Browne. Although Browne had not consented or even encouraged such a visit, Hess was proceeding with the assumption that the killer would be happy to see him.

The DOC, Hess said, had been "very positive to a transfer." Hess was also expecting a meeting to discuss Browne's demands for a medical exam. The investigator told Browne he hoped to have everything arranged by the first half of February. It was an optimistic prediction — too optimistic, as it happened.

"If I can, I will give you advance notice — I hope you're feeling well. Will see you as soon as I can get some info.

"Regards, Charlie."

Browne wrote once more before receiving Hess's letter of the twenty-ninth and he was not happy. "I'm not really concerned with who may or may not be prosecuted," he began. "I could care less."

He returned again to his usual complaints about the justice system and prison abuse before responding specifically to point three of Hess's January 16 letter. "No," he wrote, "I'll not 'just lay it all out and let the chips fall where they may.' I'll take it with me to my grave before I do such!"

The killer was signaling without equivocation that if the game did not proceed according to his rules, it would not proceed at all. In time, the El Paso County sheriff and district attorney's office would take this threat very seriously. They'd have no choice.

"Let's change the subject," he continued. "As far as needing the carbohydrates for the 'enervating' project at hand, I neither have the strength, energy, or desire to participate in a grueling interrogation. I *will not* be abused!"

The cold case squad puzzled over Browne's professed fear of interrogation. Paranoia, again, could explain it. But his performance in the marathon 1995 arrest interview with Finley — who'd skillfully hectored Browne, trying to rattle him — had struck everyone, including Finley, as smooth and poised. What did he fear?

Other serial killers, real and bogus, actually have enjoyed matching wits with the cops. Henry Lee Lucas, for example, spun his fictions in exchange for attention, helicopter rides, and steak dinners. Ted Bundy — Charlie Hess's favorite example — talked, separately, at Florida State Prison to Detective Bob Keppel of the Washington State Attorney General's Office and to Special Agent Bill Hagmaier of the FBI throughout much of the 1980s. He never told either investigator anything that was used against him in court, but they did learn a lot about serial murder from him.

When Florida Governor Bob Martinez finally signed a death warrant for Bundy in early 1989, Ted decided it might be time to tell all. He quickly invited detectives from all over the West to come visit him at the prison, hoping that if he gave them times and locations and other details of his murders, they'd intercede on his behalf with the governor. It didn't work, nor did a bizarre videotaped interview Bundy did with James Dobson, head of Focus on the Family, on the eve of his execution, in which Ted talked about the evil influence of pornography, a favorite Dobson topic, in his life.

Browne also differed from Lucas and Bundy in his aversion to the press. Once they were in custody and identified by police as suspected serial killers, Lucas and Bundy played to the media, whom Bundy, at least, held in even deeper contempt than he did the police. Browne, by contrast, had nothing to say to reporters and made it clear to the Colorado authorities that he desired as little press attention as was possible.

Charlie Hess's latest plea for more information was acknowledged and dismissed at the bottom of Browne's letter. "As far as something tangible that will convince someone that there really are cases out there, I tried before with the white Grand Am," Browne wrote. "I guess some cases (people) don't rate. Also, the sanitation companies do a great job of disposal. — There were also poems."

When Lieutenant Hilte read the Hess-Browne correspondence, their letters reminded him of a squabbling married couple. "They were both saying, 'I've given you everything and you've given me nothing,' " Hilte says.

It still sounded like a waste of time to Hilte.

On February 11, 2003, Hess countered Browne's complaints about the criminal justice system with a diatribe of his own. Hess wrote that he was "more than offended" that his daughter had to contend with frequent hearings where the possible early release of his son-in-law's killers was at issue. Hess railed against the "flaws in the parole system" that allowed murders to be released before their sentences were served in full.

"I happen to believe in truth in sentencing," he wrote. "Twenty years is twenty years. No parole, no good time, nothing. If you do the crime, do the time."

Hess reminded Browne that he did admit in court to killing Heather Church; he was not the innocent victim in this story, but the perpetrator. Nevertheless, Hess offered, if Browne were being "tortured or mistreated" and was willing to tell Hess, the investigator would report the matter to prison officials.

And speaking of authorities, a meeting with officials from the Department of Corrections was set, Hess reported, but he didn't hold out much hope unless he could say to them with complete self-assurance that Browne was the real deal. "Whatever transpires, I will pass on to you soon," he wrote.

"Robert," he pleaded yet again, "the poems, the Grand Am, etc., etc., are just over my head. I told you we are not that smart . . . I freely admit to my limitations. My successes have not come to pass because of any genius, but because I was trusted. . . ."

"You see, Robert, it really is up to you."

NINETEEN

Browne had toyed with Hess for several
months now, offering him nothing more
substantive than the hint about an eighteen-
member coven in December and cryptic
mentions of a white Grand Am. Possibly
the resigned tone of Hess's last letter
persuaded the killer that his complaints and
demands were wearing thin. Perhaps it was
time to come up with something fresh for
the cold case squad to consider, even though
he remained incredulous at their inability to
act on what they had already been told.

"I thought I would throw a couple things
your way in hopes of adding credence to
the whole shebang," he wrote on March 3,
2003. "The first is just in addition to what
has already been said about the white
Grand Am. I find it difficult to believe that
a connection has not been made in this matter. I tend to believe you are just fishing for
more in hopes of my hanging myself."

The new clue was to search the missing persons files for a young Army wife, he said. Browne was certain a case file had been opened, and he also remembered that her husband had clashed with the police over their handling of the case, as well as the disappearance of his white Grand Am, which the husband recovered on his own.

"If that doesn't ring any bells," Browne wrote, "then nothing will."

He said the second case was the 1984 or 1985 murder of a young woman in Flatonia, Texas, about ninety miles west of Houston. He chose this case, he said, because small towns like Flatonia do not forget local homicides. Browne indicated that the woman's body was found "near this town," and that her husband was an early suspect in her death. He said he was curious to learn if, and how, the case was resolved.

"Please let me know," he concluded. "Afterward, we may talk some more on this. Texas does like to kill people!"

Lieutenant Hilte personally ran down the latest white Grand Am clue, which didn't take long to exhaust. "We didn't have any missing persons who matched what he was saying," Hilte explains. "So, I went over to

Colorado Springs PD, where they maintain a combined, city-county records section. CSPD gave me three names. None matched the circumstances Browne had described to us."

Flatonia, Texas, however, looked like a far more promising lead. Located just off Interstate 10 in Fayette County between Houston and San Antonio, the little town of 1,500 or so residents tends to remember its homicides for a long time, just as Browne predicted they would.

When Fischer and Smit called to inquire on March 17, Fayette County Sheriff's Deputy Frank Hoffman recognized the case at once. Hoffman told them that on March 30, 1984, a man out scavenging for returnable aluminum cans had discovered the badly decomposed body of a young woman lying in a culvert about two miles north of town, along FM (Farm-to-Market) Road 609.

She was twenty-two-year-old Melody Ann Bush, a pretty brunette who'd recently moved to Flatonia with her husband from Houston. Melody worked sporadically as a dancer and as a cocktail waitress. She'd last been seen leaving a motel bar in Flatonia just before midnight on March 18, 1984.

At autopsy, Dr. Robert E. Bayardo, the

Travis County medical examiner in Austin, had seen no cuts or bruises or other external signs of physical assault, nor needle marks, nor were there drugs or notable concentrations of alcohol in her blood. However, the toxicology screen picked up a considerable quantity of the solvent acetone, which Bayardo listed as Bush's cause of death.

Bush's murder was reported in the April 4, 1984, edition of the *Flatonia Argus,* a local weekly, under the headline, "Woman's Body Found Near Flatonia." The article, which ran on an inside page, was a scant six sentences long, but it did provide readers with a few key details, including the body's location and the fact that Bush was barefoot. Three weeks later, the *Argus* reported Bayardo's conclusions in another short item that recapped the previous story.

Deputy Hoffman sent the cold case squad a copy of Bush's death certificate, as well as the autopsy report. Hoffman also confirmed that Robert Browne had been correct about at least one detail of the investigation. Police had questioned Melody Bush's husband, Robert Bush.

The news from Texas heartened Charlie Hess. One of Browne's typically vague clues had led them to an actual unsolved homicide. They even had a body. Whether or not they had Melody Bush's killer, however, was a whole different matter.

"We had a dead-end on the Grand Am," Fischer recalls. "That was a ghost. So there was excitement about Flatonia. There was something in Robert's letter that made Charlie think this was ironclad, that he was telling the truth."

Hilte was skeptical, though. Weary as just about everyone else in the sheriff's office was with Browne's so far useless, possibly fictive disclosures, Hilte needed something far more concrete from Browne to be convinced. As Hilte played it in his own mind, "So, 'I'll pick a small town, Flatonia' and I'm thinking, even *that* he could have gotten out of the newspaper."

Hess wrote Browne on April 4.

"The Texas authorities have provided us with some interesting details which appear to apply to the case you mentioned," the letter read. "So that no one can ever say that I fed you any details, any specifics you can add will help solidify that it is indeed a case in which you have first hand (?) knowledge."

Hess confirmed that the case was unsolved. He wrote that police had questioned the victim's husband but added that the man was "never charged."

Hess urged Browne to provide "more precise details," particularly information about the victim's cause of death.

"Still working on the white Grand Am," Hess wrote. "This is quite important, as we need one or two El Paso County cases so as to get support from the District Attorney."

In his return letter of April 30, Browne came up with a fresh tease about yet another murder, which he hinted had occurred about the time that Bush died. "A body (in parts) was discovered off U.S. Hwy 59 in the S.W. Houston area. I would think someone would remember that."

The body (in parts) Browne referred to was that of seventeen-year-old Nidia Itzel Bolivar Mendoza, whom he'd later claim to have met while working in route sales for J & H Wholesale Flower Company, a Sibley, Louisiana, distributor of silk flowers. Browne drove a van for J & H from approximately March 1984 to January 1985. His regular route took him through both Houston and along I-10 past Flatonia, where Melody Bush was murdered.

On May 4, Hess wrote to say that he had not yet followed up on this new lead from Browne; in fact, the cold case squad would receive no information on Mendoza for more than eighteen months. Instead, he raised other matters.

One was an unsolved missing person case from the late 1980s in which a person from an eastern state vanished after arriving in Colorado Springs. Someone at the sheriff's office had discovered it in the old files. A white Grand Am was mentioned in one of the case reports, and the missing person was a female. There was nothing more in the crime narrative to suggest a connection to the white Grand Am case Browne kept returning to, but Hess nevertheless raised the matter for the killer's comment.

Again he asked for hard information on local cases. Again he suggested it was a good time for them to finally meet. Hess also warned the killer that it was not "good politics" to keep prison officials waiting for substantive information if he wanted their help.

"If it was only a matter between you and me, I don't think time would be of such importance. However, since we have quite a few other players, it seems their collective patience not be as enduring as ours [. . .]" Hess wrote.

"On the other hand, Robert, if you find this whole matter too trying, I will understand. We've talked about lying, etc., and I've told you over and over that I won't lie to you. If you want to just put this whole matter aside, I'll honor your wishes . . ."

Browne didn't require consultation to plot his strategy. On May 20 he ignored, as usual, Hess's questions and pleas for closer cooperation. Instead, he reasserted control over their dialogue. "As far as the white Grand Am car goes," he wrote, "if any facts conflict with the information I've provided, then you must be looking at two separate cases."

Hess took this sentence as an indication that his correspondent probably was telling the truth. *Keep looking,* Browne seemed to say.

But Browne now was ready to push the discussion in another direction, back to the territory he'd first introduced in his second letter (and map) of March 30, 2000.

In what the cold case squad henceforth would refer to as "the trip letter," he led them on a multistate, multiyear murder itinerary. "I would like to continue the trip we are on," he explained. "We started out in Colorado Springs. From there we went to Flatonia. From there we went east to Houston. Let's continue east on Interstate

10. New Orleans was very fertile grounds."

He wrote that in 1978 or 1979 "a lady" who said she was from "South Philly" was left in a Holiday Inn room not far from the French Quarter. Moving east along Interstate 10 into Mississippi, close to the Alabama border, two men were dumped in a swamp just north of the highway sometime around 1980.

North to Arkansas, just across the Mississippi River from Memphis, another "lady" was "laid to rest" in a marsh, also in 1980.

Tulsa, Oklahoma, 1985. "A male in the muck."

Eastern Washington State, 1986. A woman dropped over the side of a highway scenic overlook.

Northern California, also 1986. The bodies of a man and a woman dumped on a sandy Pacific Ocean beach dotted with driftwood and boulders.

Finally, 1993, and an east-west highway in New Mexico. At another overlook opposite a vast rock face, "once again there is a body over the precipice."

TWENTY

Following Browne's recent disclosure of the Flatonia and Houston homicides, the cold case squad did not at first know what to make of the five-page "trip letter." "We went from 'Oh, my God,' to 'How in the world are we going to effectively run all these down?' " Fischer says.

The volunteers' intent had been to find one case, any case, they could corroborate with physical evidence, preferably Browne's DNA. Instead, the "trip letter" had raised the number of possible victims to twelve, spread across nine states. And the claims were maddeningly vague.

Still, Lou Smit had believed from the earliest days of their investigation that geography would help them prove — or disprove — Browne's claims. Now, with this trip letter, Browne was telling investigators where he had been — just as he had with the hand-drawn map he mailed to Detective Mark Finley in 2000.

The map, in fact, had been one of the things that persuaded Smit early on that Browne's claims of serial murder were worth investigating.

"I knew the [Heather Church] case so well that I knew he had been in every one of those states," Smit remembers. "That really triggered something. I thought, 'Wait a minute! This guy might be for real.' I knew he'd been in Louisiana, and he'd been in Texas and he'd been in Washington. That is what kind of kept us going."

Smit recognized that the larger numbers on the map — seventeen in Louisiana, seven in Texas, nine in Colorado — were in the states where Browne had spent the most time. Likewise, Smit knew that Browne was just passing through Washington State (1) and had only spent a short time in California (2) before he was arrested on a fugitive warrant for stealing the blue Ford pickup truck.

Conversely, if Browne had claimed a murder in a state when they could prove he'd been elsewhere at the time, they would know he was lying. Smit had been able to use just that kind of evidence to discredit Ottis Toole back in the 1980s, when he proved that Toole had been home in Jacksonville, Florida, putting new tires on his mother's truck on the very day that he'd claimed to have robbed, raped, stabbed, and burned two women — one of whom survived — in a Colorado Springs massage parlor.

So far, the investigators had not found conclusive proof to discredit Browne's alleged ramblings. And the trip letter, while vague, fit with the map.

The letter also raised red flags as to what type of killer Robert Browne really was. The great majority of serial murderers (almost always males) are motivated by sex — or, as Roy Hazelwood, the noted FBI profiler, describes it, "what they call sex." Heterosexual serial killers tend to hunt females; gay serial killers prey on males.

Sexual serial killers are driven by a private fantasy that is very specific to the individual killer and often is reflected in his victims of choice: i.e., college girls, young African American males, middle-aged female real estate agents. Each murder is an attempt, always doomed to failure, to make the fantasy real.

If a serial killer routinely preys on both females and males, he is highly unlikely to be pursuing two separate fantasies at once. Yet among the infinite variety of deviant criminals, exceptions often are the rule. The cold case squad would repeatedly confront intimations that Robert Browne was attracted to both sexes.

The immediate objective, however, was to run down the clues contained in the trip letter.

"It was frustrating," Fischer recollects, "because there was very little information, other than the ramblings of his trip, but a whole bunch of cases that you couldn't afford to ignore." The three of them divided up the list and started contacting law enforcement agencies in the towns, cities, and states on Robert Browne's long itinerary.

Beginning, as Browne did, with New Orleans, where he said that in 1978 or '79 he'd left a victim "from South Philly" inside a Holiday Inn room five minutes from the French Quarter, Scott Fischer believed he figured out exactly where that Holiday Inn had been. Maybe there was a record of the crime. He expected that a big-city police force such as New Orleans PD could have a complete investigative record, even some forensic evidence.

Not a chance.

Fischer contacted New Orleans PD Detective Sergeant Fred Austin, explained the situation with Browne, and forwarded to Detective Austin a copy of the "trip" letter. No further information in the case came to light. "I don't think we ever got anybody to take any interest and look through the files," he recalls. "We got nowhere."

El Paso County investigators continued to inquire about the body in the New Orleans Holiday Inn until Hurricane Katrina struck the city two years later. That's when a local detective informed them, "If a record of that was ever here, it's gone now."

Inquiries in Mississippi yielded nothing as well.

In West Memphis, Fischer found the local cold case expert and asked about the marshy area southwest of town. "He told me that over a twenty- or thirty-year period they got dozens of bodies out there," Fischer reports. Browne's brief description wasn't going to lead anywhere.

The same was true for Tulsa, where officers also said the location Browne described sounded like one of the city's more popular body dumping sites.

In eastern Washington State, John Turley, a Grant County investigator, recognized the scenic overlook on Interstate 90 from Browne's description. But Turley told Hess there were no homicides or missing person reports or bone discoveries to bolster the prisoner's claim. The site was searched, nonetheless. Nothing of interest was found.

They had no better luck in California, where the state police knew of three different locations — in three different counties — that fit Browne's description. They also had three or four possible missing person cases with which to work. But the scope was too broad. Furthermore, as one state trooper told Fischer, if the beach Browne described was the one they had in mind, vigorous tides were common. Bodies left in the driftwood would likely have been swept out to sea.

New Mexico, at first, was not a bit more promising.

In his May 28 reply to Browne, Hess tried to put a positive spin on the "trip letter," while he continued to dun the killer for substantive information.

"Dear Mr. Robert," he wrote, "My guess is that if 'higher powers' see your information to be credible, it may be that you would be asked to actually take us to some of these places you mentioned." Hess reasonably, but mistakenly, assumed Browne would be enticed by the possibility of a road trip and the chance at "steaks, Big Macs, tacos, and protein galore. Certainly better than those empty carbs you speak of."

Instead of asking yet again if Browne was open to a visit, Hess suggested he might consider coming to Colorado Springs "for a few days of face to face."

The bottom line, however, had not changed. The investigator urged Browne to deliver a local case or risk losing their interest.

Then he turned to the "trip letter," noting what an "incredible memory" Browne must have to be able to recall so much, while also implying that more information was going to be necessary. "We have traveled a long way together," Hess concluded, "and [I] hope that in some way we can make the rest of the trip easier on you."

Browne did not respond, prompting another short note from Hess on July 8, 2003. The investigator inquired about Browne's health and said that he would send another copy of his last letter in case it had been waylaid. The investigator also had sent a second book to the prison for Browne and he was wondering if he had received it.

Browne finally wrote again on the fourteenth of July.

He had been ill, he said, and thus was not feeling well enough for "any trips — or interrogations," rejecting Hess's invitation to a road trip, complete with steaks, Big Macs, and protein galore. Instead, Browne launched into a now-familiar litany of complains about the Department of Corrections.

Browne then added that he thought Hess should have been able to verify some of his alleged murders. What, he wondered had been the reaction? Were, he asked, the authorities "in a feeding frenzy" or had they attempted to "discredit it all?"

"I'll write again," he said, "when I'm feeling better."

Having regained control of the conversation, Browne now retired from it.

Cold case squad members Lou Smit (left), Scott Fischer (center), and Charlie Hess (right) met regularly in a small office at the El Paso County Sheriff's Office. On the wall behind the men are photographs of Robert Browne and Colorado Springs victim Rocio Sperry. *(Photo credit: Todd Heisler/Rocky Mountain News/Polaris)*

Shown in this eighth-grade school photo, Robert Charles Browne grew up in Coushatta, Louisiana, the youngest of nine children. *(Photo courtesy of the El Paso County Sheriff's Office)*

Robert Browne enlisted in the U.S. Army on his seventeenth birthday, October 31, 1969. He was stationed in South Korea, Vietnam, Texas, and Germany, earning a Bronze Star and other commendations, before being discharged in July 1976. *(Photo courtesy of the El Paso County Sheriff's Office)*

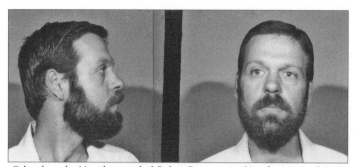

Colorado authorities photographed Robert Browne, age thirty-four, in April 1987 when he was paroled to the state upon his release from a Louisiana state prison where he served approximately seven months for auto theft. *(Photo courtesy of the El Paso County Sheriff's Office)*

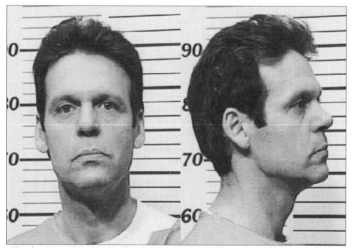

This booking photograph of Robert Browne, age forty-two, was taken after his March 28, 1995, arrest for the murder of Heather Dawn Church. Fingerprints found at the Church residence were matched to Browne's prints on file in California and Louisiana. Heather, thirteen, disappeared from her Black Forest home north of Colorado Springs on September 17, 1991. *(Photo courtesy of the El Paso County Sheriff's Office)*

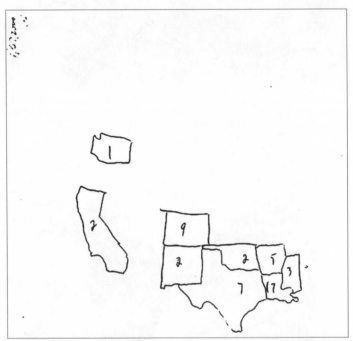

This is a copy of the map that Robert Browne enclosed in a March 30, 2000, letter to El Paso County Sheriff's Detective Mark Finley, along with the taunt, *"The score is you one, the other team forty-eight."* Browne had traced nine states from an atlas, writing a different number inside the outline of each state. Investigators interpreted the map as a guide to Browne's claim that he had killed forty-eight people. *(Map courtesy of the El Paso County Sheriff's Office)*

Heather Dawn Church, shown in her seventh-grade photo a year before her death, was thirteen years old when she disappeared from her family's home in the Black Forest area north of Colorado Springs on September 17, 1991. Her remains were found two years later in the foothills west of Colorado Springs. Browne pleaded guilty to her murder in 1995 and later said that he accidentally killed the girl while burglarizing her home. *(Photo courtesy of Diane Wilson)*

Wanda Faye Hudson was twenty-six years old when she was stabbed to death in the bedroom of her small cottage at the River Towne Apartments on May 28, 1983. Browne claims that he used a key to enter Hudson's apartment and that he stabbed her when she awoke as he was attempting to subdue her with a rag soaked in ant poison containing chloroform. As of April 2007, Louisiana State Police were awaiting the results of DNA tests on forensic evidence recovered from her body. The Hudson case remains open. *(Photo courtesy of the El Paso County Sheriff's Office)*

Katherine "Fuzzy" Hayes, a fifteen-year-old runaway from Coushatta, was last seen leaving Saline Lake, a popular swimming hole, on July 4, 1980. Her remains were found on October 17, 1980, in a dry creek bed beneath a highway bridge on U.S. Highway 71 near Montgomery, Louisiana, south of Coushatta. Browne claims he picked up Hayes at the Chicken Shack, a local hangout, took her to his mother's home where they had sex, and then strangled her with a leather bootlace. Her case remains open. *(Photo courtesy of the El Paso County Sheriff's Office)*

Faye Aline Self, twenty-six, was last seen leaving Alice's Wagon Wheel, a roadhouse on Highway 1 near Coushatta, Louisiana, on March 30, 1983. Browne claims that he found Self asleep in her unit at the River Towne Apartments later that night and inadvertently killed her by leaving a rag soaked in ant poison on her face while he searched for a rope with which to tie her. He claims he dumped her body in the nearby Red River. Her remains have not been found. Her case remains open. *(Photo courtesy of Kathy Cole)*

In 1983, Browne and two of the women he claims to have killed lived in the River Towne Apartments, now vacant. Browne's neighbor, Wanda Faye Hudson, was stabbed to death in the bedroom of her house (since torn down) on May 28, 1983. Faye Aline Self, another neighbor, was last seen on March 30, 1983, leaving a local bar. *(Photo credit: Debbie M. Price)*

Faye Aline Self was living in this tiny house, part of the River Towne complex in Coushatta owned by Robert Browne's brother, Donald Browne, when she disappeared in 1983. *(Photo credit: Debbie M. Price)*

The land around Coushatta, Louisiana, is laced with bayous, chutes, and cypress swamps like this one. Browne claimed that he dumped the bodies of some of his victims in rivers, creeks, and swamps in Louisiana, Arkansas, and Mississippi. *(Photo credit: Debbie M. Price)*

Nidia Mendoza, a seventeen-year-old exotic dancer, was last seen alive leaving Dames, the club where she worked on Southwest Freeway/U.S. Highway 59 in Houston, on February 2, 1984. Her dismembered body was found four days later, in a field near a U.S. Highway 59 in nearby Sugar Land, Texas, by a motorist looking for a lost hubcap. Browne claims he accompanied Mendoza to a local hotel, paid her for sex, strangled her, and dismembered her body so that he could carry it out of the hotel in his suitcase. As of April 2007, Texas authorities were awaiting the results of the DNA tests on forensic evidence recovered from Mendoza's body. The Mendoza case remains open. *(Photo courtesy of the El Paso County Sheriff's Office)*

Lisa Lowe, twenty-one, was reported missing from Forrest City, Arkansas, on November 3, 1991. Her body, clad in a sweaterdress, was found floating in a shallow culvert off the St. Francis River thirty miles southwest of West Memphis, Arkansas, about four weeks later. Investigators at first thought Lowe might fit Browne's description of a West Memphis prostitute he claimed to have picked up, killed, and dumped in an Arkansas river in 1980. However, Arkansas State Police decided that there were too many differences between Browne's account and Lowe's death— including an eleven-year time difference— to consider him a suspect in that case. Lowe's case remains open.
(Photo courtesy of the El Paso County Sheriff's Office)

The decomposed body of Melody Bush, age twenty-two, was found on March 30, 1984, lying in a culvert two miles north of Flatonia, Texas. Bush was last seen alive about two weeks earlier at the Stag Bar, a bar adjacent to the Antlers Inn in Flatonia. Browne claimed he stabbed Bush to death in his room at the inn and dumped her body north of town. *(Photo courtesy of the El Paso County Sheriff's Office)*

FLATONIA
ETHER/ICE PICK

Browne enclosed a scrap of paper with these cryptic words in a letter he sent to Charlie Hess in October 2004. Browne had claimed during his September 2004 prison interview with Hess that Melody Bush had died of "two very unusual circumstances" that the local medical examiner could have overlooked. Investigators interpreted the note as Browne's way of telling them that he had killed Bush with ether and an ice pick, assertions that were at odds with the findings of the victim's autopsy. *(Photo courtesy of the El Paso County Sheriff's Office)*

Rocio Sperry was fifteen years old and the mother of an infant when she disappeared from her Colorado Springs home in November 1987, while her husband was visiting family in Florida. Browne, who worked as a convenience store clerk near Sperry's apartment, pleaded guilty to killing Sperry in July 2006 and received a concurrent sentence of life without parole for forty years. He claimed he took Sperry to his apartment, had sex with her, and then strangled her, dismembered her body, and left it in a Dumpster. *(Photo courtesy of the El Paso County Sheriff's Office)*

During his tenure as El Paso County sheriff from 1995 to 2003, John Wesley Anderson created a volunteer cold case squad to organize and investigate the department's unsolved murders. *(Photo courtesy of John W. Anderson)*

El Paso County Sheriff's Detective Jeff Nohr joined the cold case volunteers on the Browne investigation in February 2005. He continues to work cold cases full time. *(Photo courtesy of the El Paso County Sheriff's Office)*

Cold case volunteers Scott Fischer (left) and Charlie Hess (right) prepare case binders with Detective Jeff Nohr (center). *(Photo courtesy of the El Paso County Sheriff's Office)*

Cold case squad volunteers Lou Smit, Scott Fischer, and Charlie Hess (left to right) pack case files for a meeting with law enforcement agencies investigating Robert Browne's claims. *(Photo courtesy of the El Paso County Sheriff's Office)*

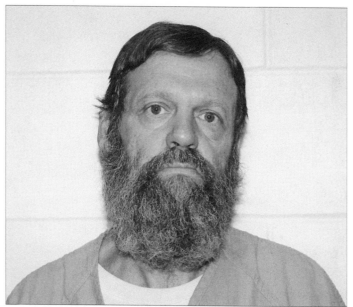

Robert Charles Browne, fifty-three years old, was photographed in the El Paso County Criminal Justice Center shortly before he pleaded guilty to the murder of Rocio Sperry in July 2006. Browne remained in the El Paso County facility for about two months before returning to Colorado Territorial Correctional Facility in Cañon City. *(Photo courtesy of the El Paso County Sheriff's Office)*

Twenty-One

Unaware that his prison pen pal had withdrawn from their dialogue, Charlie Hess kept sending letters for a time. On July 17, 2003, he wrote, "Going back to the poems and to try to solve the puzzles is really not sufficient. We need a map, specific directions or a definite location in order to effectuate [matters]."

The tone of this letter was uncharacteristically blunt, no doubt reflecting Hess's frustrations with Browne, as well as his concerns — which he shared with others within the police department — that if he couldn't deliver some sort of substantive favor soon, Browne would lose interest altogether.

Other states, Hess wrote, had shown little interest in Browne's vague claims. "They won't budge an inch without the same sort of specificity we need here," Hess wrote. "As you can appreciate, we have no control over their actions, or lack thereof. We, on the other hand, are very interested in the cases here."

A week, a month, two months passed. No reply.

On September 23, Hess tried again.

If Browne didn't want to work with local authorities, perhaps he could work through Hess to provide information to out-of-state jurisdictions? Flatonia, he wrote, was one possibility.

He assured the prisoner that he was still conscientiously working on his list of requirements, including a relocation, but as usual, "Please understand, I can't promise anything until there is positive verification."

Hess sent a copy of the letter to Kennith Hilte. Across the top he scrawled: "Lt. H — Trying to get Browne to get back in the game. C."

It didn't work.

Hess left on a long vacation. On his return, he gave it another shot.

"February 3, 2004,

"Dear Robert,

"It is good to be back in Colorado, after a three-month hiatus in the Midwest. I was hoping to have a letter from you on my return."

Hess didn't bother to hide his disappointment that no such letter awaited him. The investigator even verged on an apology for unknown missteps, telling Browne that he had looked over his last letters to try to learn if he had "in some way offended you." But he concluded that he thought they were "getting on the same wavelength."

Finally, Hess tried reheating his most recent proposal to get Browne talking.

If the killer came across with hard information, several good things might happen. If he didn't want to talk about Colorado cases, fine. An out-of-state homicide could also "get the ball rolling."

He wished Browne well, whatever he decided, and concluded with the cautionary quote from an old friend who'd spent long years in prison on multiple bank robbery convictions. "It's difficult to do hard time if there is nothing to look forward to."

Browne ignored this letter, too. His prolonged silence seemed to confirm the consensus around the sheriff's office that he'd been trifling with the cold case squad all along, just as you'd expect from a sociopath. The new sheriff, Terry Maketa, John Anderson's handpicked successor who had taken office in January 2003, so far seemed as supportive of the cold case squad's work as Anderson had been. But the cold case squad had been Anderson's creation, not Maketa's. Whether or not the squad cost the department anything, at some point the complete lack of concrete progress with Browne was bound to imperil the project. Charlie Hess, for his part, readily conceded that Browne was a manipulator, but Hess still adamantly insisted that the killer could be coaxed into a confession. After nearly two years of trying, few others agreed.

No one had a clue why Browne had suddenly given up the game. Regular checks with authorities at DOC confirmed he had suffered no physical traumas or other personal disruptions that would explain his silence, and hardly anyone much cared.

Over the coming months Fischer and Smit kept busy on several cold cases — mostly drug cases and prostitute murders — that had grown that much colder while their attention had been on Browne. Hess left Colorado for six months to manage a Midwestern motel property for a friend.

He also reflected a good bit on Robert Browne. Late that summer, Hess finally decided to pay Browne a surprise visit. There was nothing to lose.

Detective Jeff Nohr of the El Paso County

Sheriff's Office, who was soon to assume a central role in the case, made arrangements for the meeting with DOC's inspector general. On Thursday, September 9, 2004, Fischer drove Hess south to the penitentiary. They arrived at about 9:00 a.m. Since Browne had in the past explicitly and repeatedly insisted that he did not wish to meet with any Colorado law enforcement officials, Hess had no reason to be sanguine. Two years earlier, when Mark Finley and Larry Martin, a district attorney's investigator, had appeared unannounced at the prison in much the same way, Browne glowered at them and said nothing until they left.

So Hess prepared a cover story. If Browne asked, he'd tell him that they'd come to the penitentiary on another matter and had decided on the spur of the moment to see if Browne cared to come out for a conversation. Hess decided to talk with Browne alone; Fischer would wait outside in the prison lobby.

The prisoner was brought into the visiting room wearing an orange DOC inmate jumpsuit. He was in leg irons, his hands cuffed behind his back.

"Do you know who I am?" Hess asked as their eyes met.

Browne studied the small, pear-shaped old man standing before him. Hess, with his professorial goatee and stooped gait, hardly looked like the former CIA agent and Phoenix Program operative he had described in his letters to Browne.

"No," Browne replied, either disingenuously or because he did not recognize Hess from the photograph the old fisherman had sent of himself with the yellowfin tuna.

"I'm Charlie Hess," he said.

As Hess would later tell Scott Fischer, he saw what he construed to be a flicker of intrigue in Browne's eye. Suddenly they were in a new arena, contending along a new power gradient. New opportunities. New dangers. Hess would be genial, Browne very wary.

Hess asked that the inmate's restraints be removed. The corrections officers refused, explaining they were concerned for Hess's safety. Though unarmed, of course, Browne was considerably bigger, younger, and more robust than Hess, whose age and recent health problems had left him comparatively frail.

They were left alone together in the interview room for approximately an hour. The meeting was not tape-recorded. Hess told Fischer on the drive back to the Springs

210

later that morning that he was very quiet and reassuring with the killer. They talked a bit about Vietnam. Hess told Browne that he was not there to cause him any grief but, because of his own history, wished to explore the possibility of finding answers for victims' survivors.

Browne was polite and well-spoken, as he had been when Detective Finley interrogated him in 1995. He was also a broken record. Browne launched into his usual complaints about his poor health — acid reflux, fear of heart problems, aching joints — and inadequate medical care, the regular abuse he received from corrections officers, and society's shortcomings in general. Hess noted that moving his torso did seem to pain Browne.

Fischer describes it as "a bargaining session" between Hess and Browne. "[Hess] said [Browne] wouldn't give specifics about unsolved homicides until he received what he considered to be reasonable treatment."

Hess divulged to Fischer how he'd prodded for more information on the white Grand Am/Army wife case. "Look, we don't have enough specific details," Hess told Browne. "You have to give me more."

"I've given you everything you need," the killer replied. "You know the husband filed a missing persons report, and you ought to be able to track it down."

"But I can't find anything that matches the case," Hess pleaded.

Browne relented a bit. He told Hess that the victim was a young married woman who lived in an apartment complex across the street from him in the late 1980s. "I think I can point out the apartment where the couple lived," he added.

The problem with that clue was that Browne had moved fairly frequently during that time period. The cold case squad did comb the missing persons lists to see if any of those reported missing had lived in or near Browne's known addresses. No luck. It was a practical strategy, however. Had there been such a report in the files, they would have stood an excellent chance of finding the victim.

The subject shifted to Flatonia. Hess asked if Robert could give him a cause of death. He did not disclose Dr. Bayardo's conclusion that Melody Bush died of acute acetone poisoning, although the finding had been published in Flatonia's weekly newspaper where Browne could have seen it. Browne replied that Bush died of two "very unusual circumstances" which might be difficult for a medical examiner to figure out.

The killer declined to specify what he meant.

Scott Fischer says that Hess listened patiently. In the car on the way back to Colorado Springs he was pleased to announce that Browne had agreed to further face-to-face sessions — just as long as he knew at least two or three weeks in advance. Hess also told Fischer he'd cleared up one nagging question. Why had Browne stopped writing? The inmate had shrugged. No reason, he said, except that he had used up all his paper and stamps.

Twenty-Two

Robert Browne's new insistence that he'd give up cases only *after* his situation improved was not warmly received back at the sheriff's office. Lieutenant Hilte in particular questioned whether the killer had anything to trade.

Undeterred as ever, Charlie Hess turned to practical matters. On September 23 he informed Browne by mail that he'd made a modest deposit in his prison account for "stamps and paper." He also returned to the key issue between them. What did Browne have, and what did he want for it?

"I'll get down to business," Browne wrote in his first letter to Hess in eighteen months. "The two things I require are medical care and relocation."

He said he wanted a thorough examination by an outside doctor, who would see to all his medical problems from medications to any necessary therapies and surgeries, with guaranteed follow-up "once I've delivered."

Relocation, he said, did not mean freedom, since he understood that "I must remain in confinement." His first choice, he said, would be a fire watch tower in a remote wilderness somewhere. Recognizing that was a remote possibility, too, his second suggestion was a minimum-security facility where he could have some freedom of movement and an individual cell.

"If something can be worked out, I will hold up my end of the deal. If you think this is impossible, then please tell me and I won't waste either of our time.

"I hope you are feeling well.

"Robert Browne"

He added in a postscript that either Alaska or Canada would be acceptable "for the fire watch confinement," as well any number of states with large national forests.

On a separate sheet of paper, Browne made a small gesture of good faith by explaining what he'd meant by "two very unusual circumstances."

"FLATONIA," he printed in large block letters. "ETHER/ICE PICK."

Twenty-Three

There was nothing in Melody Bush's autopsy to remotely suggest either an ice pick or ether had been involved in her death, unless Browne was mistaking one highly volatile and poisonous fluid for another. He would adamantly say he did not. For the first time, the possibility of having her remains exhumed occurred to the cold case squad.

Hess and Browne met at the prison again on October 12, 2004. Browne's criminal past was not discussed. They enjoyed coffee together, and at Hess's request the killer was not shackled.

A month later, Hess wrote Browne a short note to report: "I believe that certain things you have asked about are obtainable, and I am pursuing that path." Hess already knew that Browne's choices for relocation, a forest watchtower or a minimum security prison, were both entirely out of the question, but there was no sense in disappointing the killer with this news.

Nor was Hess's upbeat report based on any reassurances from his bosses at the sheriff's office. Lieutenant Hilte, Commander Joe Breister, and the rest of the brass were as skeptical of Browne's stories as ever. Hess was thus hugely relieved to receive a report from Sugar Land, Texas, that finally seemed to bolster Browne's credibility.

After a considerable delay — Browne had first mentioned a "body (in parts)" dumped in southwest Houston in his letter dated April 30, 2003 — the cold case squad established contact with the Sugar Land PD, which seemed to have a case that matched Browne's body parts story. Sergeant Jimmie Surrat of the Sugar Land police, as a later court document explained, "advised Mr. Hess the Sugar Land Police Department does have an unsolved homicide which occurred in 1984.

"The victim was identified as a seventeen-year-old female named Nidia Mendoza. She had been reported missing to the Sugar Land Police Department on 02/02/84.

"Sergeant Surrat advised the Sugar Land Police Department received a report of a found body on 02/06/84. Sergeant Surrat advised Mr. Hess that Ms. Mendoza's body was found along Interstate 59 southwest of Houston, Texas, and she had been dismembered. Specifically, her head and legs had been cut off. Her arms remained attached to her torso."

Nidia had been employed as a dancer at Dames Nightclub on Houston's Southwest Freeway. She'd also freelanced as a prostitute.

Hess was in contact with New Mexico authorities, as well. On November 4, 2004, he telephoned the state police headquarters in Santa Fe to inquire if they had any missing person or homicide cases that might fit the scant details Browne had provided in his May 20, 2003, "trip letter." Eventually, he spoke with Sergeant Thomas Christian, who remembers hearing, very clearly, that Browne was concerned about the death penalty. "I could almost guarantee that there would be no death penalty," says Christian. "He was already doing life. They'd work a deal, let him stay in Colorado if that is what he wants to do."

The only exception would be if a child was the victim. "Even in New Mexico," Christian explains, "we don't like child killers."

Browne's single mention to date of the alleged murder didn't give Christian much to go on. But there soon would be more to come.

On December 9, 2004, Scott Fischer once again drove Charlie Hess to Cañon City for his third meeting with Browne. This conversation would be held at the DOC's Fremont Correctional Facility, where Browne recently had been moved. His new prison-issue was green pants and a pullover.

Hess asked if Browne could elaborate on the New Mexico case. For the first time by mail or in person, the killer forthrightly recounted one of his alleged crimes, complete with useful detail. Perhaps the experience with the white Grand Am and Army wife had taught Browne to be less coy if he was ever going to cut a deal with Hess.

He recalled that he had been traveling along Highway 64 out of Taos and had passed an Indian reservation, then a barren stretch, before coming to a forested area with a scenic overlook. He needed money, so he decided to pull over and wait for someone to rob. Soon, a motorcyclist who appeared to be in his thirties rode up and stopped. Browne said he shot the man with a .38 pistol, took $150 off his body, and threw him over the side of the cliff.

Christian, who at the time headed the state police cold case unit, now had a pretty good idea of the location Browne described to Hess. But there were no reports of dead or missing persons in the area, nor any information about abandoned motorcycles. As Christian asked around about the bike, however, one person did recall that a motorcycle *had* been recovered in that area, and about the time in question.

A young state trooper had been driving along Highway 64 on a summer day in 1993 when he saw a flash of sunlight reflected off a metal object resting on a hillside off the highway. Suspecting this could indicate a stolen vehicle, the trooper parked his cruiser and walked over to have a look. The object turned out to be a fairly new motorcycle, which appeared to have been recently — and deliberately — ditched.

The bike was towed to a wrecking yard. Although the registered owner was identified, he had not reported the vehicle stolen or missing, nor was he able to retrieve it personally. So the motorcycle remained, untouched, in the wrecking yard for about ten years until Sergeant Christian located it, confirmed it was the bike he was looking for, photographed it, then released it back to its new title holder, the towing company.

"We're not even sure this is the same motorcycle that Mr. Browne is talking about," says Christian. "There is a very high probability, but we don't know."

December 9, 2004, would be a day of significant, if grisly, progress in the newly discovered Nidia Mendoza case, as well. During their previous meetings and in his letters, he had been vague about the specifics of his alleged crimes, which he invariably discussed in the third person. Until this interview, he had not directly described how he killed any of his victims. His conversation had been cloaked in riddles.

This time, when Hess brought up the Highway 59 case, Browne was responsive and explicit. He said he'd met the victim — he did not remember Mendoza's name — at a strip club off Highway 59, southwest of downtown Houston. She was petite, just five feet tall and ninety-five pounds, and appeared to be Asian. Browne remembered Mendoza said she was from Guam. They struck a deal for sex and left the club in his company van when Mendoza's shift was finished.

At what Browne described as "a rather nice motel" that Nidia chose, with a large atrium and a glass elevator, she disrobed, they had sex, and then Browne manually strangled her, he said. Afterward, he put her into the bathtub and cut her up, using a dull knife he found in the room's kitchenette.

Hess described Browne's tone as even and unemotional throughout, as if he were explaining how to roast a chicken. He told Hess it required two trips to his van with a suitcase to remove all of Nidia from the room. When he was finished, he drove to an area off Highway 59 and dumped her in some tall grass, where her body parts were found a few days later by a motorist searching for a lost hubcap.

Hess listened impassively, as he would later tell Fischer. Browne had finally told the investigator exactly how he had killed a victim in very direct and personal terms. But if Hess felt revulsion or elation — they were finally getting somewhere — he was not going to let the emotion show.

Browne's brief descriptions dovetailed with the information in the 600-page investigative report Sugar Land PD had provided in most details except for one: Nidia Mendoza was from Panama, not Guam.

Browne's motive for discussing the Mendoza murder with Charlie Hess in such apparently self-incriminating detail is not clear. He may have erroneously believed Hess was responsible for his move to the Fremont facility, an improvement from the state penitentiary, and was offering Mendoza as a quid pro quo.

As usual, little or nothing of what he said was verifiable. The part about the victim's head and legs being severed had appeared in both of the big Houston daily newspapers. Browne also probably understood that since he was neither tape-recorded nor under oath, the only way this "confession" eventually could be heard in court was secondhand, as hearsay.

Still, since he openly feared Texas justice — "Texas does like to kill people!" he had written in an early letter — it seemed pointless for him to risk a capital murder indictment, unless Browne believed, as he had in the Church case, that no physical evidence linked him to Nidia Mendoza's murder. In light of his experience in the Church case, such a faith would be difficult for a rational person to sustain.

Then there was the nature of the crime. Assuming, as Charlie Hess did, that Browne was telling the truth, this was the cold case squad's first clear look at the manner in which Robert Browne went about his crimes. Nothing lyrical here, no sacred virgins tucked away in their dark and watery tomb. Browne had dispassionately admitted to sex with a tiny, teenaged hooker. Then he methodically hacked her to pieces.

There was a practical reason for dismembering Nidia Mendoza; it was an efficient, if ghoulish, way of removing her body — incriminating evidence — from the hotel. But it seems likely that something more was going on in her killer's mind as he took up his knife.

Experts in aberrant crime recognize that a common objective among sexually motivated killers is total possession of their victims. As Ted Bundy famously put it, "possessing [a victim] physically as one would possess a potted plant, a painting or a Porsche. Owning, as it were, this individual."

But just as no two deviant offenders will kill in exactly the same way, or for precisely the same reasons, they also differ in what they mean by possession, which to them is synonymous with power. Janet Warren, a professor of clinical psychiatric medicine and associate director of the Institute of Law, Psychiatry and Public Policy at the University of Virginia, has studied sexual killers extensively. Among them was a sexual sadist who found the act of murder exhilarating, so much so, that if his female victims lost consciousness too quickly, he revived them.

In a 1999 interview on Salon.com, Warren recalled this particular deviant killer. "He said, 'I wasn't going to let myself be robbed of the experience. I wanted to see in her eyes that she knew she was going to die, and that I was going to take her life.' "

For Bundy, who enjoyed sex with his dead victims, possession meant control of a lifeless female, and time to do what he wanted with her body. For Jeffrey Dahmer, a cannibal, possession meant consumption.

Possession usually requires reducing the victim to an object. J. Reid Meloy, a forensic psychologist and author of *The Psychopathic Mind,* has written extensively about the narcissistic nature of the psychopath's need to possess his victim.

In the same Salon.com article, Meloy observed, "The perpetrator cannot see the victim as a separate, whole, real, meaningful person, with her own thoughts and feelings and perceptions. She must be reduced to an object with no meaning except to gratify his desires."

It was Nidia Mendoza's catastrophic ill fortune to meet such a killer that night in

Sugar Land. His intent was her complete sexual eradication.

Warren compared a killer she studied who also decapitated his female victim with Dahmer. Both killers got a thrill, she said, by the ultimate possession of consuming and destroying their victims.

"It is interesting that Dahmer ate people, but that was part of the same thing," Warren said. "For instance, decapitating a woman. Taking off a person's head is so destructive. He is saying, 'You will be nothing. You will have no individuality.'

"These men have to take women as slaves, or as dinner or as a destroyed object. They can have no ambiguity, ambivalence, confusion, vulnerability, intense anger, fear or love in their lives. All that is fundamental to human intimacy is destroyed by what they do."

Twenty-Four

At their next meeting, on January 5, 2005, Hess again noticed something he'd first detected in November: Browne's overall mood was brightening. The constant references to his imminent demise, a feature of his correspondence, had eased considerably. The dour stare occasionally gave way to a grin. Hess attributed Browne's relative buoyancy to his recent release from lockdown.

"Charlie said he didn't come dragging into the room," Scott Fischer remembers. "He came in with a bounce in his step. You could look at him and see that he was a different person. He wasn't suicidal. He didn't talk that way anymore. He didn't look at his feet and shuffle. He walked in with a smile on his face and said, 'Hello.'

"But even when Browne was in the dumps, he ran the show. If you asked him a question he didn't want to discuss, he made it clear: You don't talk about that. If you kept pushing on that line, you had a real short interview. If you wanted to keep him talking, you had to let him control the conversation."

As usual, Browne was all business. He again complained that he'd given the authorities too much information without receiving what he needed in return. Hess pushed back. The most recent disclosures, he said, though graphic, did not shed sufficient light on matters from a law enforcement point of view, which continued to be the only point of view that mattered if Browne expected the authorities to cut a deal with him.

Hess did tell the killer that arrangements were being made to have an outside doctor examine him. Also, it was possible that he could be moved to another facility.

Browne responded that should his terms be met, he was prepared to give up three homicides in his hometown, Coushatta, one or two more in Colorado, as well as information on other killers. He also offered more substantive information about another of his victims, the "Grand Am Lady," as he called her, whose mysterious case had been hovering like a ghost in the middle distance for nearly five years now.

At the time of the murder, Browne said, he had been living in an apartment on a working-class stretch of Murray Boulevard, between Platte and Pikes Peak Avenues, near a Kwik Stop convenience store, where he worked as a cashier. The Grand Am Lady lived with her husband, a soldier at nearby Fort Carson, in a first-floor apartment across the street from him. After killing her, he added, he'd taken a very showy diamond ring from her finger and later gave it to female friend named Jan Osgood. He'd also stolen a brand-new television set from the Grand Am couple's apartment.

The meeting was not altogether collegial. The next day, Browne wrote Hess, "First, I would like to apologize for becoming testy near the end of our meeting yesterday." He explained that after sitting still for so long his joints had stiffened painfully, and the discomfort had undermined his usual self-control.

"Cold weather does exacerbate this condition," he wrote, "Again, I apologize. A warmer climate might be in order."

He added in a postscript that, "If there is anything released to the press before a deal is reached, I will be in danger. I will need to be relocated to a safe (and comfortable) location until the final deal is concluded. To put me in danger will not strengthen the hand I am negotiating with. It will only anger me."

"Thanx for the apology," Hess replied cheerily by hand a week later, "but it really isn't necessary, as I did not take it personally. We all have off days. I truly feel that you recognize that I am trying to get the things you've asked for.

"We're meeting with DOC next week. I have high hopes."

Browne's detailed recollections of Nidia Mendoza together with his much more specific information about the Grand Am lady persuaded the sheriff's office to finally take the dialogue a bit more seriously.

Hess, Smit, and Fischer, for example, at last had a substantive and local lead to run down. The three drove eastward from downtown Colorado Springs, along Platte Avenue to Murray Boulevard and the Kwik Stop where Browne had worked. Fischer photographed the convenience store with its barred front windows. They crossed the street to the sprawling complex where Browne had rented an inside apartment on the third floor. More photographs.

Working south on Murray Boulevard,

Fischer kept photographing apartment buildings until they came to a complex on the northeast corner of Murray and Pikes Peak Avenue, about a tenth of mile south of Browne's old building. It was a dreary-looking place, in need of repair and a paint job. Its only apparent asset, besides price, was a spectacular view of snow-covered Pikes Peak. It also fit Browne's description of the Grand Am Lady's complex fairly closely, so Fischer made a thorough photographic record for Hess to show Browne during their next visit.

By now, Sheriff Terry Maketa had decided that Charlie Hess's free-form approach required some structure and professional guidance.

Maketa, a sixteen-year veteran of the department, was something of a local legend for his nervy role in the 2000 capture of the so-called Texas Seven.

"Tiga-gatas" one and all, the seven had escaped together from a Texas maximum-security prison, then brutally murdered an Irving, Texas, police officer before the FBI and federal marshals chased them to a trailer park in Woodland Park, near Colorado Springs. While agents and officers surrounded the RV where two of the seven were holed up, members of the El Paso sheriff's department followed three of the other escaped killers to a nearby convenience store and gas station.

The heavily armed and obviously desperate fugitives had little to lose in a final shoot-out, but the SWAT team, led by Maketa, likely forestalled a bloodbath by converging on their stolen Jeep before the surprised outlaws could move. Maketa jumped from a sheriff's vehicle directly in front of their stolen Jeep Cherokee to draw down on the desperadoes, thus preventing their escape. His heroics helped peacefully conclude one of the largest and most urgent manhunts in U.S. history.

"That can be the high point of a law enforcement career," says Maketa of his moment in the limelight. "Then you move on, and the next thing you know you're involved in something like Robert Browne."

Maketa had grown as skeptical as anyone else in his office about the conversations with Browne. But after the killer's disclosures of early January, the sheriff took the advice of Commander Brad Shannon and tapped Jeff Nohr to assume direct managerial control of the cold case squad. "They decided we need a full-time babysitter," says Scott Fischer. "Jeff was the guy who was sent to make sure we put together the case properly."

Jeffrey Nohr, then forty-five years old, had solid investigative and supervisory credentials. He'd spent twenty years with the neighboring Manitou Springs PD — the last three as chief — before coming aboard in 1999 at the El Paso County Sheriff's Office as a major crimes investigator. He was another of John Anderson's personal selections. Nohr's strength was homicide investigation, and he was especially good at crime scenes. He had a reputation for being meticulous, thorough, and unflappable.

In 2002, when the El Paso County Sheriff's Office was asked to reinvestigate the April 20, 1999, shootings at Columbine High School in Littleton, Colorado, Anderson tapped Nohr to lead the effort. Two heavily armed suburban kids, Eric Harris and Dylan Klebold, had shot and killed twelve fellow students and a teacher before killing themselves. In the aftermath, questions had arisen about whether a lawman might have killed one of the students by accident. Nohr's team of detectives demonstrated with finality that Harris and Klebold did the shooting in question.

Nohr, a native of Wagner, South Dakota, who'd moved to Colorado in 1969, also brought a compatible mind-set to the squad.

In fact, Lou Smit was his former father-in-law, with whom he remained close. And Jeff Nohr concurred with Charlie Hess that ferreting out the truth for survivors of Browne's victims was a higher priority than exacting further punishment for his crimes.

One of Nohr's several new responsibilities was to replace Scott Fischer as Charlie Hess's driver. On an arctic, snowy February 23, 2005, they made their first trip together to the prison. This visit would differ from Hess's three previous prison interviews in several significant ways.

Robert Browne also would do his part to make the day memorable.

The visit had been arranged with Browne by mail, as usual, and DOC had signed off as well. But this time, the DOC inspector general's office took a more direct hand. They equipped Hess with a radio transmitter, taped to his sternum under his shirt. Although Browne had insisted none of the interviews be recorded, Jeff Nohr now insisted otherwise, and Hess did not demur.

The Australian-made device, called a Joey, was about the size of a double pack of chewing gum. It digitally recorded the conversation and transmitted it in real time to a receiver in another room about seventy feet away, where Nohr, along with DOC's Dave Smith and Chief Inspector Jay Kirby, would listen in.

The sheriff's detective had brought with him every pertinent investigative file he could think of, as well as crime scene photos. Jeff Nohr likes to be fully prepared.

Charlie Hess took his place at the table first. Browne, who by this point had grown a beard, was brought in about one o'clock.

"How are you doing?" Hess asked as he always did. "Are things OK?"

Of course, they weren't, and Browne filled up the first part of their ninety-minute session with his usual complaints. When he finally calmed down, Hess indicated he would like to start the conversation with Louisiana.

"OK," Browne replied quietly. "You want the three in Louisiana?"

"Holy shit!" Nohr whispered under his breath. The sheriff's office was well aware of the Hudson and Self cases but not a third one.

Hess and Browne began with Wanda Faye Hudson, whose boyfriend had discovered her murdered in her cabin at the River Towne Apartments on the morning of May 28, 1983. Robert Browne had been her next-door neighbor. Where was Wanda Fay killed? Hess asked.

In her apartment bedroom, Browne said.

How?

Browne recalled that he'd repeatedly stabbed the young woman with a screwdriver.

As he listened to Browne, Jeff Nohr pulled out the Hudson crime scene pictures of the victim lying on the floor of her cabin. Browne's description matched the photo evidence.

This was the first time Nohr had ever heard Charlie Hess conduct an interview, and Nohr was impressed with how easily Browne slipped into a confessional mode. Hess had really established rapport.

Hess asked about what time of night Browne had murdered Hudson.

He couldn't remember exactly when, but said it was late.

How did he enter the cabin?

Browne had a key, he said. There was also a chain on the door. Using a screwdriver — which doubled as the murder weapon — he carefully unscrewed the anchor plate that secured the chain to the wall. Then he silently walked in, leaving the door approximately six inches ajar to make his exit as quick and quiet as possible.

Hess asked where Hudson was stabbed.

Browne said her chest area, which was an accurate though incomplete reply. He claimed not to remember if she was dressed. He said he thought he threw the screwdriver in a trash bin.

Hess did not inquire whether Browne had sex with Hudson.

They then discussed Faye Aline Self.

In 1995 Browne had told Susan Lawrence, his prison placement counselor in Denver, that he remembered one of the two Coushatta cases, but only indistinctly and that he knew nothing about either of them, or any other homicides, for that matter. After nearly ten years in prison, his recall was much sharper.

Twenty-six years old and a mother of three, Faye Self was five feet two inches tall and weighed 100 pounds. She bleached her brown hair blond. Self also lived in a cabin at the River Towne Apartments, next door to Robert Browne. She was last seen leaving a bar outside Coushatta on March 30, 1983, two months before Wanda Hudson's murder.

"Mr. Hess asked him what happened to Ms. Faye Self," Jeff Nohr later wrote in an affidavit. "Mr. Browne said he had gone to a nightclub in Coushatta, Louisiana, known as Alice's Wagon Wheel. He said upon entering the bar, he observed Ms. Self with another woman he knew as Lacreesha. . . . Mr. Browne said Ms. Self left the bar, and he remained and danced with Lacreesha."

"Lacreesha" was Lycrecia Foster, one of Self's close friends.

The affidavit contined: "He said he returned home around midnight. Mr. Browne said he had gotten the urge to go to Self's apartment, because he did not see lights on or any cars. Mr. Browne said he soaked a rag with chloroform [actually liquid fire ant killer, which at that time contained chloroform] and put the rag in a plastic bag. He said he went to Self's apartment and found her door unlocked. Mr. Browne said the door to Self's apartment was on the side and it opened into her kitchen.

"He quietly entered her residence and found her asleep in her bedroom. He used the chloroformed soaked rag to 'put her out.' Mr. Browne told Mr. Hess he left Ms. Self's apartment and left the rag on her face. Mr. Browne said he went back to his neighboring apartment to obtain rope with which to bind Ms. Self.

"Upon his return, he found her dead. He said he placed her body in the trunk of his Datsun B210 car and drove her to a bridge over the Red River which was located approximately one to two hundred yards from his apartment complex. Mr. Browne said he dumped her body into the Red River.

"Mr. Hess asked Mr. Browne why there was a need to restrain Ms. Self. Mr. Browne replied if he was going to take the chloroform away and she was to come to, he wanted her restrained. Mr. Hess asked Mr. Browne if he had sex with Ms. Self. Mr. Browne replied, 'No, she was dead.' Mr. Hess asked Mr. Browne if he had sex with her prior to her death. Mr. Browne replied no, stating as soon as he chloroformed her, he left and when he returned, she was already dead. Mr. Browne said he left the chloroform rag on Ms. Self's face, because he did not want her waking up while he had gone to get something to restrain her.

"Mr. Browne was asked why he selected Faye Self. Mr. Browne replied it was opportunity. Mr. Browne said when he was restless, he 'rambled' and he liked nights because they are peaceful. He denied planning his crimes. He described them as being spontaneous crimes of opportunity.

"Mr. Hess asked Mr. Browne if he could explain why these things happen. Mr. Browne replied he could not, however his opinion of women is very low. He said, 'women are unfaithful, they screw around a lot, they cheat, and they are not of the highest moral value. They cheat and they are users.' Mr. Browne said in some way, he feels justified in what he has done. Mr. Browne added in his opinion, the human race was not very good.

"Mr. Hess asked if there had been a struggle with Ms. Self. Mr. Browne replied no, she was asleep. He said when he put the chloroform in her face, she started to wake, but the chloroform worked quickly.

"Mr. Hess asked Mr. Browne if any of his victims ever got away. Mr. Browne replied, 'None ever got away; never gave the opportunity. If you're going to do it, just do it.'

"Mr. Hess noted there appeared to be more female victims than male victims. Mr. Browne stated there were more opportunities with females. He said he has been disappointed with women his whole life. He accused women of being 'users,' and 'not loyal.' He said women will attach themselves to men whom they believe they can get the most from."

Then Browne came to his surprise victim: Katherine Jean Hayes, known as Fuzzy. Neither the El Paso County Sheriff's Office nor Coushatta authorities had known anything of Browne's connection to the fifteen-year-old, who had last been seen at a swimming hole near Coushatta on July 4, 1980.

Browne told Hess that he'd met Hayes — whose name he only could remember as Fuzzy — late one night at Uncle Albert's Chicken Shack, a small, casual restaurant on Coushatta's main drag where teenagers often gathered. Hayes, nicknamed for her frizzy red hair, was a waiflike child, no taller than five feet. Her stepmother, Bettie Joice Smith, describes Fuzzy as very troubled, a drug user, alcoholic, and chronic runaway. Since Fuzzy had no place to go that night, as usual, Browne said she could come home with him.

Browne was twenty-six at the time, estranged from his third wife, and staying with his mother in the family home at 1010 Carrol Street. He said that he took the girl back to his mother's house, where in his bedroom they "made out" and "had our thing." According to Browne, an argument ensued. The girl got dressed and then fell asleep on his bed.

As she slept, Browne said, he took a pair of leather bootlaces from his dresser and used them to strangle her. Then he said he loaded the girl's body into the trunk of the Datsun he was driving at the time and steered south on Highway 71 from Coushatta to a highway bridge between the little towns of Clarence and Montgomery, in Winn Parish. Browne said he then dumped the teenager's body over the side and heard it hit water. In a subsequent conversation he would explain that he hadn't planned to drive so far with Fuzzy before disposing of her, but traffic was too heavy for him to take the risk closer to home. Three months later, Katherine Hayes's skull was discovered by a hunter in what by then had become a dry creek bed. Tufts of her stepdaughter's distinctively red hair still clung to the bone, says Bettie Joice Smith. She was positively identified by means of dental records.

Twenty-Five

Charlie Hess liberally interwove personal chitchat throughout the interview, just as he had with his written correspondence. There were fishing stories and tales from his personal life.

"He always does that," says Jeff Nohr. "He was jumping all over the place."

Next jump: Flatonia.

"What do you want to know?" Browne asked.

"Anything. Anything you want to tell me," Hess answered.

"Well, I told you pretty much everything there is to tell, except the one person who could put me with her."

Hess perked up. "Let's talk about that," he said.

Browne explained that he had been staying at a place called the Antlers Inn that night. It was right on his regular artificial flower delivery route. Around back of the motel was the Stag Bar.

"I was in the bar, and this gal came in barefoot," he said. "I don't remember if she had on jeans or shorts or whatever. And she was pretty drunk. She was looking for her boyfriend or husband at the time. Anyway, the bartender didn't want her there, so she asked me if I would give her a ride to another bar down the street where her husband or boyfriend might be. That's how I got her."

"Uh-huh."

"I left the bar with her."

"OK. After you left the bar with her, where did you go?"

"I took her back to my motel room."

"Not her room?"

"No, my room."

"Then, I was going to ask this question. When she was stabbed with the ice pick —"

"Uh-huh."

"Was she alive or not alive?"

"She was alive."

"She was alive."

"I used ether to keep her quiet, you know, to put her to sleep."

"You used chloroform or ether?"

"I used ether on her."

"Did I tell you what the coroner said she died from?"

"No. You mentioned about something in her stomach."

"Yeah. Let me ask you this, since you've been frank. I'm sorry, let me back up. I lost my train of thought. You go back to the room, and after the things happened that happened in the room, was it? . . . Did you take her immediately to the place where you put her?"

"No. I left her in the room."

"Until when?"

Until Robert Browne returned from a nearby truck stop, where he'd eaten breakfast with the bartender at the Stag Bar, he said.

"So she didn't end up in the culvert or whatever until after breakfast?"

"Yeah."

"And it was still night?"

"It was. I think the bar closed somewhere around twelve or two, or whatever."

The focus then shifted to Nidia Mendoza, the Texas teenager who preceded Melody Bush on Browne's victim list by about six weeks.

Browne told Hess that he put the girl's body into the motel bathtub and began by cutting off her legs. Then, he said, he removed her head and her arms.

Scott Fischer, who later listened to the interview tape with a group of investigators, recalls the room "just went flat," when Browne said that he had cut off Mendoza's arms. They all knew that Nidia's murderer left her arms intact.

Not until the end of the interview did Browne return to this point, as though he had been puzzling over it. "You know," he said, "she was so small . . . let me correct that. I did not cut her arms off. I cut her legs off and her head off." Nidia's torso and arms, he said, fit nicely into his suitcase.

"The way he said that, it was like I've done this a dozen times and I can't remember how exactly I cut them up," says Fischer. The tape also persuaded Scott Fischer that, as far as the Mendoza case went, Browne was telling the truth.

"The location of the body and his description of how he severed her, that's when all doubt went out of my mind," he says. "This guy was either present or he did it."

Later, when Jeff Nohr joined Hess and Browne in the interview sessions, he returned to the Mendoza case, probing for details. How exactly had Browne dissected, or disarticulated, the young girl?

Browne described the work with his customary dispassion. He worked his knife into the soft tissue at the joints until he reached bone. Then, he told the investigators, he grabbed the dead girl by each ankle, one after the other, and twisted her legs. Her hips easily popped from their sockets.

"What did you do with the knife when you finished?" Nohr asked.

"I wiped it off and put it back in the drawer."

As they talked, Browne flexed and stretched his hands.

Jesus, Nohr thought as he watched, *what have those hands done?*

It was important, Nohr knew, not to show emotion or to say anything that Browne might interpret as a judgment, lest the inmate stop talking. Even so, the detective found himself wondering as the visits progressed what, if any, emotion Browne might have felt. Why did Browne do what he had done? How could anyone be so heartlessly cruel?

Charlie Hess never considered such questions and was impatient with Nohr's concerns.

"Why? Why? Why? You want to ask why?" he said when Nohr raised the subject. "Why does it matter?"

"It's for me to learn about this case and any case I deal with in the future," Nohr answered. "When I'm looking at a particular crime scene, I can relate back to what Robert said."

So Jeff Nohr continued to probe and eventually got a few answers from Browne.

Nidia Mendoza, Browne said, was one murder that bothered him.

"Why did that one bother you?" Nohr asked, not looking at Charlie sitting beside him at the interview table.

"Because I had to spend so much time with her."

"What does that have to do with?" the detective wanted to know.

"We were having sex and she said, 'Slap me.' I said, 'What?' 'Slap me.' So I hit her," he said, "and then I strangled her."

"Why did you strangle her if you felt bad about it?" Nohr asked.

"I guess I just wanted my money back," Browne said.

Mendoza had charged him $100.

The February 23, 2005, conversation returned once again to Wanda Faye Hudson. Hess asked if Browne knew that Hudson had a boyfriend. Yes, he said, a local pharmacist named Higgs. Browne also was aware that Higgs had been questioned repeatedly in the murder, while he himself had never been interviewed.

Why not? Hess wanted to know. After all, Robert lived next door to the victim, a circumstance that would not be lost on those familiar with the Heather Church case.

Browne pointed out that he was married to Rita Coleman at the time. Although their marriage was disintegrating, they most definitely were together that night. They'd been to a family gathering at the home of his brother Donald and returned late to his cabin at the River Towne Apartments. There was a lot of drinking. Rita went to sleep.

Next morning, when the police knocked on his door to ask if he'd seen or heard anything, Browne said no. He and his wife had been out late and went to bed the moment they got home.

Without pause Hess then moved to the Grand Am Lady — so abruptly that he surprised Jeff Nohr. "Charlie just jumped right into it," the detective recalls. "It took me a few moments to figure out what he was doing."

He produced a little folder containing the photos of the building exterior Scott Fischer had taken and began showing them to Browne, who reviewed the pictures one by one until he finally stopped, pointed at a building, and said, "Right about there."

He said the Kwik Stop where he worked was located just north of this, the Grand Am Lady's apartment complex. Her apartment was on the north side of the building, on the ground level, three or four doors from the end.

"How did you meet her?" Hess asked.

Browne said the woman and her husband were frequent customers at the Kwik Stop.

"Do you recall her name?"

"I don't recall her name."

"How about her husband's name?"

"Don't recall that either. They were just a young couple, and they stopped in there. They would rent the video player and movies."

"And you don't remember anything about their names?"

"I don't remember names. I'm the world's worst with names. I do remember [his army grade] was something like a Spec 4."

"Yeah. You told me that."

Browne then spent a few minutes using the photos to orient Hess to the neighborhood and the relative locations of his apartment, the Grand Am Lady's apartment, and the Kwik Stop.

"And how did she meet her demise?" Hess asked at length.

"I'm trying to remember," Browne answered. "I know I strangled her. Yeah, and I remember I strangled her that night. She . . . also I dismembered, or disarticulated or whatever you want to call it."

"Uh-huh."

"Put her in the Dumpster in the apartment complex over there. Took her out piece by piece in trash bags and put her in the Dumpster."

"You dismembered her in your apartment?"

"Yes, bathtub."

"And you put her in a Dumpster?"

"[And] the knife and plastic garbage bags."

"In your own Dumpster, right there at your own apartment?"

"Yeah."

"That's taking a pretty big chance. I'm mean, you're rational —"

Here, Browne stopped the conversation to make an emphatic point. "Rational people," he told Hess, "wouldn't do what I do."

Hess laughed. So did Browne.

"Sometimes," the killer added, "the most obvious things are the easiest things to get away with."

"Yeah, I've heard that," Hess answered. "Yeah."

"Too obvious."

Then Hess said, without prelude or further discussion, "I'm going to show you something else real quick," as he slid a stack of pictures from a fishing trip to Mexico across the table to Browne.

The conversation returned to the white Grand Am Lady a short while after.

According to the later affidavit:

Mr. Hess asked Mr. Browne how many times he had been at the victim's residence. Mr. Browne replied once. Mr. Hess asked Mr. Browne how he knew how to get to the woman's apartment. Mr. Browne replied the woman had come into the convenience store that day and had agreed to go out on a "date" and she gave him her address.

Mr. Browne said her husband was gone and had taken their baby to one of two places, either Miami, Florida, or New Orleans, Louisiana. Mr. Browne said he thought they were from one of those two places.

Mr. Browne said he and the Grand Am Lady went to a movie together. He said they went in her vehicle, a white Pontiac Grand Am, and then returned to his apartment after the movie.

Mr. Browne said after arriving at his apartment, he strangled her. Mr. Hess asked Mr. Browne where he kept the victim in the apartment. Mr. Browne advised he left her on the floor to one side of the room, where he had all of his blankets, and threw blankets over her. Mr. Browne said, "You couldn't tell anyone was there."

Mr. Hess asked Mr. Browne if he dismembered her that night. Mr. Browne said he was tired and did not do it that night; he left her there. After covering the body with blankets, he took the woman's keys and drove her vehicle, the 1987 Grand Am, to her apartment complex parking lot.

Upon entering the woman's apartment, Mr. Browne noted the kitchen was on the right of the entry way and the living room was to the left. He looked around the apartment for items of value and found nothing of interest. Mr. Browne said he knew the couple had bought a new Sony color television set. He took the television, and as he was leaving the apartment, he was confronted by a security guard for the apartment complex. The security guard asked him if the television was his. Mr. Browne replied "yes," and returned to the victim's Grand Am.

■ ■ ■ ■

Actually, the confrontation with the guard amused Browne, and he remembered chuckling to himself as he returned to his apartment with the television.

He went to work at the Kwik Stop the next day, leaving the woman's body under the pile of blankets. There was no chance she'd be discovered. Browne was living alone, and did not receive surprise visits. After work he came home, carried her body to his bathtub, selected a knife and began to cut.

"Mr. Browne," reads the affidavit, "said he reached 'in and did [his] thing.' He described how he severed her at the joints, 'just popping them' and taking the body apart. Mr. Browne said there was only a small amount of blood, but it stayed in the bathtub. Mr. Browne said the tub itself was the only thing that needed to be cleaned."

Like Nidia Mendoza before her, the "Grand Am Lady" was now more than dead; she was destroyed.

The affidavit continues: "Mr. Browne advised he took a ring from the victim. He described it as a 'big cluster ring with a lot of small diamonds.' "

Mr. Browne said he drove the victim's vehicle for a couple of days, and then parked it in the parking lot of the Dove Tree Apartments, 335 North Murray Boulevard, which was directly south of the Kwik Stop. He knew the victim's husband would find it there.

Mr. Browne said when the victim's husband returned, he came into the Kwik Stop store and used the pay phone to notify the police that his wife was missing, as well as his 1987 white Grand Am. Your Affiant showed Mr. Browne a black and white photograph of a 1987 Pontiac Grand Am. After Mr. Browne looked at the photograph, he stated it looked a "little boxy," but it may be similar to the car that belonged to the victim. He said, "It could be, because it was a two door and had a small backseat." Mr. Browne said it was a four speed and had blue cloth interior. Mr. Browne said the car was very clean and was possibly less than a year old and did not have very many miles.

TWENTY-SIX

February 23, 2005, shines in the cold case squad's collective memory as the turning point in their complex history with Robert Browne. They called it their "watershed event." It appeared to be Charlie Hess's moment of validation, too. Years of frustration and corrosive doubt suddenly gave way to cautious optimism at the sheriff's office in the wake of Browne's latest revelations. The investigation could now focus on two objectives: find and identify the Grand Am Lady. At least there was now a small store of relevant and reliable information with which to work.

With Jeff Nohr's arrival, the dynamics of the squad changed as well. Over the two and a half years of letter writing with Browne, Lou Smit and Scott Fischer had done most of the legwork and served as sounding boards for Hess, who generally liked to work the hot leads himself. These had been agreeable roles for both men, who were happy to defer to Hess and had other responsibilities to fulfill.

"Jeff just really took control of the case," Smit explains. With Nohr on board and with audiotaping begun, Smit found his greatest value to the project was to chat it up around the office, where doubters persisted. With his stellar reputation as a detective, Smit was a powerful, if quiet, voice in support of Hess's strategy.

When he wasn't out on patrol as a reserve deputy, Scott Fischer continued to serve as the cold case squad's information manager, making sure that the recorded interviews were transcribed, typed up, and sorted into evidence volumes, as well as electronic files. "A lot of what I did was grunt work," he says.

Both men shared a rising sense of anticipation as the investigation finally developed a little traction.

The sheriff's detectives knew from employment records that Browne had worked at the Kwik Stop from September 15, 1987, to January 16, 1988, when he had been fired for closing the store early one night. If he was telling the truth, that substantially narrowed his window of opportunity from a few years to just a few months. Plus they now knew how and where the crime had occurred.

The haystack was getting smaller.

The Colorado Bureau of Investigation was asked to compile a list of all Pontiac Grand Ams and Trans Ams registered in the state between January 1, 1987, and December 31, 1988. Since Browne had been hazy on the exact date of the crime, they wanted to make sure they captured information on all possible vehicles.

The list came back on March 31, 2005. There were 172 Pontiacs of these model types, with license plate and vehicle identification numbers for each.

The job of identifying and locating the owners fell to Detective Rick Frady.

Thickset, with thinning sandy hair and a ruddy complexion, Frady was a retired Army officer and a relative newcomer to local law enforcement. Before joining the major crimes division of the sheriff's office, he had worked in the jail, on patrol, and then for three years chasing down stolen cars. In 2004, he led a team that cracked a major theft ring. They recovered $750,000 in stolen equipment, including a trailer full of fossilized dinosaur bones.

Meticulous by nature, Frady hadn't spent twenty-one years in the military — including three years as an instructor at the United States Military Academy at West Point — without learning to dot and cross and check and cross-check his facts until every piece fit.

His critical tool was VINs.

VINs, or vehicle identification numbers, are seventeen-figure alphanumeric codes issued to every automobile or truck built in the United States after 1980. A car or truck's VIN is as unique to that vehicle as fingerprints are to a human.

Each letter and number in a VIN codes for a specific piece of information about the car, from its manufacturer to its engine size. For example, if a vehicle was made by General Motors, the first two numbers should be either 1G or 2G. Anything else, and something's wrong. Rick Frady could tell at a glance if a VIN had been corrupted, accidentally or otherwise.

Frady scanned the computer list and instantly spotted an anomaly. One of the VINs was only sixteen figures long. It read: 1G2NE14WHC926030. He sent the faulty code off to the National Insurance Crime Bureau and went to work on the 171 remaining Pontiacs.

Although computers have speeded the process considerably, it still took several

days for Rick Frady to compile a list of owners' names and addresses from the Colorado
Crime Information Center (CCIC) database. Of course, the list was limited to
Colorado Grand Am and Trans Am owners
and where they'd lived in 1987 and 1988.
Who knew where these people might be
fifteen years later — or if they even were
still alive?

He would need to search yet another
database, this time person by person, to find
current addresses and phone numbers or in
some cases, relatives who might tell him
where a missing owner was, or wasn't. Over
the next two weeks, Frady made more than
a hundred phone calls, each time posing the
same set of queries.

"Did you ever own a white Pontiac Grand
Am? When did you own it? Where did you
live when you owned it? Do you still have
the vehicle? If not, what happened to it?"

Most people were cooperative, though at
least a dozen seemed apprehensive and
evasive, setting off bells in Frady's cop
brain. These folks had something to hide,
though it probably had nothing to do with
Robert Browne's alleged murder victim.
Cars had been sold and resold, stolen and
recovered, parted out, wrecked. At least a
dozen of the Pontiacs had gone to the

crusher. But none of the cars or their owners fit Browne's scenario.

In a nearby room in the plain brown brick building on Costilla Street that housed the sheriff's department investigators, Lieutenant Ken Hilte and Jeff Nohr set about trying to find people who had lived in the sprawling apartment complex on the corner of Pikes Peak and Murray Boulevard in the late 1980s. For this part of the search, Hilte turned to the dusty old Coles Directories, fat blue volumes from the pre-Internet age that listed city residents by address. He pulled four years' worth, from 1985 to 1989.

Then, as now, the stucco-sided apartment buildings in Browne's old neighborhood were home mostly to servicemen, young couples, and people looking for work and cheap rent. The view of Pikes Peak looming over its namesake avenue was indeed spectacular, but that was about the only good thing anyone could say about the grim buildings with thin, Sheetrock walls and peeling paint on the metal stair railings. No one stayed for long at the Grand Am Lady's address, which in any event had changed owners. Rental records from the 1980s no longer existed.

The old address lists then were compared to up-to-date databases as the investigators searched again for matches. Once more, they worked the telephones, which once again was frustrating. Most of the numbers they dialed had been disconnected.

Their big break finally came courtesy of the National Crime Insurance Bureau. The NCIB had reconstructed Rick Frady's faulty VIN and figured out the likely cause for the glitch. Some clerk, probably when the car was first registered, had mistaken *UI* for *W* and accordingly had incorrectly entered the VIN in the CCIC records. The correct VIN was 1G2NE14U1HC926030. The car's then and current owner, Frady quickly learned, was a Florida man named Joseph Anthony Sperry.

They were partway home.

Jeff Nohr then scanned his list of neighborhood apartment renters, looking for a Joseph Sperry. Sure enough, he found one.

"A little light came on and I said, 'Damn!' " Frady recalled. "It was one of those things where you go through dozens and dozens of things and it looks like nothing is going to pan out, and then, all of a sudden, you hit that thing, and you think, 'This might really be something.' "

But where was Joseph Sperry?

Nohr tapped into every database he could think of and came up with but a single, out-of-date factoid: Joe Sperry had done time in a Florida prison. There was no current phone number or address listed for Sperry, though he was last known to be in West Palm Beach. The police in West Palm had no information. All Nohr had was a $5.50 Accurint report that listed Joe Sperry's "known associates," including a person named Amie Charity. He called her number.

Based on his experience to date, Nohr was not optimistic. The few former Murray Boulevard residents he'd been able to find by telephone had been uniformly unhelpful, even hostile. One, whom he found in New York, even berated him for taking so long to investigate the case.

A woman answered his call. Nohr asked to speak to Amie Charity. He was told she wasn't in.

"Actually, I'm looking for a man named Joseph Sperry," the detective said, expecting to be told that no such individual lived at that address.

Instead, he heard the woman call out, "Hey, Joe! It's for you."

She in fact was Joe Sperry's wife. Amie Charity was his mother, who lived in another state. Her son, for his own reasons, kept his telephone in her name.

Before Jeff Nohr knew it, Joe Sperry was

on the line.

"I was shocked," the detective says. "There was no way this was going to happen. I'm thinking I'm going to be making a dozen phone calls to find this guy and now, he's on the phone and I'm thinking, Is he the one? Am I going to tell this guy we have a guy in prison who says he murdered his wife?"

Nohr began gingerly, asking the standard questions. "Did you ever own a white Grand Am?"

Yes, said Sperry. It was outside in the yard, though it didn't run.

Were you in the military?

Yes. Stationed at Fort Carson.

Did you live at 4410 Pikes Peak Avenue?

Yes, from August to December of 1987. Apartment number 109.

Nohr felt a surge of excitement.

When Hess had shown Browne pictures of the apartment building at Murray and Platte, trying to pinpoint where the Grand Am Lady lived, the killer had focused on a row of doors. Might have been here, here, or here, Browne had said, pointing to apartment numbers 107, 108, and 109.

The detective hesitated, then asked Joe Sperry, "Did you have a wife or a girlfriend who disappeared then?"

A pause. Then, in a breaking voice, Joe Sperry said yes, Rocio, his wife and the mother of his daughter, Amie. She vanished in November 1987. The story burst from him in a torrent of tears.

TWENTY-SEVEN

Joe Sperry had never stopped mourning his beautiful child bride.

The deep emotional pain of losing Rocio was as fresh in Sperry's voice in April 2005, over the telephone from West Palm Beach, as it had been in his heart eight years earlier when he'd flown home to find his wife had vanished with no trace, no explanation, and with apparently no hope of ever unraveling the awful mystery. The surprise call from Jeff Nohr had simply released in a sudden flood the wrenching agony that Joe Sperry, and later his daughter, Amie, lived with every day.

Over the course of several conversations, Sperry told Nohr that he met his future wife in a mobile home park in south Florida, where he was visiting friends. Rocio was just thirteen years old, and he was eighteen, a high school dropout from New Orleans. She was Cuban and had immigrated to the

United States with her family on an Ecuadorian passport.

Rocio's girlhood so far had been difficult. Not long after arriving in the U.S., her abusive mother had beaten her so violently, on a beach in front of dozens of witnesses, that authorities placed Rocio into a foster home, where the abuse continued, though in a less public way.

She was on her third foster home when Joe met her. They talked about their families and their childhoods — Sperry's had been chaotic, as well — and they bonded.

Rocio was gorgeous, a tiny girl only five feet, four inches tall and 104 pounds, with long, shiny black hair and happy ways, in spite of everything she had endured. Joe fell for her at once, even though he realized Rocio was much too young for him. Within a few months, they were living together, and Rocio soon was pregnant. They married.

Joe enlisted in the Army, looking for a better way to support his family. Rocio, he would later say, inspired him to get his act together, to make something out of himself.

In August 1987, Joe was transferred to Fort Carson. Rocio and Amie, then an infant, came with him, and the little family settled into an apartment at 4410 Pikes Peak Avenue. It was the only place Sperry could find that he could afford, and then just barely.

Rocio by now was fifteen, in many ways still a child, trying to take care of a baby, and not always succeeding. At the same time, Joe's heavy training schedule kept him on base, away from his wife and daughter, more hours than he liked. Money also was a problem. He called his mother, Amie Charity, in Florida. She was eager to see her namesake granddaughter, and Joe needed to borrow some money. They arranged for a visit.

Sperry flew with little Amie to Florida on November 7, 1987. Two days later, Rocio telephoned Joe's aunt, Barbara Carbo, with whom she was close. Rocio said she was calling from the apartment of a man she identified as a "GI from Shreveport." She giggled and joked that the man was cute. He had a "golden bed," she said.

Carbo also spoke briefly with the GI from Shreveport. She'd recall that he had a faint Southern accent. He told her that Rocio "was a very naive girl," and that he did not want her in his apartment. He thought she could cause problems. In the background, Carbo thought she heard Rocio making smooching sounds.

Rocio telephoned her husband in Florida

just before dawn on November 10, 1987 — the day that investigators believe was her last. Something was wrong.

"I could tell that she was upset," Joe Sperry recalls. "I asked her what was wrong and she said, 'Nothing. I just wanted to call and tell you that I love you and miss you. And tell the baby that I'll always love her.'"

They agreed to talk again that evening. But when Joe called as arranged, there was no answer. He telephoned again, repeatedly, over the next few days. Nothing.

When his plane landed in Denver in the midst of an early-season blizzard on November 14, Sperry expected to find his wife and his friend, George Gonzales, waiting at the airport to meet him, as they previously had discussed. Neither Gonzalez nor Rocio showed up. When he telephoned Gonzales from the airport, he was told that both Rocio and their new, white Pontiac Grand Am were gone.

Sperry found his wife's clothes piled into garbage bags in their apartment. A ten-inch hank of her hair, still in a ponytail bound with a rubber band, lay on the dresser. His new Sony TV was missing, although Rocio's purse, which contained her birth certificate and passport, was still there.

He called the Colorado Springs police.

According to police department policy, he was told that officers would not take a report until Rocio had been missing for seventy-two hours. Sperry hung up and called back to report a domestic disturbance.

"I need the cops out here right now," he said, fear and agitation in his voice.

When an officer arrived at his apartment, Sperry showed him the hank of Rocio's hair. In his heart, Sperry has always believed that the person who took Rocio cut off her hair and left it for him to find.

The officer, horrified by the hank of hair, agreed to file a missing person report, along with theft reports for the car and TV. He seemed sympathetic and concerned, and told Sperry to talk to detectives the next day at the police station.

Even so, Sperry had a hard time getting the Colorado Springs Police Department to take his wife's disappearance seriously. And when they did, he soon found himself atop their suspect list.

Almost two weeks after he returned to the Springs, walking back to his apartment along Murray Boulevard from the grocery store, Sperry spotted his missing Grand Am. The car was parked along the fence between the Kwik Stop and a neighboring apartment complex.

He raced back to the Kwik Stop and asked the clerk — Robert Browne — if he could use the store telephone. While Browne listened, Sperry unleashed his anger on police.

As he later recalled, "I'm saying, 'You ain't doing your blankety-blank job! I have to find my own car.' I'm cursing at them, telling them that they don't want to do anything."

When a uniformed officer finally arrived to make a report, Sperry lost it again, this time hurling racial epithets at the policeman, an African American.

"I was begging him to tow the car, fingerprint it, open the trunk," Sperry recalls. "I didn't want to touch it until they went over it, 'cause I thought, whoever took my car has my wife. And he's saying, 'No, I'm not going to do that.' So I called him a stupid nigger."

The police officer threatened to arrest Sperry.

"I *want* you to arrest me!" Joe shouted, "because then you'll have to tow the car."

In the end, Sperry walked back to his apartment, put on gloves, and drove the car home. He'd later recall noticing the imprint left by what looked like a heavy box that had rested on plush upholstery of the passenger's seat. Jeff Nohr guesses the indentation was the last trace of Sperry's missing TV.

The Colorado Springs Police Department did not distinguish itself in the Rocio Sperry matter. Perhaps they assumed that either Joe had killed her, which Sperry vehemently denied, or that Rocio had not come to grief but was just another runaway teen, tired of the married life and motherhood.

Apparently little effort went into canvassing the local neighborhoods or interviewing those who possibly had information. The police knew from Joe, for example, that Rocio and her friends often walked with the baby up Murray Boulevard to the Kwik Stop to buy candy. A Sperry acquaintance volunteered that she last saw Rocio on the afternoon of November 10, walking north on Murray toward the Kwik Stop. Another neighbor told police that he heard someone enter the Sperrys' apartment just after midnight on November 11. Then the door to 109 slammed shut, and there was the sound of footsteps moving away from the apartment a few minutes later.

But there's no indication that officers ever asked the Kwik Stop clerk what he might know or looked at his criminal background. Had they done so, they would have seen that Robert Charles Browne was a parolee from Louisiana with auto theft and burglary charges on his record.

If they tried to trace the call that Rocio made from the Shreveport GI's phone to Barbara Carbo or any of her other calls to Joe in Florida, there's no record of what they found out. Seventeen years later, when Jeff Nohr tried to determine whether Rocio had in fact called Carbo from Browne's apartment, it was too late. The phone records were long gone.

On January 22, 1988, a volunteer cleaning out Colorado Springs Police Department files inexplicably wrote on Rocio Sperry's missing person report that she had been found. Five years later, the report was removed from the system and archived. All the physical evidence collected in the case was thrown away. Neither her case nor Rocio Sperry herself existed any longer in fact or file. By the time Robert Browne started hinting about a murdered wife and a missing car, only the vehicle retained any vestigial existence.

Following Rocio's disappearance, her grief-stricken husband quickly spiraled out of control. Not only had Joe Sperry lost his wife, but members of his own family, including his mother, thought he had something to do with Rocio's disappearance. He argued with Army buddies and had a hard time focusing on his duties.

Within weeks of losing her, Sperry was discharged from the Army and left Colorado for Florida. An aunt who lived in Mississippi agreed to assume care of Amie. Joe then shattered another man's eye socket in a brawl and went to prison on assault charges. He married again and divorced. His father, the one person who had believed unequivocally in Joe's innocence, died.

Joe lost his job, got hooked on heroin. Then he finally straightened up, married again, and put some order in his life for the first time in a long, long while. Then Detective Jeff Nohr called, and the black pit of memory threatened to swallow him up once again.

Sperry told Nohr that he still had his copy of Rocio's meager missing person report, which he promptly mailed to the detective. Nohr later noticed that Joe had scribbled the El Paso County sheriff's current phone number on the missing person flyer, along with these words: "Bad news. Closure. With love."

"If he had killed his wife and now, after all these years, another guy was taking credit for it, do you think he would have written, 'Bad news?' " Nohr says. "That note told me that this is a guy who never stopped grieving for his wife."

Nohr hung up the telephone absolutely certain that Robert Browne had murdered Rocio Sperry as he said he did. Joe's story had matched Browne's account in every detail; the missing Army wife, the husband's trip to Florida with the baby, the first-floor apartment, the stolen television, the husband's outrage with police, the white Grand Am found exactly where Browne said he left it. The car also was nearly new, with few miles on the odometer. And it had a blue-cloth interior, too, just as Browne had said it did.

Now all Jeff Nohr had to do was corroborate Browne's story with physical evidence, anything tangible to link Browne to his crime. It wouldn't be easy. Nothing was.

TWENTY-EIGHT

On March 14, Charlie Hess steered Browne back to Melody Bush's murder.

"He said the woman and her husband or boyfriend were having an argument," Jeff Nohr later noted in an affidavit, "and the woman thought her husband/boyfriend may have gone to another bar down the street. He said the bartender asked him (Mr. Browne) if he would take this woman to the other bar. Mr. Browne said, 'At first I said no, but then I said okay.'

"Mr. Browne said as he was driving the woman to the other bar, she began to 'make out' with him. He said he took her back to his motel room where they had sex. He said after '. . . then I used ether on her. Put her out. And then I used a ice pick on her.' Mr. Hess asked Mr. Browne how much time he had spent with Ms. Bush. Mr. Browne replied 'Before I killed her? Twenty minutes maybe. If that. Wasn't long. She was just actin' like a slutty, low-life woman, wantin' to "fuck." ' Mr. Browne said the woman was, 'slobbering drunk, behavin' like the slut she was.' Mr. Browne said, 'and so what the hell. Opportunity arose again.'

"Mr. Browne said afterwards, he returned to the bar where he had met the woman. He said he remained at the bar for a little while and then returned to his motel room to make plans. Mr. Browne did not describe what those plans were. He said he returned to the bar yet again, around closing time. Mr. Browne said he was not sure if plans were made prior to him leaving the bar earlier, but he and the bartender were going to go to breakfast. He said when the bar closed, he and the bartender went to a local truck stop to have breakfast. Mr. Browne said they drove the bartender's vehicle to and from the truck stop. Mr. Browne said after having breakfast, he returned to his motel room where Ms. Bush's body was still located on the bed.

"Mr. Browne told Mr. Hess after a while, he loaded the body into his van and drove north across the Interstate to a bridge or culvert. He could not remember, but did recall there were rails. He said he stopped his van and dumped the body over the rails and heard the body hit water. Mr. Browne described the area as having tall grass and water.

"Mr. Hess asked Mr. Browne about using ether. Mr. Browne replied he used ether a number of times. Mr. Hess asked Mr. Browne if he ever used acetone. Mr. Browne replied he never used acetone on any of his victims."

Although Browne had insisted to Hess that he breakfasted with the Stag Bar's bartender after murdering Melody Bush and before he disposed of her body, the bartender (or manager, as she described herself) could not corroborate his memory.

According to the affidavit, "The Fayette County Sheriff's Office interviewed Florine Rutkowski, the manager of the Stag Club, on 04/02/84. Ms. Rutkowski advised investigators Melody Bush had come into the Stag Bar at approximately 11:30 p.m., on 03/19/84. Ms. Rutkowski remembered Melody Bush was having trouble walking. Ms. Rutkowski said Melody Bush was dressed in a black sweater with red heart designs around the chest area, silver pants and no shoes. She said Ms. Bush was carrying a black purse. Ms. Rutkowski said Melody Bush left the Stag Club alone. The Fayette County Sheriff's Office reports do not mention anything about Ms. Rutkowski asking anyone to give Ms. Bush a ride to another bar, nor was Mr. Browne mentioned in their report."

Twenty-two years later, Texas Ranger Otto Hanak, then assigned to the still officially open case, relocated Ms. Rutkowski, now Mrs. Florine J. Troquille.

The former bar manager told Hanak she still remembered Melody, her marital problems, and how drunk and "spaced out" she was the night she disappeared. Hanak showed her pictures of Browne, whom she recognized as a silk flower salesman who regularly stopped by the bar over the six months prior to Melody's murder. Sometimes he handed out his flowers to women in the bar. One time, he gave her eight-year-old daughter a silk daisy. However, Troquille did not remember the salesman present on the night in question, and she denied ever seeing him together with the victim. She also said she had never gone anywhere with him.

Melody Bush's husband, Robert Stewart Bush, also was interviewed at the time of his wife's homicide. He told investigators, according to reports, that two friends had come to their motel room to party with him and Melody. When the Bushes began to argue, which reportedly was common for them, Melody stalked out of the room, headed for the Stag Bar. Robert Bush said he then went to sleep and did not wake up until six the next morning.

From the outset, Texas law enforcement officials had resisted the possibility that Robert Browne murdered Melody Bush as he claimed, and the Stag Bar manager's inability or unwillingness to corroborate Browne's recollection of her actions the night Bush disappeared only reinforced those doubts. Fayette County investigators discounted Browne's accurate description of the victim — tall and slim — and his knowledge that her husband was questioned by police. This was information anyone could have picked up. Indeed, Browne told Hess that he'd heard about the authorities' interest in his victim's husband on a subsequent visit to the Stag Bar.

J & H Wholesale Flower Company had since gone out of business, so there were no employment records that might at least put Browne in the Flatonia vicinity on the night of March 19, 1984. One of the late owner's daughters did remember Browne, but she could not say with certainty when he had worked for the company. In fact, the only available dates to confirm Browne's employment with J & H were the ones that he had supplied in 1987 on an employment application for the Kwik Stop job. Since he always paid in cash while he was on the road — or so Browne claimed to Charlie Hess — he'd left no paper trail at credit card companies.

Another source of doubt was the business about the ether and the ice pick; it simply was not supported by the facts at hand, i.e., the autopsy report. And though there were serious misgivings in Flatonia and around Fayette County over Dr. Bayardo's theory of acute acetone poisoning, that didn't make Browne look any more credible. Without any hard and reliable forensic information to go by, it was broadly assumed by authorities that Melody Bush — who'd made heavy recreational use of both alcohol and drugs — had died of a drug overdose.

Browne himself conceded that he was describing "very unusual circumstances," in his version of her death. A chary Jeff Nohr pressed him hard to see if the killer might trip on his own invention.

On April 12, 2005, the detective asked Browne where he kept his ether.

In his company van, he said, for cold days when it was hard to fire up its diesel motor. Nohr, a farm boy from the upper Midwest who knew something about starting vehicles in the wintertime, recognized the application. He also knew you could buy spray cans of ether for this use in many auto supply stores.

"Was it liquid ether?" he asked.

Browne wrinkled his forehead at such a question. "No," he answered. "It was in an aerosol can."

And what was Browne doing with an ice pick that night?

Browne replied matter-of-factly that he'd purchased a block of ice and needed something with which to break it up.

As Browne explained it, his story sounded somewhat less far-fetched, though clearly "very unusual." It sorted well with his other disclosures, particularly his description of how Wanda Faye Hudson was murdered. But it just did not square with the autopsy findings.

Skepticism in law enforcement circles over the quality of the work done at the Travis County Medical Examiner's Office stemmed in large part from some highly publicized and deeply embarrassing mistakes. Dr. Bayardo resigned as Travis County medical examiner in 2006. In one case highlighted by the *Austin American-Statesman*, a pathologist on Bayardo's team mistook the badly burned body of an eighty-one-year-old woman for that of a twenty-three-year-old man, even going so far as to note the presence of the deceased's "penis" in the report.

Bayardo's autopsy of Melody Bush noted that the victim was clad in light pink party pants — Rutkowski had remembered they were silver — and a black pullover sweater with red hearts on it. Her pants were unzipped and torn at the crotch. There was also a tear in the sweater over Bush's right breast. She was wearing a gold wedding band and a gold ring with a black stone on her right hand.

Bayardo found no sign of major trauma and recorded that Bush's body had decomposed to a degree consistent with being left exposed in a culvert for several days at that time of year. The toxicology screens were negative for Quaaludes, which some investigators surmised Bush had taken that night, as well as for barbiturates, salicylates (aspirin), cocaine, morphine, codeine, and a list of prescription medicines. Reports that she was very drunk the night she vanished — something that Browne and the bartender certainly *did* agree on — were not supported by the autopsy. Tests showed only a trace amount of alcohol in her system.

Tests for sperm were negative, also; another finding at odds with Browne's story.

Dr. Michael Doberson, a forensic pathologist and chief coroner for Arapahoe County, Colorado, reviewed Bush's autopsy report and found it curious in several respects. Doberson did agree with Bayardo that there was nothing to suggest that Melody Bush had sustained any gross physical injury — such as a stab wound — that might account for her death. "I would think," he says, "that if there were puncture marks you would see them and you would see the hemorrhage that is caused by the wound."

Yet another reason to question Robert Browne's story.

However, Doberson noted some key omissions in the autopsy, gaps that call into question the autopsy's thoroughness and accuracy. For instance, the autopsy notes maggots on the corpse but not maggot holes, which were presumably present and normally command a pathologist's close attention. Maggot holes — traces of their movements through decomposing tissue — can mimic gunshot and puncture wounds. As a result, says Doberson, they are individually and carefully dissected for just that reason.

"When we have a decomposed body, we're

extra careful," he explains. "You're even more attuned to the possibility that there is potential stuff that you could easily miss."

Dr. Doberson further noted there was no discussion in the autopsy of the sweater tear; no description of it and no indication whether the garment had been tested for the presence of blood.

The Travis County medical examiner seems to have settled on acute acetone poisoning as Melody's Bush's cause of death by a process of elimination. "The only thing they're hanging their hat on is the acetone," says Doberson. "That's the only thing they found."

But the autopsy's conclusion raises more questions than it answers. The toxicological report found 0.1 percent of acetone in Bush's blood and a similar concentration of the solvent in her gastric contents. Zero point one percent acetone in the blood generally is not lethal, certainly not acutely so. But even such a comparatively small amount of this highly volatile and irritating solvent would gag just about anyone. So how did it get there?

Werner Jenkins, the chief toxicologist with the El Paso County Coroner's Office, thinks he may know the answer.

According to Jenkins's research, there are

only three plausible ways for acetone to have turned up in Bush's body:

1. Diabetics who suffer from a condition called ketoacidosis often have elevated acetone in their blood. There's no available evidence whether Melody Bush was diabetic, but ketoacidosis in any event would not explain the acetone in her gut.
2. If Melody had drunk a huge amount of acetone or rubbing alcohol (which metabolizes into acetone). But, says Jenkins, "We can't imagine the scenario in which someone would drink enough of that to get a legally intoxicated level."
3. The acetone was an artifact of the autopsy itself. Jenkins explains that the glass pipettes used to collect autopsy specimens can become contaminated by acetone residues. Laboratories often use acetone to rinse their glassware because it evaporates quickly. But if a pathologist uses a freshly rinsed pipette before it has time to dry, he or she can contaminate the specimen. It is not a common occurrence, but it does happen, Jenkins says, and seems the most likely explanation.

TWENTY-NINE

Jeff Nohr joined Charlie Hess in the interview room with Browne beginning in March 2005. Up to that time, Hess had never read Browne his Miranda rights — essentially a person's constitutional protections against self-incrimination — a circumstance Nohr had to remedy.

The Miranda warning is short and direct. "You have the right to remain silent. Anything you say can and will be used against you in a court of law. You have the right to an attorney. If you cannot afford an attorney, one will be provided for you. Do you understand the rights I have just read to you? With these rights in mind, do you wish to speak to me?"

Given the informal character of the Browne conversations thus far, the trick was to put them on a firmer legal footing without destroying the chemistry Hess had worked so hard to establish. It was agreed that suddenly reading his Miranda rights to Browne could easily dry up the flow of information just as the killer was getting started.

So Nohr consulted with the district attorney's office, where he explored Colorado's legal alternative to Miranda called the Denison standard, established in 1996. According to Denison, just because a suspect is in custody on one charge does not necessarily mean that he is "in custody" for the purposes of questioning about a different, unrelated offense. In other words, Browne was in the custody of the Department of Corrections for the murder of Heather Church, but he was not in the custody of El Paso County sheriff's detectives who wanted to talk to him about the other deaths he claimed. The prison, was, in effect, Browne's home.

The El Paso County detectives could interview him there, as long as they met certain conditions outlined in the law. These begin with the language used to summon an inmate from his or her cell. It must be clear that the prisoner can say, "No." The surroundings in which the interview takes place must not be coercive. The suspect cannot be confronted with evidence of his or her alleged crime. And the interviewee cannot be unduly pressured.

Accordingly, Hess and Nohr began each meeting with a specific set of questions. "Are you here voluntarily? Would you have to answer my questions if you didn't want to?" And the DOC served coffee, which Browne savored. With these guidelines in place, the interviews continued.

Beginning in April 2005 they moved again to another venue. Browne's transfer in late autumn 2004 from lockdown at the Colorado State Penitentiary to the general population at the Fremont facility had been a temporary arrangement to permit him to attend some therapy sessions. Under normal circumstances, he would return to CSP once he'd completed the Fremont program.

But there was nothing normal about Robert Browne's circumstances, and so the sheriff's office approached the DOC with an unconventional request. Instead of sending Browne back to maximum security at CSP, could he be transferred to the Colorado Territorial Correctional Facility, a medium-security unit, also in Cañon City?

There were several arguments in favor of this arrangement, all having to do with the nature of their enterprise. The DOC headquarters staff, of course, was aware via its inspector's office that Browne was cooperating in a humanitarian effort to bring his victims' survivors some comfort in knowing the details of their loved ones' fates, which in some cases were total mysteries. They also knew that Browne had asked for certain perks in exchange for his information. One was a doctor visit, which he finally received in spring 2005. The other was a permanent transfer out of CSP and outside the state altogether if that could be managed.

In light of his expectations, returning Browne to CSP, the state's meanest, loudest, roughest joint, wasn't likely to encourage further cooperation. What was more, if the inmate population learned he was talking to the El Paso County authorities, possibly snitching on his brother cons, it would be very difficult to protect Browne's life at CSP.

Similarly, if other inmates anywhere knew that Browne was getting special treatment in return for his information, the news would spread instantaneously throughout the prison system, creating a prisoner-control debacle of gargantuan dimensions and ugly consequences.

After the cold case squad made its proposal to a sympathetic headquarters staff, Bill Zalman, director of inmate services, was delegated to contact Major Linda Maifield, custody and control manager at Territorial.

Once Maifield's boss, Warden James E. Abbott, blessed the idea, she eagerly went to work on the details.

"We're brothers and sisters in law enforcement," says Maifield, a former police officer. "I've always believed that. Our doors were wide open. Whatever we could do to help them, within our boundaries, we were willing to do."

Maifield's paramount consideration was the need for absolute and reliable secrecy. Her answer to that problem was to let just three other staffers at Territorial, including the warden and associate warden, in on the project. She declines to say just how she managed to get Browne back and forth, undetected, to a specially designated interview room more than twenty times in the coming months — "I don't want to tip my hand" — but admits, "Things like that don't normally happen. It was just highly unusual."

Territorial was a welcome lifestyle upgrade for Browne, who was soon also rewarded with a plum job in the prison's license plate plant. For a serial killer, he was doing very well behind the walls, and for the time being seemed fairly content with his situation. The upside for law enforcement, Hess and

Nohr were quick to point out, was a continued, if strictly controlled, flow of further information from Browne.

The night before each visit, Nohr says, he'd take a little time to mentally prepare for the ninety-minute session with Browne. "My thing," he says, "was 'Robert's my neighbor. Robert's my friend. Do not be judgmental. The point is to gain information and develop trust.'

"It's not something you can teach a new investigator, or the average person. I think it only comes with time and maturity. You split your mind in half; one side stays in reality and the other, well, whatever."

The morning ritual didn't vary much, either. Nohr would pick up Hess at his house, and then they'd stop at a McDonald's for Egg McMuffins and coffee somewhere along the fifty-five-mile drive.

Most of the Territorial conversations in the spring of 2005 were devoted to the murders that Browne had first hinted at almost two years earlier in his "trip letter" of May 20, 2003. The killer also disclosed yet another possible victim in El Paso County, the so-called "Cowboy Lady" whom Browne said he met at Cowboys Night Club on Palmer Park Boulevard in Colorado Springs.

He first saw her "making her rounds," as he put it, at the nightclub on a spring or summer night sometime between 1990 and 1994. As usual, Browne could not remember her name, and was uncertain of the date. He described Cowboy Lady as thirty-five or so, tall and slender, about five feet six inches to five feet seven inches and 120 pounds. She was a bit taller, bigger, and older than most of the other victims he claimed, and her hair was bleached blond, a feature found elsewhere in the victim pool only with Faye Aline Self.

She was, Browne said, very drunk and flirtatious with men in the bar. But Cowboy Lady did not appear to be a prostitute, he added. As he was driving home later, Browne said, he saw her hitchhiking on Academy Boulevard, north of the bar. He picked her up and drove her in his red Ford Ranger to another nearby nightclub on Academy and North Carefree Boulevards. There, Browne said, they danced and drank, and she agreed to go home with him to the trailer on Eastonville Road. Diane Browne was out of town visiting relatives in Florida.

Browne told Hess and Nohr that he had sex with Cowboy Lady several times before strangling her. Afterward, he said, he wrapped her body in a large sheet of plastic and left it in a second bedroom.

Hess asked Browne if he had sex with the woman after he killed her.

"No," Browne said with annoyance. "She was dead."

Two nights later, the prisoner continued, he loaded Cowboy Lady, still snug in her plastic sheet, into the back of his pickup and drove westward from Colorado Springs on Gold Camp Road. The rutted, gravel track leads up and over the mountains to the old mining town of Cripple Creek. Like Rampart Range Road, where Heather Church's remains were found, Gold Camp Road is locally popular for body disposal.

Browne said he came to a high spot in the road. On the left was a sheer rock face. To the right, he could see a steep drop-off. Perfect. He said he took Cowboy Lady from the back of his truck, unrolled the plastic, and tossed her down the hillside. He put the plastic sheet back into his truck and continued westward for a short distance before turning around to return home. Heading east, he said, he saw the glint of moonlight reflecting off a body of water north of the road.

Nohr immediately began a check of missing person reports from Colorado Springs and the surrounding jurisdictions, as well as from the Colorado Bureau of Investigation. In the wake of the Sperry case screwup, Colorado Springs police pulled every missing person report for the sheriff's investigators, even those that had been cleared. One missing woman, who fit the description of the tall blond Cowboy Lady, turned out to be in Germany, where she had fled to escape a bad marriage. Investigators also checked with the management of Cowboys Night Club to see if any of their former employees had failed to collect a paycheck. No one had.

On their next visit to Territorial prison, Nohr and Hess took along topographical maps of the Gold Camp Road area, hoping that Browne could use them to pinpoint where he claimed to have dumped the woman's body. Because Browne described moonlight shining on water, the investigators initially believed he could have dumped the body near Skagway Reservoir, the only body of water shown on the maps. The reservoir, however, is about three miles from Gold Camp Road. Browne studied the maps but couldn't say whether he had been near Skagway Reservoir or not.

Mindful that the Grand Am had been the

key to unlocking the Sperry case, Nohr asked Browne if the Cowboy Lady had a car.

Browne scowled, as though he wasn't sure whether the investigator was trying to trick him or was just plain stupid.

"She was hitchhiking," he said.

Nohr later combed Gold Camp Road with a county search and rescue expert who was familiar with the area. Skagway Reservoir, it turned out, was too far away to be the body of water Browne had claimed to see. About eight miles up the road, however, they came to a stretch that did fit Browne's description: a high cliff to the left and a steep drop-off to the right. A debris field of boulders was piled on the hillside. Below that, shining in the distance, was a private lake. The lake was not on the topo maps.

In September 2005, Nohr and about fifteen members of the El Paso County Search and Rescue team carefully searched the hillside. Amidst the bottles, cans, and other debris tossed from the roadside, they found the leather sole and shank of a cowboy boot. From the cut of the leather and the shape of the heel, Nohr guessed the boot could have been made for a woman. On the hillside, they also encountered a large colony of ferrets, notoriously efficient scavengers, who devour even the bones of carrion.

"If there ever was a body, the ferrets would have taken care of it," Nohr says. "Everything was to no avail."

Hess tried to jog Browne's memory for the other murders he claimed to have committed in his early correspondence. He slid across the table a copy of the crudely drawn map Browne had included with his second letter, and pointed to the number seventeen Browne scrawled inside the outline of Louisiana. So far, Browne had discussed only four killings with them, three in Coushatta and one in New Orleans.

Browne obliged Hess with a fifth case. The woman, he said, had a pronounced Cajun accent, short, dark hair, and dark eyes. She was wearing a skirt and blouse and a wedding ring. He thought she was in her late thirties.

He remembered meeting her in a Morgan City bar sometime in the late 1970s. According to the sheriff's later narrative, Browne said they left the bar together and drove in his Ford Maverick to a place near the Atchafalaya River, where they had sex. As with his other victims, Browne claimed that the sex was consensual. Afterward, he said, he strangled her and then drove onto a high bridge over the river and dumped her body into the water.

Hess asked Browne if he dismembered this victim.

No need to, Browne said. No one was around. It was easy to get rid of her.

Once again, investigators would ask Louisiana authorities about missing person reports. Once again, they would find nothing that fit Browne's story.

During an April interview, Browne returned to the Memphis prostitute he claimed he killed in 1980. He described her as a light-skinned black woman, very pretty, and approximately twenty-five to thirty years old. She was wearing a short sweater-dress, he said.

He met her in a blues club. They drove together across the Mississippi River, through West Memphis, and westward along Interstate 40 until she directed him to turn south off the interstate. They followed this road for a few miles before coming to an area near what he thought was a small lake.

Browne paid for oral sex, then throttled her. He thought that he also might have shot her, although he could not be certain. Her body went into the water, too.

After the cold case squad passed on these sketchy recollections, Arkansas State Police

Sergeant Barry Roy believed he found a case that fit at least some of the details Browne had provided. The victim was Lisa Lowe, a young, light-skinned black woman whose body had been found floating in a culvert off the Saint Francis River, about thirty miles southwest of West Memphis. She was wearing a sweater dress, much like the one Browne described. The only problem was a big one: timing. Lowe was murdered in 1991, eleven years after Browne claimed he killed the Memphis prostitute. Browne *was* often vague or wrong about dates, but more than a decade was a stretch, even for him.

Browne also added details about the "two males in the muck" mentioned in the trip letter. He said that he was parked in a Mississippi highway pull-off when two men started walking toward him in a threatening manner. Browne said that he thought these "tough guys" and "bullies" wanted to rob him.

Without waiting for them to try, Browne said, he pulled out the .44 Magnum revolver he was wearing in a shoulder holster and shot both strangers in the chest, then dumped their bodies in a swampy area.

Hess and Nohr probed without luck for details that would help them narrow their search. Their best guess puts the double murder somewhere along Interstate 10 in Jackson County, Mississippi. However, authorities there have no unsolved homicides or missing person reports that fit Browne's story.

Nohr approached each of Browne's revelations in his usual orderly way, burrowing in with questions about highways, landmarks, dates, cars, clothing, anything that might yield an investigative lead. Did Browne turn left or right when he departed the highway? Was the road paved or gravel? How long did he drive? Did he remember anything unusual about the area?

Hess stuck with his much more random, ad hoc approach to the interviews. Nohr remembers that Browne took amused note of their contrasting styles. "He said, 'Charlie, you are a fly-by-the-seat-of-your-pants kind of guy, and Jeff is the kind of person who has to dot every 'i' and cross every 't'."

After a time, the murder stories developed a sameness. None of the killings seemed to have made much of an impression on Browne. If he was telling the truth, he had crisscrossed America, cutting a swath of bloody havoc for two decades. Forty-eight or even fifty-one victims was not out of line for such a killer. But as he discussed them, their violent deaths seemed to have little or no meaning for him, either individually or collectively. They moved through his mind like so many half-remembered vignettes, fragments from his past, or his imagination.

"When he talks about killing someone," Nohr says, "it's just like he's talking about changing lanes on the highway, or going to the grocery store. Very matter-of-fact. No emotion whatsoever."

For one so exceedingly bright — Browne reportedly scored 140 on a prison IQ test — he had absolutely no insights to share about what he did and why he did it. Browne reduced his behavior to a question of urge and opportunity joining to produce action, usually "a spur of the moment thing."

It was clear that he generally chose his victims from among those least likely to be missed or mourned — Heather Church was a noteworthy exception — but he had no explanation for his apparent success over the years, except to link it to self-control, a handy trait for any serial killer. "He told me, 'I have the urge a lot, but I fended it off,'" Nohr says. "If I hadn't been able to fend it off, you would have hundreds."

Browne described the majority of his victims as somehow complicit in their own deaths, and deserving of them, as well; as if he, by implication, were some sort of avenging angel, the self-appointed scourge of morally deficient, *worthless* whores, horny housewives and all other loose women everywhere. As rationalizations went, it was pretty thin stuff.

No one as yet has satisfactorily worked out the origins of sociopathy, only its symptoms and its often dire consequences for the rest of humanity. Ted Bundy, who gave the subject considerable thought, believed that two factors work to create the sociopathic serial sexual killer, and that both must be present for this particular form of deviant offender to develop. One is a predisposition, possibly genetic, to antisocial behavior. Two is a trigger, some condition or event in a person's life that frees or opens the predisposition to full expression.

While it is impossible to know what trigger, if any, turned Robert Browne from a narcissistic child with a possible touch of paranoia into a heartless sex killer, there is a candidate event that he has discussed openly. It was his first murder, or at least the murder that he claims was his first. Like almost every violent act he's attested to, this one is wrapped in enigma.

The victim, he says, was a fellow soldier

he killed while stationed for a time in South Korea. The year either was 1970 or '71.

When Robert Browne returned to Coushatta from the service, he told his mother that he had killed a GI in a fight over a girl. His sister Mary and his brother Donald told Mark Finley in 1995 that they, too, had heard that their younger brother claimed to have killed a man. Donald Browne didn't necessarily believe the tale was true.

Browne ultimately repeated the story to Charlie Hess. Again, as nearly always, there was no way to verify his story. The Army searched hard through its records and could find no homicides or other deaths or even missing person reports that remotely fit the facts as Browne described them. Since the U.S. military customarily keeps very close track of where its soldiers are and assiduously notes when they are not where they should be, Browne's story has its doubters.

After first hearing about it from Charlie Hess, Jeff Nohr was intrigued, even after the Army failed to find a trace of the supposedly slain soldier. He returned more than once to the subject with Browne, searching for some way to prove or disprove what Browne said, or at least to understand it.

Browne told him while he was stationed

at Yongsan Army Garrison in Seoul, he picked up a prostitute at a nightclub. As they were leaving the club together, another American soldier came at him with a knife.

According to Browne, he kicked his attacker and took him to the ground. As they fought, he grabbed the man by his scalp and hoisted him up. Then, with a swift, hard motion, Browne brought the man's head and neck down onto a metal fence rail.

"He said he heard the bones in his neck pop and he dropped him and there was no more movement," Nohr said. "He said he broke his neck."

Browne could offer no further detail. He said he didn't know the other soldier's name and never heard any report of the incident's aftermath. It was like the guy just vanished. Browne wasn't even clear on why the fight had started but guessed his dead adversary maybe was "jealous over the prostitute."

"Was that really your first murder, Robert?" Nohr asked.

"Yes."

"When that happened, how did you feel? Were you upset by it?"

Browne shook his head.

"No," he said. "What really bothered me was that it didn't bother me."

■ ■ ■ ■

Browne provided sufficient information about the killing he claimed to have committed near Tulsa, Oklahoma, to lead investigators to yet another possible victim.

He said he met a gay man at a truck stop outside Tulsa, and that together they had driven to a riverside park. While they were still in his car, Browne said, he strangled the man and then dumped his body into the water. He recalled that there was a boat launch or dock nearby.

Two weeks later, Browne changed his story. Now he remembered that when his gay acquaintance got out of the car at the park, he shot him. In his trip letter, Browne pegged the date of the murder as 1985. He denied having sex with the man, even though sex would clearly have been the ostensible reason for their trip to the park.

Whether, in fact, Robert Browne is gay or bisexual was a common topic of speculation in cold case squad conferences, in part sparked by the fact that he killed both women and men. Additionally, when Fischer and Hess had interviewed Jack Mason, Browne's friend told the investigators that the killer had come on to him sexually, a claim a fellow inmate repeated as well. But the question never was pursued in the interview room. It was one of several topics, including whether Heather Church was his youngest victim, that were "off the table" with Browne, as Nohr puts it. Raise one of these issues, and the discussion was over.

In July 2005, the Tulsa police reported to the cold case squad that an open case of theirs matched Browne's account in key ways. The victim was a homosexual named Timothy Warren, whose seminude body had been found in a shallow creek in Mohawk Park. Warren was known to frequent local truck stops. He had been shot three times in the head with a .22 caliber weapon. The cold case squad instantly snapped on the weapon. Jack Mason had told them Robert Browne preferred .22s of any sort to almost any other firearm. The date of Warren's murder was 1992, seven years later than Browne remembered. But the case bore a closer look.

By May 2005, Browne's relatively good humor had begun to sour as he started to question whether the transfer he demanded would ever materialize. On May 10, Hess and Nohr came to Territorial hoping to talk about Colorado victims. Out of the nine Browne had indicated on his map, only three — Heather Church, Rocio Sperry, and the Cowboy Lady — had been addressed with any specificity. Of particular interest to Hess and Nohr this day was Browne's previous disclosure that he killed two people at a scenic overlook on Interstate 70, somewhere west of Denver. The investigators thought Browne might be talking about the Glenwood Canyon area. However, again, they knew of no dead or missing people who were possible victims.

Charlie Hess asked Browne if he remembered any more details about the I-70 killings. Browne shrugged and brushed aside the question. Hess persisted. Not in the mood to be pressed, Browne finally said he wasn't sure if the murders had occurred in Colorado, or if they had occurred at all. He might have been thinking about something he read. The details were "just not real clear."

Hess had had enough.

"So what is real?" he challenged Browne.

"Flatonia," the killer replied.

"Sugar Land?" Hess asked, not bothering to hide his irritation.

"Clear."

"Self?"

"Clear, real clear."

"Hudson?"

"Clear, real clear."

"Hayes?"

"Clear, real clear."

Hess continued ticking off the shorthand names they had given to the cases: New Orleans, Clarence, Washington State, West Memphis, Grand Am Lady, Cowboy Lady. Browne answered, "clear, real clear," each time.

The tone of the discussion was headed downhill fast.

"Cut it off," Nohr wrote and slid his notepad over to Hess.

"His medication might have been off that day," Nohr says. "We never knew what we were going to get until we got there — which Robert was going to show up."

The little set-to effectively ended this productive phase in their relationship with Browne. In early July, he and Hess again grew short with each other. The killer was impatient for a transfer to an out-of-state institution. Nohr and Hess told him that they were working on it but that matters took time to resolve. Furthermore, Hess said, no one would be willing or able to accommodate some of Browne's more extreme requests.

For example, he reminded Browne that at

one point he had unrealistically proposed to be sent to a remote island, possibly off the coast of Alaska, where he would live alone and keep watch for fires. Browne angrily denied that he had ever suggested such an idea. Hess said he had, and could produce the letter to prove it.

Nohr watched Browne's eyes. When he was angry, they shifted from hazel to steel gray, and that meant Robert Browne was done for the day. It was happening now. Nohr kicked Hess under the table. *Knock it off.*

Hess did, but Browne stayed angry.

Two days later came a letter. "Hello Charlie Hess," he began as usual. "Upon our next meeting, *bring* a copy of my letter which discusses the *fire-tower* and other conditions!!!" If Hess couldn't or wouldn't produce the letter, and be ready to discuss it, "then we are both wasting our time!!!"

He didn't give Hess a chance to reply. On July 12, 2005, Browne shut down all communication. "I have decided to end this whole affair," he wrote. "As of the above date, I terminate all discussions, negotiations, etc."

THIRTY

Well before the Grand Am Lady was identified as Rocio Sperry, the sheriff's investigators knew of only two objects that might yield them useful physical evidence in her case: the TV that Browne said he'd stolen from her apartment and the diamond ring he'd taken from her dead hand. Once they located Joe Sperry and learned that all the physical evidence in his wife's missing person investigation had been discarded, Jeff Nohr's *only* chance of slamming the circle shut seemed to hinge on the television and the ring.

According to Browne, the stolen TV still was working in 1995 when he was arrested for murdering Heather Church. Ten years later the set would be eighteen years old, but perhaps his fifth wife, Diane, still had it.

Nohr found Diane, who had remarried, changed her name, and moved to another county. Yes, she said, she had the old machine, and the sheriff's office was welcome to it.

According to the sheriff's affidavit filed later, when Nohr and another detective visited Diane in March 2005, they found the set sitting on her dining room table. She said her ex-husband had told her that he'd "obtained the television from a couple who were breaking up and needed money."

That certainly corroborated the story Browne had told Hess.

Diane told Nohr to take the TV, and she didn't want it back. Mere mention of Robert Browne left her shaken and in tears. Like most of his ex-wives, she deeply feared him.

The Sony's model number, serial number, and date of manufacture were stamped on the back of the television. Nohr called the Sony Corporation to see if any warranty papers had been filed by the person who bought the TV. No luck. Not only was there no warranty issued for that set, there was no way to determine who bought the television set, or even where it had been sold. That left the serial number. If Nohr could match the number from the stolen set with the one entered on the original theft report, he had the case nailed. Unfortunately, the original theft report seemed to have vanished, permanently.

Nohr was able to locate the original crime scene photographs that had been archived with the missing persons report and sifted through them in search of anything that might help. One, he noticed, depicted the Sperrys' double bed, with papers and an envelope lying on top. "Fred Schmid Appliance" read the envelope. The detective also could make out a sales receipt for the missing television.

Maybe, just maybe, he thought. But even though he had the picture carefully enlarged, nowhere on the envelope or receipt was that elusive serial number. What's more, Fred Schmid Appliance had long since gone out of business.

Yet another blind alley.

Next, Nohr went in search of the diamond cluster ring that Browne claimed to have given to his former girlfriend, Jan Osgood. When interviewed 1995 in connection with the Heather Church case, Osgood told Detective Michele Hodges that she'd met Browne at a singles dance at a local hotel sometime in 1987. Around Christmastime that year, he stayed at her residence for about three weeks. She told the detective she gave him a coffeepot because she thought he might not get any other gifts.

Shortly thereafter, Browne was fired by Kwik Stop and began working at a furniture outlet called Beds Unique.

Osgood told Hodges that Browne could be "a scary person." She remembered once driving up to her house with her mother. With Jan's permission, a former boyfriend had temporarily parked his eighteen-wheeler out in front. As the two women watched, Browne raced furiously from the front door, forcefully dragged her old beau through the big truck's window, and beat him soundly. When she asked Browne why, he said the guy was "bothering him."

Her mother observed that Robert Browne seemed to be "a mean, angry person," Hodges noted.

Jan Osgood also explained to the detective that her relationship with Browne ended with the advent of his future wife — number five, Diane — whom he met at another singles dance at the same hotel where he'd met Osgood. Robert told Jan he was a gigolo. "Ms. Osgood stated that Robert Browne had told her that Diane Browne was rich and he was going to marry her," Hodges wrote. "She stated that the marriage had happened very quickly."

In 2005, Jeff Nohr tracked Jan Osgood to Jackson Hole, Wyoming. Yes, she said,

Browne had given her a ring. She remembered it as a "wedding set"; two rings, soldered together, with lots of small diamonds. Osgood had given it to her daughter when she married in 2000.

Jan's daughter lived in Boulder, a ninety-minute drive from the Springs. She was surprised to learn from Jeff Nohr that the ring her mother gave her originally came from Robert Browne. She told the detective that she had used the setting's central diamond to make a new wedding ring, but she still had the original setting. He was welcome to borrow it. She also said her now ex-husband had pawned her wedding ring, but she had saved the small diamonds, which were folded in a piece of paper with the original set.

The young woman, Nohr noted in a later affidavit, "did provide Your Affiant with a small clear plastic bag containing a two-piece, 14K gold wedding ring set. Upon closer examination of the rings, Your Affiant noted all the diamonds had been removed from the ring. Each piece of the ring contained five small chip diamonds and one large solitaire diamond in the center."

Nohr photographed the empty setting.

On April 12, 2005, Charlie Hess showed Nohr's photograph to Browne. He studied the picture for a moment, then shook his head.

No, the inmate said. That wasn't the ring he took from the Grand Am Lady. That ring was "gaudy" with a large, round cluster of small diamonds, and no center stone.

Jeff Nohr was now oh for two, and running out of innings.

Joe Sperry sent a picture of Rocio, smiling tentatively into the camera, to the sheriff's office. Hess and Nohr showed the photograph to Browne.

"You know, that could be, that could be, that very well could be, because it's been a long time," Browne said.

They told him about Joe Sperry.

"Could very well be her," Browne said. "If everything fits, then it probably is."

Browne was curious to know if the Sperrys were from Louisiana or Florida. Joe Sperry, Nohr told him, was born and raised in Louisiana and was visiting his mother in Florida when Rocio disappeared. So they were from *both* Louisiana and Florida.

Browne nodded. "That must have been why Louisiana and Florida stuck in my mind."

On July 27, 2005, Nohr met Joe Sperry in Jackson, Mississippi, where his eighteen-year-old daughter, Amie, lived.

"As I'm flying to Jackson," Nohr recalls, "I'm looking out the window, thinking, *What the hell am I doing? Am I going to tell this girl what happened to her mother, that Robert choked her mother to death and put her in the bathtub and cut her up and put her in trash bags and put her in the Dumpster?*"

No, Nohr decided. This was not the time or the place for that discussion.

Instead, he would remain focused on the search for evidence, any evidence.

Nohr showed Joe Sperry the police photograph of the envelope lying on his rumpled bed. Sperry identified it. Then he showed Sperry a photograph of Diane's Sony, the one that Robert Browne said he stole. Sperry said it looked just like his missing TV. Both had side speakers and an antenna plug on the top, toward the back of the set. There was only one problem. Sperry remembered it as a twenty-seven-inch television. Diane's was a twenty-inch model. According to Sony, in 1987 the company did not make a twenty-seven-inch TV in the same style as their twenty-inch model. Joe Sperry was mistaken either about the size or the design of his missing set.

He did confirm that the 1987 Grand Am shown in the old police photos was his. He said he found his stolen car in a parking lot immediately south of the Kwik Stop, parked along a wooden fence, next to a Dumpster. He identified the spot in one of the pictures Scott Fischer had taken. It was the exact location where Browne said he left the vehicle.

Once a locksmith had let him into his locked car, Sperry had noted that the odometer read 3,165 miles. Before he left for Florida he'd written down his mileage: 2,853 miles. Someone had driven the Grand Am 312 miles. Again, Browne's story matched Sperry's. He'd told Charlie Hess the vehicle had low mileage, and that he'd driven it around for a while himself.

Next, Nohr showed Sperry photographs of Browne. In one picture, the killer was clean-shaven. In another, he wore a beard. Sperry did not recognize Browne in either photograph.

Nohr now wanted to probe whether Browne could have pieced together his story from snippets he picked up in the neighborhood or behind the counter at the Kwik Stop.

Had Sperry told anyone at the Kwik Stop about finding his car or about any other personal matters? Joe said he didn't think so.

Had he ever told anyone at the Kwik Stop about taking his daughter Amie to Louisiana or Florida? No.

As he flew home to Colorado from Mississippi, Nohr could consider his glass half full: He now had two independent stories that dovetailed in every important detail. Or he could see it as more or less empty. Despite a confession and a strong circumstantial case, he still had no hard physical evidence connecting Robert Browne to the murder of Rocio Sperry.

He had one long-shot possibility left. Jan Osgood had a pretty large collection of jewelry. What if she somehow gave him the wrong ring?

In late September 2005, Jeff Nohr and Charlie Hess traveled to Wyoming to speak once again with Osgood and to examine the jewelry she kept in her bank safe-deposit box. This time, she had a much sharper recollection of Browne than she had ten years earlier with Detective Hodges.

As the investigators later reported in the affidavit, Osgood said Browne lived with her for nine months, not three weeks, as she'd formerly recollected.

During this period, they went on two rather bizarre road trips. One was a five-hour drive to a lake in Nebraska, where

Browne fished all night while she slept in the car. At least, Browne said he'd gone fishing. Osgood couldn't remember if he'd brought along any tackle.

On the second outing, they drove all night from the Springs to Grand Prairie, Texas, near Dallas, where Browne met a friend of his whom Osgood did not know. She told the investigators that the men left together — ostensibly to go fishing — and she waited in the car for four hours.

According to the affidavit, "Ms. Osgood said at approximately 3:00 p.m., she walked across the street from where they were parked to a restaurant. She said at approximately 3:30 p.m., Mr. Browne returned to the restaurant by himself. He was upset with her because she was not at the car and ordered her back to the car."

They drove straight back to Colorado Springs, a trip of more than fifteen hours.

Osgood, like Jack Mason, said Browne loved target shooting and had taken her with him to go target shooting. He'd also brought her out to the land in Fremont County near the old mining areas, the same property Diane Browne had described to investigators ten years earlier.

Osgood remembered Browne taking measurements around his acreage, without explaining his purpose. He did tell her, without elaboration, that he liked underground houses, the investigators reported.

Among the personal details that Osgood shared with Nohr and Hess was her recollection that Browne had often disappeared in the night and wouldn't return for several days. He told her he had a job folding laundry at a hotel or a hospital.

Her recollections were all useful to Jeff Nohr, as he sketched in more detail to the personal portrait of Robert Charles Browne that the detective refined in his head. The jewelry angle didn't work out, however. At the bank, where Nohr and Hess examined several pieces of jewelry from her safe-deposit box, the detective noticed a yellow gold ring with a round raised cluster of diamonds, set in the middle with a larger marquis-cut diamond. Osgood said that she couldn't remember where she had gotten that ring.

Nohr photographed the ring to show to Robert Browne and Joe Sperry.

Neither man recognized it.

THIRTY-ONE

In August 2005, the cold case squad and their supervisors contacted the FBI's Behavioral Science Service (BSS), headquartered at Quantico, Virginia, which specializes in the analysis of aberrant crime. "To their credit," says David T. Resch, a special agent at the BSS, "they did not call us and say, 'Hey, this guy's telling us a bunch of stories, and we believe every one of them.' They said, 'We think there might be some truth to some of this. We want your help looking at it.'"

Resch, along with Supervisory Special Agent Mary Ellen O'Toole and Kirk Mellecker (a retired homicide detective with the Los Angeles Police Department who'd hired on as a major case specialist at the BSS), first reviewed a packet of documents they received from Colorado. The fat file included police reports, copies of the cold case squad's correspondence with Browne, as well as reports on their direct, tape-recorded sessions with him. After conducting an initial analysis, the FBI team flew to Colorado Springs to meet directly with the sheriff's office investigators.

For a full day, Hess, Nohr, and the others briefed the federal agents on the many cases Browne had discussed, going through them one at a time. Then Resch, O'Toole, and Mellecker shared their observations.

The Bureau continuously gathers information on deviant crimes and deviant offenders from all 14,000 law enforcement agencies in the U.S. and has amassed a vast and up-to-date repository of information on types of criminals that a local detective may encounter no more than once, if ever, across a twenty- or thirty-year career. In the Browne case, Agent Resch recalls, they immediately were put in mind of a similar and recent case in Alabama. "They had an incarcerated serial offender," says Resch. "He was reaching out much the way Browne reached out. [We explained] this is the path they went down with him. Some of the things they reported were positive and helpful, and there are some lessons learned that they said they wouldn't repeat."

The Bureau team also broadly endorsed the cold case squad's approach to Browne, particularly Charlie Hess's patient handling of the killer. "Much of what we were doing was validating the path they'd already gone down," says Resch. "I'll tell you it's not unusual for incarcerated offenders, especially long-term incarcerated offenders, to reach out and talk about their crimes. What is unusual is to find a law enforcement agency that will approach one of these cases, and exhibit the perseverance that El Paso County did.

"It can be very frustrating. He may be lying. He may just want attention. He may just want to make his situation a little bit better in prison. For departments that have a whole lot of crimes happening every day, to spend a whole lot of time conversing with incarcerated offenders about what they may, or may not have done — especially when you think they may be giving you a line of bull — that takes some dedication."

The agents also provided the cold case squad with perspective on a trait with which they already were intimately familiar: Browne's need to control and manipulate.

The controller doesn't lose that urge when he's locked up, Resch explains. "And he's going to look for opportunities to do that. It could be a cell mate, a guard, a former paramour whom he controls using threatening letters. If it's law enforcement, he will look for opportunities to control and manipulate the detective. This could take the form of agreeing to talk, then canceling the appointment at the last minute. At that point, he's manipulated the detective's whole day."

Resch reminded Hess and Nohr to "be very cognizant of Browne's attempts to manipulate you. Without calling him on the carpet — saying, 'You're just manipulating me here' — let him know that you're not going to be manipulated. This could be as simple as waiting a couple of weeks to return a letter."

From what he saw, the interviewers handled this issue with skill. "They did a good job of walking the fine line between keeping him engaged and not allowing him to manipulate them," says Resch. "That's important. They had to give him enough to keep him talking but not so much that he was calling all the shots."

On the central issue of Browne's motivation for murder, Resch equivocates, in part because the available physical and behavioral evidence is fragmentary. Although sex clearly was involved, at least with the female victims, Resch is unwilling to speculate whether sex was Browne's *exclusive* reason for murder. Reason: Browne also was a thief. Also, in some instances he might have killed simply to avoid detection.

What about his claim of killing both female and male victims?

"It does happen," says Resch, even when females are the victims of preference. "You have what might be desired," he says, "and then you have what is available. He may desire a female of a certain body type and certain race and occupation at a certain time of day. But what's available to him might be someone at the opposite end of the spectrum. It isn't unusual to see victims of all races, all ages, and both sexes."

There can be other dynamics at work, as well. "When you're dealing with someone who has routinely used violence as a means to whatever end, it won't be unusual to find them using violence against males as well as females," Resch explains. "It's also not unusual for them to lie about it. When you are in that interview and you're talking about the kids they've had sex with, or the women they've controlled and killed, at some point in time he'll start feeling that you feel that he's not a man. So then he'll say, 'Yeah, and then there was the time that I beat that guy to death outside the bar because he pissed me off when he bumped into me.' At times the offender has a need to reaffirm his manhood."

Resch believes the manliness issue might explain why continued efforts to identify the GI whom Browne claims to have killed in Korea has so far yielded nothing. He advised Hess and Nohr to press Browne on his claims of killing male victims, to see if he offers as much substance as he does when he discusses his female victims.

Resch spent little time thinking about Browne and victim dismemberment, even though it was a central feature of two cases. If the killer was unknown to officials, the fact that he cut up some victims would have investigative value, the agent says. But since the killer already was identified and imprisoned, Resch concentrated on Browne's interactions with Hess and Nohr.

As part of that analysis, he discounted Browne's references to the occult and supernatural. "As you look through some of the writings about serial killers, you'll see that they will often go in this direction," he explains. " 'This wasn't about me and about my desires. This was about something outside of me, controlling me. This was something bigger than just me and my paraphilias.' They're latching on to something they think people will believe in. So I didn't put a lot of thought into the high priestess and the virgins and the cult aspect of this."

Finally, what might explain Browne's hatred for Lou Smit? A possibility, says Resch, is the killer's need to preserve some shred of self-respect. "He could be looking for one small victory," Resch surmises. " 'While I'm going down for committing murders and being completely depraved, I'm going to take down the reputation of that one detective, so I have some small victory to hold on to when it's all said and done.' "

The FBI team urged the sheriff's office to cultivate communication and cooperation among the various other police agencies around the country who also had an interest in these cases. This was an excellent suggestion. Successful serial killers take advantage of the fact that local law enforcement jurisdictions often do not share information effectively with one another. Initiatives such as the FBI's ViCAP (Violent Criminal Apprehension Program), a vast computer database of serial murder cases gleaned from detectives all over the U.S., make it easier these days for local investigators to check for information and leads outside of their jurisdictions. But the ideal of reliable, open, real-time cop-to-cop communication around the country still remains far out of reach.

Since the El Paso sheriff's office was the de facto lead agency in the Browne case, it was decided that Jeff Nohr would undertake what became known as the goodwill tour, a circuit of the interested agencies with whom he'd share and, it was hoped, receive information about Browne as well as discuss both investigative strategies and legal options going forward.

Besides Nohr's time and considerable effort, however, the goodwill tour and related efforts were also going to cost money. In the middle of the budget year, that meant that Sheriff Maketa would need to go directly to the El Paso County commissioners to ask for extra money. This was never fun. The commissioners were generally reluctant to authorize additional spending outside the budget process, and they almost never OK'd extra outlays without first demanding a detailed explanation of how the money was to be spent. Yet Maketa, who was very concerned with keeping Robert Browne's name out of the press, could not explain in public why he needed the money. So he met privately with four of the five commissioners.

It happened, luckily, that the sheriff's office had recently brought a major project in $40,000 under budget, and Maketa asked to keep the extra money. "I need the $40,000, but I can't tell you why," he told the commissioners, and without a question or demurral, the commissioners OK'd it. Maketa says he was still able to return half the sum to the county treasury and remained under budget.

Nohr decided to limit his visits to jurisdictions with actual unsolved homicide cases for which Browne might be responsible. Regrettably, that meant skipping Mississippi, Washington, New Mexico, and California, where there was no information developed yet that would support or compromise Browne's claims.

Nohr's first stop, on September 19, 2005, was Tulsa, Oklahoma, where he met with police Detective Eddie Majors. Majors took Nohr to the park where Timothy Warren's body was found, and the investigators reviewed crime scene photos together. It was clear that Warren had been shot and his body dragged to the water, much as Browne described. But there was no boat launch or dock, as Browne remembered, in Mohawk Park.

Jeff Nohr's next stop on the goodwill tour

was Texas. On November 14, 2000, he flew to Houston, where Sugar Land police detective Billy Baugh met him at the airport. They drove together past Dames Nightclub where Nidia Mendoza worked, to the intersection of State Highway 59 and U.S. 90, near where her dismembered body was discovered. In 1984, the two roads had intersected in an open field covered in tall grass, but by 2005 the old prairie had been swallowed up by a bustling industrial strip and acres of warehouses.

Then it was on to the Embassy Suites on Southwest Freeway. Based on Browne's descriptions of his night with Mendoza, local investigators pinpointed this hotel as the likeliest site of the murder. Nohr walked through the entrance with Baugh, and with one look at the Embassy Suites lobby felt certain that the Sugar Land detectives were correct.

"I go in," he remembers, "and there was the front desk and there was the glass elevator. It was just as Browne described it."

Nidia Mendoza's remains had been still fresh enough when they were found to yield reliable physical information, which the cold case squad hoped would help them prove (or disprove) Browne's confession. For example, they were interested to learn whether Browne's descriptions of how he'd dismembered Mendoza were consistent with the autopsy findings.

Browne had told Nohr that he worked the knife into the soft tissue at the joints until he reached bone. Then he grabbed Mendoza by the ankle and twisted her leg to pop the femur from the hip joint. The cold case squad shared Browne's recollections with an official who was familiar with the Mendoza autopsy. "He said, 'That's exactly how she was cut up; not close, exactly,' " Scott Fischer recalls. " 'You've got the right man.' "

Since the Sugar Land police still hadn't been fully briefed on all that Browne had said, they were excited for the chance to learn about their suspect firsthand from Jeff Nohr. Besides Billy Baugh, Chief Steve Griffith called Captain Gary Cox into the meeting, along with an assistant district attorney and Cliff Brothers, who had been the original investigator on the case. Brothers, now a DEA agent in Houston, still carried a photograph of Mendoza in his wallet.

Nohr recounted how Browne first mentioned "a body, in parts" in his letter of April 30, 2003, then offered nothing more of substance until his third meeting with Charlie Hess at the Fremont Correctional

Facility in December 2004. That day, and during the "watershed event" of February 23, 2005, as well as later, Browne made a very persuasive case for his guilt. The Sugar Land investigators were especially pleased to hear that their suspect seemed to know details about Mendoza's murder that had not been released.

As they talked over the crime, it became clear that Browne had deviated in an interesting way from his usual, more thorough, body disposal strategies. Instead of putting Mendoza in the water — there was a nearby stretch of the Brazos River — he chose to dump her along a major highway where her remains were likely to be found fairly soon. Browne had said he'd been "bothered" by killing her, because he and the girl had spent so much time together. That could explain why he left her somewhere she'd be found.

"Our case is one of — if not *the* — strongest cases outside of Colorado," says Captain Cox. "We were pretty much on board and feel pretty strongly about the information that was given to us. It was credible. In our mind, he's definitely the person who is responsible — unless the evidence dictates otherwise."

Unlike some of the other agencies, Sugar

Land police had preserved the entire Mendoza investigative file plus all the physical evidence in the Mendoza case. These include fluid and body swabs, nail clippings, and bloodstained clothing — all potential sources of the killer's DNA.

Although the samples are more than twenty years old and, in some cases, fairly degraded, the Sugar Land police have submitted them for laboratory analysis, hoping that DNA tests, unavailable in 1984, can finally sort out the question of who killed Nidia Mendoza. Right now, Robert Browne is the prime suspect. "But if the tests rule him out," says Cox, "obviously he got his information from somewhere, and we'd be interested in knowing where it came from."

From Sugar Land, the goodwill tour headed west on Interstate 90 toward Flatonia, where Jeff Nohr would confer on the Melody Bush case with local authorities. Detective Baugh drove Nohr to LaGrange, the seat of Fayette County, where he met at the courthouse with Rick Cole, a sheriff's detective and a young assistant district attorney. In contrast to the huge Mendoza investigative file assembled over the years by Sugar Land investigators, there were few reports in the original Bush case file that

Nohr was shown, and no physical evidence. Cole and the assistant district attorney had little to say about the case, as well.

Jeff Nohr, of course, had every available detail at hand. "I told them when, how, where he dumped the body, how far it was from Flatonia," the detective recalls. "I think they were a little overwhelmed by the level of detail."

After their meeting in LaGrange, Baugh and Nohr drove south to Flatonia. They stopped along the way to examine the site where Melody Bush's body was recovered.

"Robert said that two miles north of Flatonia there was a guardrail and a drainage ditch or culvert," Nohr recalls. "Exactly two miles north of Flatonia, there was a guardrail — the only guardrail for miles — and a culvert. It was just as he described it. I think the Flatonia authorities were surprised by that."

But not persuaded.

The Colorado detective continued on to the town of Flatonia itself, where he inspected the Antlers Inn, now a Carefree Inn. The Stag Bar had become a motel storeroom, though the bar itself was intact. Nohr tried to picture the scene that night as Browne described it: the inebriated, barefoot Melody Bush staggering around the room;

Browne seated at the bar; and the bartender behind him, asking him to get this sloppy drunk out of her place and go look for her husband. Then opportunity rose again.

Nohr walked along the backside of the motel to examine the layout. He wanted to see for himself if Browne, in a first-floor room, could have backed his diesel van up to his door in the dark and loaded up a body without anyone noticing.

Yeah, Nohr decided, it could be done.

The local authorities' reluctance to look any harder at Browne frustrated the cold case squad. They conceded that Browne *might* have based his recollections on things he'd read and heard, but wondered why anyone would so steep himself in second-hand information and retain it for twenty years. Nohr adds that Browne continued to insist he stabbed Bush multiple times, and that he'd himself suggested exhumation to verify his claims.

"Dig up the body," Browne told the detective. "Tell the coroner to look for nicks on her ribs."

According to Texas Ranger Otto Hanak, that won't happen. "The evidence," Hanak insists, "doesn't suggest that he was the person who committed the crime. He tells the El Paso County Sheriff's Office that he did certain things, and those things were not detected in the autopsy or during the investigation."

Hanak also says that Texas will have nothing to do with Browne's insistence, relayed to him by Jeff Nohr, that he requires a letter guaranteeing immunity from prosecution before he talks.

"We're not going to get on an airplane and fly up to El Paso County to be told, 'You're not interviewing me without the letter,' " says Hanak. "We're all in agreement that he's not getting a free ride on a murder in Texas."

So why not exhume Melody Bush, as Browne advised, and possibly resolve the controversy one way or the other?

"Her family wants her to rest in peace," the ranger says. Second, any exhumation order would require a strong argument — "probable cause" — for disturbing Bush's grave. "And probable cause," Hanak says, "is not there."

The first week in December 2005, Nohr flew to Shreveport, Louisiana, where he met with a group that included Louisiana State Trooper Michael Allen. Trooper Allen had taken over as lead investigator in the Coushatta cases at the invitation of Johnny Norman, sheriff of Red River Parish, soon after Browne's disclosures during February's "watershed event." Allen's boss, state police Sergeant Darrell Mills, also attended the meeting, as did Scotty Fletcher, an investigator for the Red River Parish district attorney's office, and a sheriff's detective from the parish.

Jeff Nohr laid out the information that Browne had provided for Wanda Hudson and Faye Aline Self, his neighbors at the River Towne Apartments, as well as Fuzzy Hayes, the teen runaway whose skull had been recovered to the south of Coushatta in a creek bed under a highway bridge. Nohr remembers that his hosts were polite and reserved, though they offered little information about the three Coushatta cases. Much of the time, he recalls, was given over to discussion of the Browne family, particularly how Robert's father and older brother had been such respected lawmen in the community. It was pretty clear that the Louisiana lawmen, who were acquainted with former state trooper Donald Browne, didn't think much of Robert's confessions.

If Robert Browne's descriptions of the murders of Faye Aline Self, Wanda Faye Hudson, and Katherine "Fuzzy" Hayes of

Coushatta took the cold case squad by surprise in February 2005, their amazement was nothing compared to the shock and disbelief that Browne's stories occasioned in his hometown. Despite his arrest in the Church case, he had never been a suspect in the three killings, nor had local authorities considered the murders connected in any way. They didn't even know about Fuzzy Hayes, a Coushatta resident, because that homicide had been handled by the sheriff's office in Winn Parish, where her skull was discovered. At the time of the crimes in 1983, about the only people in Coushatta who considered Robert Browne capable of killing anyone seem to have been his own ex-wives. Based on their personal experiences with him, they had few doubts.

But even those who were inclined to question Browne's claims in the Hudson and Self cases admitted that the Hayes case was different.

Chief Deputy Gregg Davies of the Winn Parish Sheriff's Office, the original investigator in the case, believes that some of Browne's confessions are fiction, but not his claim to have murdered Hayes. "I don't have a doubt that he probably did do this one," says Davies, who recently handed off responsibility for the case to the Louisiana

State Police and Trooper Mike Allen. "I think that everything fits pretty good."

Davies is especially sensitive to sham confessions: He remembers Henry Lee Lucas trying to take responsibility for the Hayes murder back in the 1980s before Davies put a stop to it. "I interviewed him," the investigator recalls. "He wanted to know all about it, and we wouldn't tell him. He'd ask questions until he got in the neighborhood of a yes, and then he'd try to come up with a story that would explain how he did it. I told the people in Texas, 'Henry Lucas is making a fool out of you people.' "

Skeptics question parts of Browne's story, particularly his insistence that he brought Fuzzy Hayes to his mother's house that July night in 1980, had sex with the girl, killed her, and then carried her out without Beulah Browne ever hearing or seeing a thing. She must have been a heavy sleeper.

But Davies says that the little Browne has shared about Hayes is both consistent with what the detective learned about the girl during his investigation and was neither common knowledge around Coushatta nor ever mentioned in the newspaper. Nor could Browne have picked up the details through his Coushatta law enforcement contacts; they were ignorant of the case.

Particularly persuasive to Davies was Browne's recollection that he killed Fuzzy Hayes at home and then dumped her over the parish line. The investigator always guessed that it happened just that way.

The girl was last seen by family friends on July 4, 1980, at Saline Lake, a popular swimming hole south of Coushatta. Sketchy reports put her at Uncle Albert's Chicken Shack, the hangout where Browne claimed to have met her, later that night.

The clincher was Browne's memory that he killed Hayes with a leather shoelace ligature. Such a strip of leather was discovered near her skull. No one outside the immediate investigation knew about it. At the time, Davies said, investigators thought the leather strand might be part of a "hippie style" necklace. The strip doesn't prove that Browne killed Katherine "Fuzzy" Hayes, but it's certainly consistent with his version of events.

Faye Aline Self presented a much different investigative challenge. On Wednesday night, March 30, 1983, the twenty-six-year-old single mother of three met her friend, Lycrecia Foster — phonetically *Lacreesha* in the sheriff's affidavit — at Alice's Wagon Wheel, a cinderblock honky-tonk on Highway 1, across the Red River and a couple of miles north of Coushatta. Self and Foster worked together at the Armistead Restaurant, also on Highway 1, which Lycrecia's family owned.

Foster arrived at the bar about eight forty that evening and found her friend sitting in a truck in the parking lot. Aline told Lycrecia that she and the two men with her had been drinking at a bar called the Watering Hole. At the moment, Self and the men were sharing a joint.

Self was very drunk already, Foster remembers, and in a mood to get drunker. "They were all pretty well lit," she says. "Aline definitely had a buzz on. She was really too drunk to drive."

As it turned out, she apparently didn't.

At about nine o'clock, Foster recalls, Self left the bar with the two men. The larger one, called Daniel, seemed to be escorting her. His friend, she says, was of medium build, dark-haired, quiet, and good-looking. "I had my eye on him," she says. Today, she believes this person was Robert Browne.

Another witness that evening, the bartender, told Red River Parish Sheriff's Deputy Ricky Griggs that he saw Foster and Self with a man he knew as Daniel and a second male whose name was Robert. When Griggs interviewed the man, according to a

1983 investigative report, he did not remember seeing Self at the bar and said that he did not know anyone named Robert.

The next day, Self's car was found in the Wagon Wheel parking lot. She was missing and never reliably reported seen again.

Browne's narrative of the evening begins at the Wagon Wheel, too, where he remembers seeing Faye Aline Self and Lycrecia Foster, with whom he says he danced. Foster disagrees, saying the man whom she believes was Browne did not dance with her. When he got home around midnight, Self had somehow gotten back to the River Towne Apartments, as well. According to Browne, she was asleep in her cabin. With no lights on, no cars around, and the urge upon him, Browne said, he entered Self's unlocked apartment with a rag soaked in liquid ant killer that he placed over her face before departing to find something with which to bind her. If Browne is to be believed, Self then accidentally — or prematurely — expired from chloroform inhalation during his brief absence.

He also told Charlie Hess there was no sex, pre- or postdeath.

His story prompts questions. In all his other narratives, voluntary sex — free or paid for — is consistently the prelude to murder. Surely he didn't expect Self to awaken from the chloroform, find herself bound, and still be in the mood. Browne never mentions binding other victims, and there's no known evidence that he did. The answer to these inconsistencies may lie in what Robert Browne considers "sex" — one of his "off the table" topics. Or maybe he's lying altogether.

Bill Jones, who has been the Red River Parish district attorney since 1980, says there was never an arrest made in the Self case. Nobody alive today remembers if there was even a suspect, including Robert Browne. In fact, the Coushatta authorities appear to have been about as alarmed by Faye Aline Self's disappearance as the police in Colorado Springs were when Rocio Sperry vanished. Neither woman's body was ever found. And interestingly, both were new mothers at the time of their disappearances. Aline had left her baby girl with her mother that night, promising to fetch her home early so she could get a good night's sleep for work in the morning.

Her other children, a ten-year-old daughter named Karrie and a son, were living with their father in Houston at the time. When her mother vanished, her father at first reassured Karrie that Aline probably was OK, and surely would return soon. When she didn't, he sat his children down at the kitchen table and said: "Your mom is missing, and chances are she won't be back."

Karrie remembers rising from the table and walking outside. She looked up at the vast Texas sky and decided that no God she'd worship would countenance this. "I thought," Karrie recalls, "if he's so powerful, he wouldn't have allowed that to happen to my mother. I didn't know what *that* was, just that it had to be awful."

When she was sixteen, Karrie says that Red River Parish authorities told her family that the ubiquitous Henry Lee Lucas had confessed to killing her mother. Lucas allegedly told Major Larry Rhodes, the parish's chief deputy at the time, that he cut up Self and scattered her pieces along the Red River near a Civil War battlefield memorial. The specious tale sounded closer to Robert Browne's modus operandi than did Browne's own account of the homicide.

In 1994, when Karrie was twenty-two, she visited Coushatta, where she met with Major Rhodes. "He informed me that my mother was wild," she remembers, "and that she had disappeared from a bar and did I know that?

"I asked him, 'Did that make her

expendable?' "

She met also with Sheriff Buddy Huckabay, who conceded what Karrie long had understood in her heart: that local law enforcement had done next to nothing to solve the mystery of her mother's disappearance. Huckabay gave her a copy of the minimal case file. He'd found the file tossed in the trunk of one of the sheriff's department cruisers when he took office in 1984, a year after Faye Aline Self disappeared.

The Hayes and Self cases hadn't produced so much as a ripple of concern around Coushatta; outside the victims' immediate families, hardly anyone even noticed. But Coushatta's third case, the bloody Saturday, May 28, 1983, murder of Wanda Faye Hudson, also at the River Towne Apartments, was both especially brutal and deeply terrifying to the inhabitants of the sleepy little town.

Hudson, just shy of her twenty-first birthday, was a vivacious, dark-haired beauty, about five foot six and 125 pounds. She worked as a cashier at Bam's Handy Dandy, a locally owned convenience store, in the same small town where she'd graduated from high school, and dated John Higgs, a local pharmacist.

The police and townspeople would later puzzle why, with the little whitewashed clapboard cottages at the River Towne Apartments spaced so closely, no one heard a thing the night of Wanda Hudson's murder.

On the Friday night before she was killed, Higgs picked Wanda up at work about nine o'clock, as was his custom, and they went back to her bungalow. They had been dating about four months. Although the local press would later describe Higgs as her fiancé, they were not yet officially engaged.

Higgs, then twenty-eight years old, had been back in Coushatta only a short time, after obtaining a post-graduate degree and graduating from pharmacy school. He was working two jobs, at the hospital and Bates Pharmacy, trying to build a career and save for the family he hoped to have. Wanda was part of that plan.

"I did want to marry her. Things were going in that direction, but I never got the chance to ask her," he says.

That night, as they talked, Higgs said, Wanda told him that she thought Robert Browne, who worked as a maintenance man for his brother Donald, might have a key to her front door. Browne had changed the locks earlier in the day. Higgs said he suggested that Wanda spend the night with her mother until they could have the locks changed again, but she refused.

Higgs was not overly concerned at the time. He knew Browne and his family well. One of Browne's brothers had dated his older sister. Higgs, his sister and Browne's brother had eaten many meals together. Browne and Higgs, though two years apart, had known each other at Coushatta High School before Browne dropped out to join the Army.

"He was just a nondescript guy, sort of hanging out, doing who knew what," Higgs says. "He was very quiet. Not at all a creepy guy that you'd worry about."

Even so, Higgs said, he made sure that Wanda locked the door and fastened the security chain behind him as he left that night sometime around midnight.

The next morning, a Saturday, Higgs began trying to reach Wanda by phone. He wanted to firm up plans for the evening. He knew that she planned to do laundry that morning, but as call after call went unanswered, he grew alarmed. He ate a hasty lunch at his parents' home and then, on his way back to work, stopped at Wanda's cottage.

As he stepped onto the little covered

porch, Higgs noticed that the front door was slightly ajar. He peered through the living room windows, unable to make out much in the gloom. When Wanda didn't answer his call, he pushed through the front door.

He saw the blood splatters on the wall at once and found Wanda's body sprawled on the floor next to the bed. The mattress was soaked with blood, as if his girlfriend had been attacked while she slept. He could see that she had been stabbed repeatedly and knew immediately that she was dead.

The images seared themselves into his memory in an instant. When he later saw the crime scene photos, he was certain that her body had been moved. The pictures showed her positioned much differently than he remembered.

Stunned and shaking, Higgs backed out of the room, careful not to touch anything but the telephone, which he used to call first his father and then the sheriff.

"I just found Wanda dead," he told the sheriff's deputy who answered his distraught call.

Later, suspicious police would point to the sequence of Higgs' phone calls — his father first, authorities second — to cast doubt on his innocence.

"My parents' house was about three hundred to four hundred yards away and I knew my dad was at home. I knew he could get there quicker than the police," Higgs says, by way of explanation. "I wanted my father there with me."

He remained at his dead girlfriend's little cabin, waiting outside first for the sheriff's deputies and then for the Louisiana State Police crime lab to finish its work. He was there to watch the coroner to remove Wanda's body, too.

Word spread quickly, as a crowd gathered on the sidewalk, gawking and gossiping. Higgs says he was appalled at the time by the lax manner in which the crime scene was handled. "Too many people traipsed in and out of there that day," Higgs says. According to what he later heard, evidence from the case eventually was found in the trunk of a patrol car, just as the Self case file also was discovered in a car trunk. Higgs says there was a rumor around town that Sheriff Kerwin Brown, since deceased, kept pictures of the crime scene at his home in a photo album.

Richard Hanna, a local doctor who also served as the Red River Parish coroner, told the *Citizen* that Hudson had been stabbed twenty-five times. "There was only one weapon used, a knife with a blade of about two and a half or three inches long," Dr. Hanna told the local newspaper.

Hanna placed the time of death between two and four o'clock in the morning. There were no signs of forced entry, leading police to speculate publicly that Wanda Hudson knew her killer. "It's highly irregular to let someone in your apartment at two in the morning," one anonymous official told the *Coushatta Citizen*.

According to the Louisiana State Police report, the crime scene evidence suggested that Hudson's killer washed her blood from himself in the bathroom. The report confirmed Hudson had had sex that night; DNA testing was not then available, but semen recovered by forensic technicians matched her partner Higgs's blood type.

"I told them up front that we were together that night," Higgs said. "I didn't have anything to hide."

The hair recovered from her bed and her hands could not be positively matched with that of her boyfriend, who was blond.

From the first day, Higgs says, authorities treated him like a suspect — their only suspect, in fact. He says he met willingly, at first, with the Red River Parish sheriff and with Louisiana State Police, certain that the authorities, several of whom he knew personally, would realize that he had nothing to do with Wanda's murder.

"I didn't get much time to grieve over this," says Higgs. "I loved her. I felt bad. I felt the loss. I attended the funeral, but when people are trying to put you in jail for something you know you didn't do, you have to be defensive."

As the investigation became more serious and police seemed intent upon charging him with the crime — Higgs was read his rights — he hired a prominent criminal defense attorney, Mike Small of Alexandria, whose clients have included former Louisiana Governor Edwin Edwards. Ultimately, Red River Parish authorities dropped their active pursuit of a case against Higgs — he was never charged or taken before a grand jury — but they also never publicly cleared him either.

"They never used their peripheral vision to look at anything other than me," Higgs says. "They locked in on me and that clouded their judgment."

Although the murder weapon was publicly reported to be a knife, rumors traveled fast through the tiny town. Within days, it was common knowledge that Wanda Hudson had actually been killed with a screwdriver.

"This is a little town and anytime anything happens, it really gets around," says Vickie Woods, who still works at the same Nettles Flower & Gift Shop where she'd been working the morning Wanda was killed. "It was shocking to think that someone could be in Coushatta who could do something like that."

Woods, who also lived in the River Towne Apartments with her young children, remembers that a woman ran into the flower shop, screaming that Wanda had been killed. People poured out into the grassy common area between the flower shop and the cabins, where they waited in horror while police worked and the local ambulance operator removed Hudson's body. Later, Woods would see for herself the blood on the walls of the apartment.

Robert Browne, she remembers, was a good friend and proved particularly helpful in the tense days after the killing. Browne went door to door in the evenings, telling women and children to stay inside and lock their doors.

Vickie and Robert grew up together, and they shared lots of childhood memories, from Easter egg hunts to Halloween parties. Robert loved to dress up in ghoulish costumes and scare children on October 31, his birthday. In the early 1980s, Vickie often went dancing with him at local clubs, when they both lived in the River Towne cabins. Their relationship was never romantic. "He would walk me to the door, kiss me on the forehead, and say, 'Good night,' " said Woods. She also remembers Browne frequently saying to her, "Vickie, you're my true friend."

She wonders today why he said such a thing.

Rusty Watson, Wanda's cousin, had been out drinking at a local bar that Friday night. As he happened to drive past the River Towne Apartments, Watson considered stopping for a moment to check on her. Wanda was like a sister, he says. However, the hour was late, so Watson turned instead for home. He's since been tortured by that decision, wondering if he had stopped, could he have saved her?

The day before she was killed, Wanda also told Rusty's father that Robert Browne, had changed the locks on her door. Wanda's uncle, Robert Paxton Watson, told police in 1983 that his niece was worried that Browne had kept a key for himself. Even that information apparently did not make Browne a suspect in the case.

"My father just brought it to their attention, but nobody ever done nothing," says Rusty Watson, still angry almost a quarter century later over the authorities' inaction. "If my dad told them that, and they were so worried about who done it, why didn't they go check him to see if anything of his matched up?"

And the police did knock on Browne's door that Saturday in May 1983, after Hudson's body was found, just as the two searchers knocked on his door in September 1991, the morning after Heather Church vanished. A sleepy-eyed Browne then told them that he and his estranged wife number four, Rita, had been out late drinking and then had gone to bed. No, he'd said, they hadn't heard a thing.

When Detective Mark Finley came to Coushatta in 1995 to conduct background interviews in the Heather Church case, Rita Coleman told him essentially the same thing.

Although they were separated at the time, Rita told Finley, Robert had invited her to a cookout at Donald's home, where they stayed until about two o'clock in the morning. She said she followed Robert in her car to the River Towne Apartments, where they stayed up late drinking coffee and talking about getting back together. He made breakfast for her later that day.

Although Rita had suffered frequent and vicious abuse at the hands of her former husband, she would be the one to provide an alibi for him on the night Hudson was murdered.

In a spooky twist on the story, the task of cleaning up the blood in Wanda Hudson's cabin and also repainting it fell to Browne, as the complex's handyman. And when his older brother could find no one to rent it, Robert moved in. For a brief time, Rita, too, lived with Browne in the apartment where Wanda Hudson was killed. Eventually, the cabin was torn down.

Beyond the interest in John Higgs, authorities never developed any suspects in Wanda Hudson's murder. And physical evidence recovered from the scene, including strands of hair wound around Hudson's fingers, apparently did not conclusively match to Higgs. Louisiana State Police have sent several samples of the 1983 crime scene evidence to the Northwest Crime Lab in Natchitoches, Louisiana, for DNA testing. According to Trooper Mike Allen, if a coherent DNA sequence can be extracted from the samples — and this is a big if, given the age and condition of the samples — authorities will then compare the results with DNA samples taken from Browne, as well as from Higgs. This is at least the second or third time such forensic analysis has been attempted in the Hudson case. (It is unclear just where everything was sent. Some evidence was sent to the FBI lab in the 1980s.) However, Red River Parish authorities and the state police have declined to discuss the earlier test results. Now that the work is being done under the auspices of the Louisiana State Police, there is at least hope for a coherent set of facts to emerge for consideration.

Pending those results, however, there is little enthusiasm in Coushatta law enforcement circles for Robert Browne as a suspect in either of the two River Towne Apartments cases that he claims to have committed. His failure to offer a more complete description of Wanda Hudson's wounds is cited locally as one example of why his confessions are not to be trusted. Her killer knows what he did to her.

What Browne has said so far could be simply street knowledge, says current Sheriff Johnny Ray Norman, information that just about anybody in town would have about the cases. Husky and good-natured, Norman explored several careers. including a brief stint in the National Football League as a Dallas Cowboy, before he joined the sheriff's office in 1996. He therefore has no official connection to the investigations of the Hudson and Hayes murders or of Aline Self's disappearance.

Today, he operates out a cluttered courthouse office where a sticker affixed to the glass front of his well-stocked gun cabinet — "Walk with Jesus and you'll never walk alone" — sums up the sheriff's approach to life, he says.

In one of his earliest professional incarnations, on the faculty of Coushatta High School, Norman was Robert Browne's PE teacher, and remembers Browne in his driver's ed class, too. He recollects Browne was neither an athlete nor a very good driver. The boy was standoffish, but generally unremarkable — except for his temper.

"He wasn't a push around," says the sheriff. "He stood up for himself. If you did something that he didn't like, he'd get back with you."

Norman says he has a hard time reconciling the Robert Browne he has known with the serial killer Browne now claims to be. The sheriff was acquainted with Browne's father — "Mr. Ron," as he calls him — and knows Robert's brother Donald, the former state trooper, who still lives south of Coushatta.

Norman, like everyone else connected with the Hudson and Self cases in Coushatta, thinks a satisfactory resolution will be tough to achieve. "Our problem (is that after) twenty-four years, everybody we want to talk to is dead and gone," he explains. "Key witnesses, people that could really make this thing go one way or another are gone. All the people who investigated it are dead."

Hard evidence, he says, is needed to corroborate Browne's confessions.

"We need to get something that will really tie him into it," says the sheriff. "He may be the one who did it. He may be. I can't say he didn't. But right now I can't say that he is the one who did it."

THIRTY-TWO

Once he returned to Colorado Springs from the goodwill tour, Jeff Nohr set to work at further cultivating his coalition of the willing, as well as the less-than-willing. The FBI agents had suggested that the Colorado investigators sponsor a meeting of all the agencies with potential cases against Browne. Best to pick a neutral location, preferably closer to the away teams, the FBI team suggested. Accordingly, Dallas was chosen.

The plan had a dual purpose. Certainly, El Paso County wanted to encourage dialogue and a mutual exchange of information about Browne. But more than that, the sheriff's department was ready to seek a guilty plea from Browne or prosecute him for the murder of Rocio Sperry. If other states planned to make cases against Browne, they reasoned, it would make sense for all of them to coordinate their prosecution announcements.

On February 12, 2006, Sheriff Maketa, Undersheriff Teri Goodall, Commander Brad Shannon, Lieutenant Ken Hilte, Jeff Nohr, and Charlie Hess traveled to Dallas, along with a representative from the Colorado Department of Corrections.

The Sugar Land and Tulsa police departments, along with the Arkansas, Louisiana, and Washington State police, plus Red River Parish authorities, including Red River District Attorney William Jones, accepted invitations to the two-day meeting. California and New Mexico authorities declined, saying they didn't have any known victims. To Nohr's disappointment, no one from Fayette County or Flatonia came to hear what Browne had told him and Charlie Hess about Melody Bush.

The detective had toiled for weeks, building casebooks for each victim: twenty-three, three-inch-thick binders in all. Like his former father-in-law, Nohr says the tedious work suits him. The detective vigorously affirms that he cannot tolerate a disorganized casebook.

The binders for the Louisiana delegation alone weighed more than ten pounds. By now, Browne had discussed with Nohr and Hess six of his supposed seventeen Louisiana victims, all women, including the Coushatta cases of Hudson, Self, and Hayes. Although Louisiana State Police had not yet found evidence to corroborate the other three claims, Nohr had prepared casebooks for the "Cajun Lady," the "Hilltop Bar Lady," and the "Holiday Inn Lady," all the same.

If the detective expected the Louisiana authorities to be grateful, however, or more in a mood to share, he was mistaken. Unlike other agencies who presented the facts of their respective cases, the Louisiana delegation said little.

"At that time when we went over there, nobody from Louisiana had interviewed Robert Browne," says DA Bill Jones. "I was going over there more to learn. I was not going over there to necessarily discuss what evidence or information that we might have had, because I didn't think it pertained to the investigation in other cases. We didn't know if we shared it [whether] it would get back to Robert Browne or get around or whatever."

Jones was and is openly skeptical of Browne's claims. "I expressed my opinion at that time that we need more than just him saying 'I did this,' " he complains. "I'm not sure how much more I came out of that meeting with than I went into it with."

Louisiana's resistance struck representatives of some of the other agencies as odd. For them, the meeting was a collegial get-together, nothing more, nothing less.

"The guys from Louisiana, I could never understand what burr was under their saddle," says Jim Hansen, an investigator with the Washington State Attorney General's HITS (Homicide Investigation Tracking System) program.

Although Washington authorities had not been able to find a body or otherwise corroborate Browne's story that he'd shot a man whom he encountered on an Interstate 90 overlook in eastern Washington, Hansen said he found the meeting worthwhile.

"I thoroughly enjoyed it," he says. "For me, that type of thing is great. The networking and learning about the other cases and all that. That's what it's all about."

David Resch and Kirk Mellecker attended the meeting as well. They shared a time line they had built for El Paso County that juxtaposed what was known of Browne's movements with his claims. Resch also repeated for the gathered investigators some of the highlights of the analysis the FBI had presented to the El Paso County investigators the previous August. "I remember talking about how El Paso County had done the right thing," Resch recalls. "The rest of the show really was theirs."

"The one thing I remember [about the FBI presentation]," says Jones, "they said, 'You can't believe everything Robert Browne is telling you. You've got to verify it.' "

Browne himself struck one deeply discordant note with his insistence, relayed by Jeff Nohr, that he'd talk to police agencies about their cases only under the protection of an immunity letter. Anger and derision closely characterize the various detectives' response to this condition, which in any event Browne has yet to enforce. Louisiana, Arkansas, and Oklahoma all spoke with him without guaranteeing him a thing.

Finally, Nohr told the assembled agencies that El Paso County was close to making a case against Browne. He said he expected to be ready to file charges by May. It would be good, he urged, if "everyone could break at the same time."

"We gave them three months to get their cases together. We thought it could be done," Nohr said.

The Sugar Land police, alone, were receptive and supportive. Even they were cautious, though. The DNA tests in the Nidia

Mendoza case remained incomplete. Captain Gary Cox noted that they preferred to wait to see whether they had "a slam dunk or something else."

When the time came, none of the other agencies were ready to move, which created yet another set of headaches for the El Paso County Sheriff's Office.

THIRTY-THREE

"Robert Browne was and is very knowledge-able of the system, very intelligent," says El Paso County District Attorney John Newsome. "He knew that he held all the cards. Only he had the information that we needed to secure anything close to resembling a prosecution. Only Robert Browne could turn this missing persons case into a homicide."

After the watershed event of February 2005, it occurred to the El Paso County Sheriff's Office that they needed to consult with Newsome, who had taken office as the new DA just one month before. Although Jeff Nohr, Rick Frady, and the rest of the investigative command would work hard to find an evidentiary connection between Browne and the Grand Am Lady, it was going to be impossible to tell the full story without the killer's cooperation.

Newsome, who had joined the DA's office

straight out of law school a decade earlier, remembered the Heather Church case, with all its horrifying implications, well. He knew that there were people in Colorado and across the country who would not readily countenance another deal to save Browne's life, some of them his colleagues and associates inside the criminal justice system. They wanted the child killer to pay for his crimes with his life.

Yet to Newsome, a strong supporter of the death penalty, cutting a deal for information with Robert Browne in exchange for not pursuing the death penalty was his only logical choice under the circumstances. "Without the cooperation of Robert Browne, there was no case," says the district attorney. "I viewed that as no decision. There was only one correct course of action — to get the information, bring peace to the family, and close a missing persons case."

After the Grand Am Lady was identified as Rocio Sperry, Newsome's office consulted with her husband, Joe, and daughter, Amie. "I tried to put myself in their situation," says Newsome. "I know that is what I would want. I would want to know what happened to my wife and to my mom."

Rocio Sperry's two survivors agreed to

endorse the deal, should it come to pass.

Then things fell apart once again. Browne broke off communications altogether — "I have decided to end this whole affair" — and remained silent for several months. Not until Nohr and Hess arrived unannounced at the Territorial Correctional Facility in October 2005, carrying with them a birthday card for Browne, did the prison conversations finally resume. Charlie Hess noted during the meeting that Browne's mood seemed to have improved again, and said so. "They changed my meds," Browne explained.

The flow of case information, however, did not resume. Browne did not repeat his impatience with the lack of progress toward a transfer out of state, but the subject hung over every meeting. "He wasn't receiving what he wanted," says Nohr, and so Robert Browne had taken further disclosures off the table.

When Nohr told the Dallas conference in February 2006 that he hoped to have charges against Browne filed by May, he was offering them the rosiest scenario possible. Unless Browne somehow emerged from his latest funk, there'd be no charges, no deal, no information, and nowhere to go with Robert Browne other than back to zero —

not a viable option. Yet again the whole project seemed to be in deep jeopardy.

Then came the April 14, 2006, meeting in the interview room at Territorial. The session had begun routinely enough. Charlie Hess had asked how things were going at the license tag plant. Browne replied that he was now punching out the license blanks. He'd been asked to be a team leader but declined. Hess then said he was still working on the out-of-state transfer. Minnesota was looking like a possibility. He also said that the sheriff's office was talking with the Department of Corrections about providing the ever-misanthropic Browne a single cell. Nothing definitive yet.

The conversation then turned to out-of-state cases. Hess probed Browne to determine if he might be willing to plead guilty to any of the cases he claimed. The investigator told Browne that some of the other states might be willing to take a guilty plea from him, if he was also going to plead guilty to the Sperry case. As yet, however, Browne had made no firm offer to do any such thing.

Aware that Browne wanted as little press attention as possible, Hess told him that, theoretically, a plea deal could be done in a day. Come to the Springs. Go to court. Back at Territorial by nighttime. But, Hess added, the out-of-state plea arrangements all would depend on Browne sharing more details in each case, enough information so the various police agencies could corroborate his confession.

Browne replied that if he pled guilty, he didn't think a return to any Colorado DOC facility was in his best interest. His life would be endangered. He further said that besides immunity from the death penalty, any deal had to specify that any new sentence would run concurrently with his life sentence for murdering Heather Church. In the exceedingly rare chance that he someday might go free on a technicality, Browne did not want his sentences stacked. After some more discussion of how the out-of-state plea bargains might work, Browne insisted he needed to talk directly with the appropriate individuals and that he was not prepared at the time to put anything in writing for them. Then, in an almost offhand way, Browne said, "I'll plead."

He would plead guilty to the murder of Rocio Sperry.

Nohr and Hess, taken totally by surprise, managed not to betray their elation, or so they hoped. The three men then calmly started going over the details together.

"While we were sitting there with Robert, we were like, 'Oh, OK,' " Nohr recalls. "Then when Charlie and I left and drove out, we were like, holy shit! That was a major breakthrough. A major accomplishment."

Nohr and Hess were so inured to disappointments by this time that when they returned to Territorial on May 11, 2006, they almost expected Browne to have changed his mind and withdrawn his plea offer. Instead, he walked into the meeting ready to iron out the last few details of the deal. As usual, Browne was in charge.

In the previous meeting, he had refused their advice that he consult with an attorney. Now he agreed to do so, but only for the purpose of reviewing the documents to ensure they said what they were supposed to say.

John Newsome was all for that. The DA wanted to be certain that Browne knew he wasn't getting anything in exchange for his guilty plea, other than a promise from the DA's office not to pursue the death penalty. Whether Browne received a transfer or other accommodations in prison would be strictly up to the Department of Corrections.

"We said we would not object, but the

point was expressly made to Mr. Browne in open court by a district judge that this DA's office does not control the DOC," Newsome recalls.

Then came another tricky part. It would be a violation of Browne's constitutional rights for a judge to accept his uncorroborated guilty plea. So, in the absence of any physical evidence connecting him to Rocio Sperry's murder, Newsome directed the sheriff's office to produce an affidavit, as detailed as possible, that spelled out every shred of information they had, including Browne's statements, that tied him to Sperry as well as to all the other cases, both in and outside of Colorado. By the preponderance of this evidence, Newsome hoped, a judge would accept the likelihood that Browne was telling the truth.

Jeff Nohr went to work on the critical document under Lieutenant Hilte's direction, and in time produced a forty-four-page affidavit to accompany the arrest warrant. Hilte questioned whether Browne ought to be called "Mr. Browne" in the narrative. Nohr insisted, and the honorific stayed.

The first nineteen single-spaced pages discussed the facts of the Sperry case in extraordinary detail. This information alone would likely have satisfied a judge to accept

Browne's guilty plea. But acting on Newsome's explicit instructions, Nohr plowed on through seventeen other homicides that Browne had described to him and to Charlie Hess. In eight of the out-of-state cases, the sheriff's office was also able to supply the victim's name, too.

In the affidavit, Hilte and Nohr meticulously documented Browne's accounts of his alleged crimes and then compared — or contrasted — the killer's information with what was officially known about the crimes. The investigators were careful not to reveal any previously unreported information about the cases unless that information had come from Browne himself.

Nohr did not balk at Newsome's instructions. "We needed the information about the other cases for support and credibility," the detective says. "We had to show what he had given us versus what we had learned from talking with the other agencies."

Law enforcement officers in some of the other jurisdictions were upset by the document, which disclosed some previously unreleased information about their investigations.

Red River Parish DA Bill Jones was one of them.

"I did not see the need," he says angrily,

"for information that they had gotten — I understand from the Louisiana State Police — to be displayed in an affidavit to get an arrest warrant for Robert Browne on a case in Colorado. Now you tell me how that serves as probable cause to get an indictment on a murder in Colorado?

"I didn't think that was appropriate, I certainly didn't."

El Paso County authorities maintain that Jones was informed and did not respond to a letter that they sent to all the jurisdictions in advance of the guilty plea. Furthermore, they say, all the new information about the Red River Parish cases came from Browne, not Louisiana authorities.

The Sugar Land police say that while they were concerned with maintaining the integrity of their case, they had agreed that El Paso County could use the information in the affidavit. Captain Cox said that Nohr had called him in advance to review the document.

"Colorado communicated with all of us before they released anything and gave us the opportunity to be present [at the press conference]," said Cox. "From our standpoint, there wasn't anything in [the affidavit] that would hamper our investigation. The information came from him. It didn't come from us."

The Flatonia and Fayette County authorities, doubtful as ever that Browne was responsible for killing Melody Bush, made no comment at all.

Thirty-Four

On July 24, 2006, just a little after six o'clock in the morning, Nohr left Colorado Springs to meet Browne at Territorial prison. This time, instead of driving with Charlie Hess, the detective rode with a uniformed deputy in a marked cruiser equipped for prisoner transport with a steel cage between the front and back seats. When Nohr returned from Cañon City, Browne would be with them.

At the prison Browne was wearing an orange jumpsuit and full restraints, with his hands cuffed to a belly belt and irons on his legs. A small, clear plastic bag held a toothbrush and toothpaste, his only possessions. His medications, however, were not ready, as had been promised. Browne was nervous about leaving without his pills but reluctant to raise the issue.

"I don't want to ruffle feathers," he said.

"We're not leaving without the meds,"

Nohr responded.

It took three phone calls and about twenty minutes to resolve the matter and get the small brown envelope full of pill bottles. "I think he kind of enjoyed that someone was sticking up for him," Nohr said. "He told me thank you."

It was an absolutely gorgeous Colorado summer morning: crisp, clear, and not too hot. As they drove north on Highway 115 through the pine-covered mountains past deep gulleys and rushing streams, Browne relaxed.

"What," Nohr asked, "do you miss the most about not being out?"

"The green and the trees," Browne said, nodding toward the window and the scenery flying past the cruiser.

Driving into the Springs, past Fort Carson, the prisoner took note of the strip joints and bars that line the highway near the base.

"I was hoping that we'd get to go to some of those girlie bars," Browne quipped.

"Now, Robert, you know we can't do that."

"I know."

At the Criminal Justice Center, El Paso County's jail, Nohr signed Browne in and then served him with the arrest warrant for first-degree murder in the death of Rocio

Sperry. Browne showed no reaction.

Three days later, in a quiet room at the sheriff's office, Commander Brad Shannon, Charlie Hess, a victim's advocate, and Nohr sat down with Rocio Sperry's daughter, Amie. Then a nineteen-year-old college student, Amie Sperry had been only four months old when her mother disappeared. She was raised by her aunt and uncle, and had grown up believing that her father was to blame for her mother's death. The previous July, when Jeff Nohr flew to Jackson, Mississippi, to tell her about Browne, she had been relieved and grateful. A huge, lifelong burden of suspicion and mistrust had been lifted.

When Amie Sperry flew into Colorado Springs to attend Browne's court hearing, Nohr picked her up at the airport. She had asked to see the apartment where her mother and father had lived. Nohr drove her past the Kwik Stop and Browne's former apartment, as well. She was silent throughout the trip.

Now he watched Amie carefully, worried about how she would take the news.

Commander Shannon told her as gently as he could what Browne said he did to her mother. Amie listened stoically and said little. The district attorney had delivered the same news to Joe Sperry, Rocio's husband, the day before.

At 8:38 a.m. on July 27, 2006, District Judge Theresa M. Cisneros called case number 06CR3041, *People v. Robert Charles Browne.* The accused, again clad in an orange jail jumpsuit and full restraints, was brought into a courtroom crowded with people waiting for their cases to be called on the docket. Unlike the other defendants, buffed and polished by their lawyers into a semblance of respectability, Browne, with his wild, untrimmed beard and sunken eyes, had the look of a man who had been living apart from civilization for decades.

District Attorney John Newsome and Deputy District Attorney Amy Mullaney sat at the prosecutors' table. Public defenders William Schoewe and Peggy Ransom represented Browne.

In the back of the courtroom, Charlie Hess, Jeff Nohr, and their supervisor, Joe Breister, now chief of the Law Enforcement bureau, waited, along with a reporter from the *Gazette.* News of Browne's claims of multiple murders had not yet reached the rest of the media.

Scott Fischer came to court where, he would later say, he paid more attention to Joe and Amie Sperry than he did to Browne, even though it was the first time he had seen the killer in person.

Lou Smit did not enter the courtroom, although he wanted to. "I didn't want to take the chance that Browne would see me," he explains, "and suddenly decide not to go through with it. I didn't want to screw things up."

Judge Cisneros accepted a copy of the written plea agreement from Mullaney and began to review it aloud. Browne, she noted, would be entering a guilty plea to one count of murder in the first degree.

The district attorney's office, according to the plea, also had agreed not to seek the death penalty. Instead, the DA asked the court to impose a life sentence without the possibility of parole for forty years. This sentence, the judge read out loud, would run concurrently with Browne's sentence for the murder of Heather Church.

"And then there's an agreement that Mr. Browne — that the prosecution has agreed to support Mr. Browne's request to serve his sentence in Minnesota Department of Corrections' facility," Cisneros read from the plea agreement.

The judge summoned Browne and his lawyer to the podium.

"Mr. Browne, your lawyer tells me that

you would like to plead guilty this morning," Cisneros began.

"That is correct."

Jeff Nohr listened with deep satisfaction. "I was pleased," he says. "The man had done something very horrific, very mean, very cold, time after time after time, and he stood up in front of the judge and admitted what he had done. I have to give him credit for doing that. Does it excuse it? No. But I knew all this work and time spent, him with us and us with him, had paid off. It was well worth it."

The judge repeated the terms of the plea bargain: a life sentence with no chance of parole for forty years, to run concurrently with his present sentence in return for a pledge from the DA not to seek the death penalty.

The first portion of the plea agreement was standard; the second half, however, was not. The district attorney could not force Minnesota or any other state to accept Browne; nor could the DA force the Colorado Department of Corrections to make any special arrangements for Browne. Whatever happened in that regard was entirely up to the prisons. Cisneros wanted to make sure that Browne understood that fact.

She was very careful and very thorough.

"It also says in the plea agreement that the prosecution has agreed to support your request to be transferred from a Colorado Department of Corrections facility to a Minnesota Department of Corrections facility," Cisneros said. "I need you to understand that they can recommend that, but no department of corrections facility — they cannot bind any other — any department of corrections facility. Do you understand that?"

"I understand that. Yes, I do," Browne said.

"Does that change your mind about pleading guilty?"

"No, it doesn't."

Mullaney reminded the judge that an additional provision in the plea agreement specified that El Paso County could not bind any other jurisdictions, either.

"So, in other words, if you're being investigated for any additional crimes, those other jurisdictions will still have the ability to prosecute you for any additional crimes that they believe they can prove," Cisneros said. "Do you understand that?"

"Yes, I do."

"So this agreement right here that you're pleading guilty to takes care of only El Paso County and this particular first-degree murder charge. Do you understand that?"

"Yes, I understand that."

"Does that change your mind about pleading guilty?"

"No, it doesn't."

Cisneros confirmed that Browne could read and write English, that he had read and understood the charge, and that he was not under the influence of drugs, alcohol, or medication that would affect his ability to make a decision. In response to her questioning, Browne told the judge that he was not suffering from mental health problems that would affect his ability to make a decision and that he had had ample time to confer with his attorney and was satisfied with his advice.

"Do you believe that you're entering this guilty plea voluntarily and of your own free will?" Cisneros asked.

"Yes, I do."

Browne affirmed that he was not pressured to plead guilty.

"Do you understand, Mr. Browne, that when you plead guilty, you are telling me that you committed this crime?"

"Yes, I understand."

"Do you understand that this is a final plea on your part?"

"I understand that."

"So, in other words, you won't be able to come in at any point in the future and change your mind about this plea; it's final. Do you understand that?"

"I understand."

Cisneros reminded Browne that the court was not bound by any promises regarding his sentence, beyond what had been presented. Furthermore, she stressed that by pleading guilty Browne was giving up his constitutional right to a trial and the right to question witnesses against him. Additionally, he was giving up his right to an appeal and his right to a preliminary hearing, at which time a judge would decide whether there was enough evidence to hold him for trial.

As Fischer listened to Cisneros question Browne, he worried that the killer would grow impatient. Browne had told the investigators that he didn't want a major production in court. And here he was, enduring just the sort of repeated questioning that he despised.

To Fischer's relief, however, Browne remained calm and compliant.

Addressing the plea itself, Cisneros told Browne that if he went to trial, the prosecution would have to prove that he killed Rocio Sperry.

"They'd have to prove that you acted after deliberation. And after deliberation means not only intentionally but also that the decision to commit the act has been made after the exercise of reflection and judgment concerning the act . . . ," the judge continued. "And in this case you caused the death of Rocio Sperry."

The judge also reminded Browne that without the plea he could face the death penalty. She paused, evidently mindful of Browne's previous guilty plea and subsequent challenge.

"Was the death penalty declared unconstitutional during that time frame? I don't think it was," Cisneros said.

Browne's lawyer confirmed that the death penalty was, in fact, in effect in November 1987 when Rocio Sperry disappeared. No one wanted a repeat of Browne's 1996 attempt to withdraw his guilty plea in the Church case.

Finally, after questioning Browne for more than twenty-five minutes, the judge requested his plea.

"I plead guilty," Browne said.

"Tell me what you did that makes you think you're guilty."

"I caused — caused the death of the individual."

"I'd like you to tell me, in plain English, what happened," Cisneros requested.

"In plain English, we were in my apartment and I strangled her," Browne replied.

"And the *her* that you strangled, was that Rocio Sperry?"

"Yes, it was."

Cisneros had more questions for Browne to confirm that he did, indeed, kill Sperry in November 1987, in El Paso County, before accepting the plea and finding him guilty.

"And I'll find that you've been represented by competent counsel with whom you're satisfied; that you understand the nature and the effect of pleading guilty; that there's a factual basis for the plea," the judge added.

After Browne was finished, Joe Sperry took the stand. The detectives seated in the back watched nervously, worried how Sperry might react when he came face-to-face with Rocio's killer.

He limited himself to vituperation. "I'd just like to say that finally it's over, nineteen years," Sperry told the courtroom. "I knew some scumbag murdered my wife, I knew it from the beginning, but nobody would listen, but now I'm okay with it. I see the scumbag the way he's going and that's it.

That's his life."

"Mr. Sperry," Cisneros began.

"I'm going to live on now," Sperry continued.

"I'm sorry all of that happened to you," Cisneros said.

Amie was next. Poised and calm, she spoke softly.

"Your Honor," she began, "I'm here today on behalf of my mother, Rocio Sperry. And I'd like to say my deepest gratitude to the State of Colorado and the entire department because after nineteen years of not knowing, justice has finally come. And, as for Mr. Robert Browne, I would like to say, may God be with his soul. Thank you."

Bill Schoewe reminded the court that the case had been solved only once Browne came forward.

"He gave the information first without prodding, without investigation, without interrogation. It was his decision to contact law enforcement and put this case to rest," Schoewe said. "Based on that, I would ask the court adopt this plea agreement and sentence Mr. Browne accordingly."

Cisneros read Browne's sentence, and the hearing was over thirty-four minutes after it had begun.

In the hall outside the courtroom, Amie

Sperry thanked the detectives again and then slipped into the women's restroom to cry alone for the mother she had never known.

THIRTY-FIVE

For more than four years, the cold case squad's conversations with Robert Browne had remained a closely held secret, and luckily so. Any public mention probably would have had fatal consequences for the project and possibly for Browne, as well. A few reporters and editors at the *Gazette* had been aware of the project, but as city editor Sue McMillan explains, the sheriff's office had persuaded the newspaper to hold the story indefinitely. The embargo expired with Browne's guilty plea. The *Gazette* immediately broke the story online, guaranteeing a huge media turnout for the sheriff's press conference that afternoon.

Soon Costilla Street, in front of the squat, brown brick sheriff's office in downtown Colorado Springs, was crowded with TV satellite trucks. Reporters from all over Colorado and much of the West were inundating Lieutenant Clifton Northam, the public information officer, and members of his staff with telephone, fax, and e-mail queries.

At two o'clock that afternoon Sheriff Maketa stepped up to the microphone to begin his press conference in the largest available space in the building. It was packed with reporters, photographers, and television crews elbowing one another for position. Lieutenant Northam and his staff had prepared a fat press packet with information about Browne and his alleged victims for each of them. A copy of Browne's arrest affidavit and a media summary already were posted on the sheriff's website.

Flanked by the members of the cold case squad, as well by Newsome and members of his staff, Maketa presented a twenty-minute PowerPoint overview of the story, complete with photos of Browne and some of the female victims he claimed. Then the sheriff took questions. The reporters were most interested in Browne's claim to have killed forty-eight people, and whether or not Maketa believed him. "I don't think we can conduct business assuming he's exaggerating," the sheriff told the *Denver Post*. "We'll hold the number forty-eight until he tells us otherwise."

Joe and Amie Sperry also attended the

press conference. Rocio's widower raged against Browne. "I wanted to jump over the railing and kill that guy," Joe told *Denver Post* reporter Kirk Mitchell.

In an interview with the *Gazette,* Mike Church said the announcement was "resurfacing a lot of old memories," none of which were welcome. "He feels like he has control over us," Heather's dad said of her killer. "He's wanting to become a Charles Manson or a Ted Bundy. He wants us all to think how smart he is. But he's nothing but a coward."

Church told the *Gazette* that he, for one, had no interest in knowing the details of Heather's murder. He had never read news accounts of the crime, and he'd covered his ears in court back in 1995 when Browne had pled guilty to Heather's killing.

Charlie Hess was talkative that day. He explained to reporters how he'd shared personal details of his life with Browne, such as his son-in-law's murder and the dangerous heart surgery that his wife, Jo, had undergone. Why? "If I want to look into his soul," Hess told the *Post,* "I know he has to feel like he can look into mine."

Hess also spoke freely about the special considerations Browne enjoyed, a bit of candor that the sheriff and the Department of Corrections could have done without. The authorities had hoped to keep discussion of the information-for-favors arrangement to a minimum.

"What made us willing to consider this doctor and relocation was that Robert Browne stated, 'If you can have these things happen, I will give you three murders in Louisiana, unsolved, and enough information to solve or prove I killed a lady in Colorado Springs,' " Hess told *Gazette* reporter Pam Zubeck.

"Most of the people I talk to who have committed multiple murders are looking for something that can't be achieved, like getting out of prison," Hess explained to the *Los Angeles Times.* "His requests were reasonable."

As anticipated, Browne was big news back in the joint. "There was a real shock wave," says Major Linda Maifield at Territorial. "You would have comments such as, 'Man, that guy was sleeping in our pod.' And, 'Here I was talking to a serial murderer the whole time!' "

Browne had suddenly become the last thing a prudent inmate hopes to be: famous and a target of his fellow cons' anger. Snitching, though very common, is also violently discouraged inside the walls, even if you're only snitching on yourself. He already had to deal with his fellow inmates' disgust with a child killer; now he'd drawn unwelcome attention to himself once again.

The story was headline news around the country. "Colorado Killer Claims He Murdered 49 Others in 25 Years," reported the *New York Times.* "Retired Sleuths Heat up Old Cases," topped the story in *USA Today.*

Before the day was out, Lieutenant Northam personally fielded calls from more than sixty media outlets, including Japanese, Dutch, Czech, and Russian news organizations. In the coming days, Nohr and Hess were interviewed on CNN, MSNBC, and Fox, which assigned Geraldo Rivera, the old tiger of tabloid television, to the story. NBC's *Today* show did a live, 5:00 a.m. interview at the sheriff's office with Hess and Nohr on the following Saturday.

The news generated so much media interest in the Houston area that the Sugar Land police held their own press conference the next day. "At this point," Captain Cox told reporters, "we're hopefully optimistic that Mr. Browne is going to be [proved] responsible" for Nidia Mendoza's murder.

Several hundred miles away in Coushatta, Bill Jones sounded a different note with the *Los Angeles Times.* "They ought to let us finish before they start making comments," said Jones, still angry about the details of the Louisiana cases revealed in the Sperry arrest affidavit. "I'm not saying Robert Browne did do it, or didn't do it. I just don't need to reveal some of our stuff that's going on right now. But there will be an appropriate time for us to make a comment on all this."

The Red River Parish DA's public annoyance notwithstanding, the flood of news stories was welcome at the El Paso County Sheriff's Office. "We wanted as much coverage as we could get," says Clif Northam, "so hopefully other people might see the story and come forward with information that might help solve other cases that we had little information on."

And it worked.

Down in Albuquerque, an FBI agent investigating missing persons cases heard on the news that New Mexico authorities were searching for one of Browne's possible victims, the motorcyclist. The agent telephoned Sergeant Thomas Christian at the state police with a tip. An unidentified skull, she said, had been sitting in the office of the state medical investigator ever since 1994. It had been discovered by hunters along Highway 64, about the same time that the motorcycle was recovered.

The skull was believed to be that of a Hispanic male, thirty to forty years old. Though much of the bone was missing, the forensic experts were certain of one thing: the victim had taken at least one bullet to the head. They found a quantity of bullet fragments embedded in the bone. Unfortunately, no one could be certain of the slug's caliber.

It was not altogether clear why the skull had never been properly logged into the system. The trooper who'd found the bones and brought them to the state medical investigator had left the state police soon thereafter. He'd apparently neglected to send a DNA sample from the skull to the FBI for listing in the Bureau's CODIS registry. His former employers had no record of the skull or even knew of its existence until the FBI agent discovered it while working on other cases.

Sergeant Christian has since made certain that the FBI has a DNA sample from the skull. The New Mexico State Police are looking for the motorcycle's owner to see what he may know, and they've issued a call for help from the public. Christian says there is sufficient dentition left in the skull for a dental identification to be possible.

As for the bullet hole in the victim's head, while Browne said he shot the man in the chest, Lieutenant Hilte is not overly concerned. "Sometimes Robert Browne won't tell you," he says. "Sometimes he's lying. Sometimes he's mistaken."

In the aftermath of his guilty plea and press coverage, negotiations to send Browne to Minnesota to serve out his time went off track, possibly permanently. For his own safety, the killer was kept in a single cell at the Criminal Justice Center in Colorado Springs until September 2006, when he was returned to Territorial and placed back in a single cell under twenty-three-hour lockdown, again for his own protection. Jeff Nohr reports that Browne seems reconciled, for the time being, to this arrangement. He's happy to have no cell mates. As ever, Browne likes to be alone. He's also taking a course in electronics.

The cold case squad has disbanded.

In early 2007, Scott Fischer and his wife left Colorado Springs to live in Breckinridge, Colorado. Lou Smit has moved on to form other cold case units. Charlie Hess is working on a book.

Their parting was bittersweet. The men remain friends. "Keeping us together for six or seven years was a good run," says Fischer.

"We've almost run ourselves out of business," adds Smit. "All the old cases are in the books and completely organized. And Jeff has taken over with Browne."

Jeff Nohr is now assigned full time to the pursuit of cold cases for El Paso County, work that he loves, in spite of its inherent frustrations. He is driven by the need to find answers for families, to speak for the victims, as Lou Smit, his onetime mentor and former father-in-law, taught him to do.

The flurry of publicity surrounding Browne's confessions in July brought fresh waves of pain and sadness for the family of Heather Church. Mike Church, who has been remarried for fourteen years, still lives in Colorado Springs. He spends time with his sons, now grown, and still sobs unashamedly when he recalls his funny, smart, loving daughter. He takes comfort in his faith.

Heather's mother, Diane Wilson, after working in Colorado Springs area schools for several years, now teaches abroad, most recently in China. Heather's murder, she says, rocked her sons' world "on a cellular level. It has touched everything in their lives." Losing a child, or a sister, she says, "makes for a lot of loneliness." Others walk a wide circle around your personal pain, unable to address it. She has thrown herself into her work with other people's children, and it has helped. The heartache never really goes away, but she can laugh now when she recalls the happy moments with Heather. "As time went on," she says, "it got to be, 'I'll be damned. He's not taking me down, too.' "

In spring 2007, law enforcement agencies continued to investigate homicides Browne claims to have committed. Sugar Land police awaited results from a second, more sophisticated round of DNA tests in the Nidia Mendoza case. Because the twenty-three-year-old samples were degraded, the first DNA tests yielded no conclusive results. But authorities were hopeful that more precise tests for mitochondrial DNA might yield the results they sought.

In Coushatta, where authorities also still awaited the results of DNA testing, former sheriff Buddy Huckabay suffered a stroke and died, severing one more connection with the original cases. Wanda Hudson's uncle and her stepmother have also died. John Higgs reports that his parents and his older sisters, who remained steadfast in their support of him, also have passed on.

"My greatest regret is that they died

without seeing me vindicated," Higgs says.

Higgs moved away from Coushatta not long after Hudson's murder. He has continued to work as a pharmacist in another state.

"It killed my life in Coushatta," he says. "You really find out who are your friends and who aren't."

After the news of Browne's confessions broke in July 2006, one of Higgs's longtime friends called from Coushatta to say that he hoped the doubters would realize that they had been wrong about him and apologize.

"I didn't get a fair shake with the Red River Parish sheriff and I didn't get a fair shake with the Louisiana State Police," Higgs says. "But what I'm really angry about is that if someone had gone the extra mile to find out about Robert Browne . . . then maybe they would have saved a few other people and their families."

With no body and no evidence, Louisiana authorities had even less to work with in the case of Faye Aline Self. Reinvigorated by Browne's confession, Self's daughter, Karrie Bateman, ramped up her twelve-year effort to force authorities to investigate her mother's murder. She continues to seek witnesses and regularly telephones police with bits of information and questions. Having grown up believing — falsely — that Henry Lee Lucas killed her mother, Karrie remains skeptical about Browne's confession.

"Everybody else gets stabbed or strangled or hacked up, and my mom just falls asleep from ant poison?" Karrie says. "My own personal instinct — and I have felt this since 1994 — is that my mother is lying somewhere around that bar, in those woods and swamps."

Louisiana State Police say they are still investigating the Self case but will comment no further.

Red River Parish District Attorney Bill Jones and Sheriff Johnny Ray Norman acknowledged in late 2006 that of all Browne's alleged confessions, his claim to have killed Katherine "Fuzzy" Hayes is most credible. Still, without concrete forensic evidence to corroborate Browne's claims, authorities had yet to file charges against Browne by May 2007.

For Hayes's stepmother, Bettie Joice Smith, Browne's confession twenty-six years after Fuzzy's remains were found brings little solace. "Fuzzy did not deserve what she got," says Smith, now seventy-two. "She was just a kid going down a wrong road and she . . . went so far that it was hard to bring her back, but I tried."

Texas authorities gave the Melody Bush case a second look, even going so far as to ask a police agency in Colorado to track down and reinterview her husband. Texas Ranger Hanak said that Robert Stewart Bush's story remained consistent: he and his wife had partied together in their motel room; he fell asleep and awoke to find her gone. As far as Hanak is concerned, the Bush homicide remains open.

Tulsa police Detective Eddie Majors visited Colorado in May 2006 to interview Browne himself. Browne continued to insist that there had been a boat launch or ramp near the water where he dumped the body of the man he claimed to have killed in 1985. Majors decided that there were too many discrepancies to consider Browne a prime suspect in the 1992 murder of Timothy Warren. That case, too, remains open.

Browne's connection to the murder of Lisa Lowe, an Arkansas woman whose body was found floating in the Saint Francis River in 1991, appears the least likely. Lisa Lowe fit the physical description of a West Memphis, Arkansas, woman whom Browne claimed to have killed in 1980, and she was found wearing a short sweaterdress, much like the clothing Browne claimed his victim wore. But the eleven-year difference in the dates had always been a problem. After interviewing Browne in October 2006, Arkansas State Police Sergeant Barry Roy decided that there were too many other differences in the location Browne described to consider him a suspect in the Lowe case.

New Mexico authorities also are waiting on results of DNA analysis that they hope will help them identify the skull found in a remote area near Highway 64. FBI agents have joined their search for the registered owner of the motorcycle, which was found in the same area as the skull.

Browne's other claims — a couple killed on a beach in California, two males dumped into the Mississippi muck, women picked up in Louisiana bars and killed, a "South Philly" prostitute slain in a New Orleans Holiday Inn — remain uncorroborated. Beyond a few scraps of boot leather on a hillside near Gold Camp Road west of Colorado Springs, authorities have yet to find anything that would support Browne's claim of killing the "Cowboy Lady." Nor have they found a missing person report to suggest a possible victim.

Four of the named victims — Heather Church, Rocio Sperry, Wanda Hudson, and Faye Aline Self — have one thing in common. They lived and died where Browne lived and worked. The Church home was a quarter of a mile down an isolated country road from Browne's trailer house and tree farm. Rocio lived a longish block away from Browne's apartment and the convenience store where he worked in Colorado Springs. Wanda and Faye were his next door neighbors in Coushatta. A fifth victim, Katherine "Fuzzy" Hayes, also lived in Coushatta while Browne was there. Melody Bush disappeared from a Texas motel where Browne often stayed when he traveled on his silk flower sales route. Nidia Mendoza worked as a dancer in Houston, also one of the cities along Browne's delivery route. The geography, the Colorado investigators say, is more than coincidence. It is the key.

"Robert Browne, I believe, is a serial killer. He claims to do all these things, and so far, I can't prove that he hasn't," says Lou Smit. "And he is the one who put the numbers in the states."

As for the numbers scrawled on the hand-drawn map — nine in Colorado, seven in Texas, seventeen in Louisiana, five in Arkansas, three in Mississippi, two in Oklahoma, two in New Mexico, two in California, and one in Washington — these remain tantalizing clues hinting at mysteries yet to be solved.

Charlie Hess continued to visit Robert Browne at Territorial with Jeff Nohr through the winter of 2007. The sessions were no longer taped, although Jeff Nohr kept notes. They didn't talk about cases. The sheriff's office had cut off all discussion of crimes outside El Paso County, and Nohr and Hess felt there was no point in trying to talk about local cases as long as Browne still hadn't received all that he wanted out of the Sperry plea. The purpose of the visits was simply to keep the communications channel open. Browne, who remains an avid reader, was always grateful when they brought him books. He likes almost anything by Ernest Hemingway.

One of these calls, in January 2007, remains vivid in Nohr's memory. Browne was in an especially good mood, so Nohr thought it seemed a good time to explore a subject that he'd often wondered about.

"Robert," he said, "I have something on my mind. What does *urge* mean to you?"

Out of the corner of his eye, Nohr noticed Charlie Hess stiffen. He ignored him.

"To go, to get out and, you know . . . ," Browne said, stammering. He seemed to be searching for the right word. "It's a wanderlust," he finally said.

Did he still have those same urges, here

in prison?

"They're stronger than ever."

"What do you do about your urges?" Nohr asked.

"There's not much I can do," Browne answered. "I'm locked up."

An impatient Charlie Hess interrupted and changed the subject before Nohr could ask if Browne meant the urge to ramble or the urge to kill.

"I never did get the word *kill* out of him," Nohr says. "But he did say that his hatred of the human race is stronger than ever, too. I don't have a doubt that Robert would kill again if he could distance himself from the victim."

The detective, who visits Browne alone these days, is only partway down his long list of subjects to take up with the killer, and he has lots of unanswered questions to ask, chief among them the mystery of the seven virgins.

"I can't let it go," he says. "I have spent time reading it, studying it, trying to figure it out. What does it mean? Beat it up. Dissect it. Put it back together. And I still don't know. So I hope that someday, sometime, Robert will say what it means."

In the meantime, Jeff Nohr is willing to be patient.

"Robert's mind is his bank," he says. "What's in his mind is how he survives. So if he needs something, he's going to provide information. Such as: 'I want a single cell. I want a job. I want a warmer climate. I want a pair of long johns.' That is how he's going to pay for his stuff. When he feels that he's received what he's paid for, then he'll give us more. I'm confident of that."

TIME LINE OF KEY DATES[*]

October 31, 1952. Robert Charles Browne is born in Coushatta, Louisiana.

October 1969. Enlists in the U.S. Army.

September 1970. Marries first wife, Terry Ward.

1970–1971. Claims first murder, an American GI in South Korea.

October 1973. Marries second wife, Tuyet Minh Huynh.

January 1976. Divorces Tuyet Minh Huynh.

July 1976. Is discharged from U.S. Army.

[*] Dates in italics denote Browne's claimed victims.

September 1977. Marries third wife, Brenda Gayle Ware.

Circa 1977–1979. Kills "South Philly" prostitute in a New Orleans Holiday Inn.

Late 1970s. Kills "Cajun Lady" in Morgan City, Louisiana.

October 1980. Divorces third wife, Brenda Ware, and marries fourth wife, Rita Coleman.

1980. Claims left "two males in the muck" in Mississippi.

1980. Says "killed two people" on I-70 west of Denver.

1980. "Lady laid to rest" in marshy area near West Memphis, Arkansas.

July 4, 1980. Katherine "Fuzzy" Hayes is last seen alive at lake near Coushatta.

October 17, 1980. Remains of Katherine Hayes are found in Winn Parish, Louisiana.

March 30, 1983. Faye Aline Self is last seen

at Alice's Wagon Wheel near Coushatta.

May 28, 1983. Wanda Faye Hudson is stabbed to death in her Coushatta apartment.

February 6, 1984. Dismembered body of Nidia Mendoza is found outside Houston.

March 1984–January 1985. (Approximate) Works in route sales for J & H Wholesale Flower Company.

March 30, 1984. Body of Melody Bush is found near Flatonia, Texas.

November 18, 1984. Divorces fourth wife, Rita Coleman.

1985. Claims "dumped male in the muck" near Tulsa, Oklahoma.

January 23, 1986. Steals Ford pickup truck from Quality Ford in Coushatta.

1986. Throws "lady over the precipice" in Washington State.

1986. Kills "a couple on the beach" in

California.

March 30, 1986. Is arrested in California on a fugitive warrant for stolen truck.

September 1986. Pleads guilty to auto theft, resisting arrest. Is sentenced to eighteen months in Louisiana State Penitentiary.

April 13, 1987. Is paroled to Colorado.

September 15, 1987–January 6, 1988. Works at Kwik Stop on Murray Boulevard in Colorado Springs.

November 10, 1987. Rocio Sperry is last seen alive in Colorado Springs.

September 25, 1988. Marries fifth wife, Diane Babbitts.

September 1990. Moves to Eastonville Road.

Circa 1990–1994. Kills "Cowboy Lady" in Colorado Springs.

September 17, 1991. Heather Dawn Church disappears from her Eastonville

Road home.

1993. Claims "shot motorcyclist" in New Mexico.

September 17, 1993. Authorities announce that skull found in foothills is that of Heather Church.

March 28, 1995. Browne is arrested for the murder of Heather Dawn Church.

May 24, 1995. Browne pleads guilty to first-degree murder in Church case; is sentenced to life without parole.

March 17, 2000. Browne writes first letters from prison to El Paso County district attorney.

May 9, 2002. Charlie Hess begins correspondence with Browne.

September 9, 2004. Hess visits Browne in prison for the first time at Colorado State Penitentiary.

February 23, 2005. Browne gives details of several claimed murders in "watershed" interview.

July 27, 2006. Browne pleads guilty to the murder of Rocio Sperry; is sentenced to concurrent life without possibility of parole for forty years.

September 22, 2006. Browne returns to solitary confinement at Colorado Territorial Correctional Facility.

ACKNOWLEDGMENTS

We are indebted to Sheriff Terry Maketa and the staff of the El Paso County Sheriff's Office for their patient help. Special thanks also to sheriff's legal advisor Charles Greenlee, and Robin Wilson of the records unit, for the many hours they spent reviewing and copying investigative reports for us. Lieutenant Clif Northam, the sheriff's information officer, was especially helpful, too.

Many others contributed their expertise and time to this project, including Ronald Arndt, agent in charge of the biological science unit of the Denver lab of the Colorado Bureau of Investigation, Coushatta historian Joe Taylor, El Paso County Coroner Robert C. Bux, Deputy Coroner Chris Schweer Herndon, and William Richards, our researcher in Houston.

Our agent, Doris Booth, believed in this book from the start and charged full speed ahead to get it off the ground. Our editor,

Shannon Jamieson Vazquez, improved the manuscript in countless ways, both large and small.

And finally, thanks to our families for their support and understanding.

ABOUT THE AUTHORS

Stephen G. Michaud is a *New York Times* bestselling author who has written extensively on criminal justice topics. He has authored or coauthored more than a dozen books, including *Ted Bundy: Conversations with a Killer* and *The Only Living Witness,* which *New York Daily News* selected as one of the ten best true crime books ever written. He lives in Texas.

Debbie M. Price is an award-winning journalist who has worked as a staff writer for *The Washington Post, Philadelphia Daily News, The Baltimore Sun,* and *Fort Worth Star-Telegram,* where she was also executive editor. Her freelance articles have appeared in numerous publications. She lives in Colorado.